T0334540

FRENCH REVOLUTION

THE BASICS

French Revolution: The Basics is an accessible and concise introduction to the history of the revolution in France.

Combining a traditional narrative with documents of the era and references to contemporary imagery of the revolution, the book traces the long- and short-term causes of the French Revolution as well as its consequences up to the dissolution of the Convention and the ascendancy of Napoleon. The book is written with an explicit aim for its reader to acquire understanding of the past whilst imparting knowledge using underlying historical concepts such as evidence, continuity and change, cause and effect, significance, empathy, perspectives, and contestability.

Key topics discussed within the book include:

- The structure of French society before 1789.
- The long- and short-term factors that contributed to the French Revolution.
- How ordinary French people, including women and slaves, participated in the revolution.
- What brought about the end of the *ancien régime*.
- The major reforms of the National Assembly, 1789–1791, and how they led to the division and radicalisation of the revolution.
- How the alternative visions of the new society divided the revolution and what were the internal and external pressures on the revolution that contributed to its radicalisation.
- The forms of terror which enabled reality to triumph over idealism.
- The rise of Napoleon Bonaparte as military leader and Emperor.

This book is an ideal introduction for anyone wishing to learn more about this influential revolution in the shaping of modern Europe and the world.

Darius von Güttner is Principal Research Fellow (Associate Professor), School of Historical and Philosophical Studies, The University of Melbourne, Australia.

The Basics

The Basics is a highly successful series of accessible guidebooks which provide an overview of the fundamental principles of a subject area in a jargon-free and undaunting format.

Intended for students approaching a subject for the first time, the books both introduce the essentials of a subject and provide an ideal springboard for further study. With over 50 titles spanning subjects from artificial intelligence (AI) to women's studies, *The Basics* are an ideal starting point for students seeking to understand a subject area.

Each text comes with recommendations for further study and gradually introduces the complexities and nuances within a subject.

ACTING (SECOND EDITION)
BELLA MERLIN

ANIMAL ETHICS
TONY MILLIGAN

ANTHROPOLOGY OF RELIGION
JAMES S. BIELO

ARCHAEOLOGY (SECOND EDITION)
CLIVE GAMBLE

ART HISTORY (SECOND EDITION)
DIANA NEWELL AND GRANT POOKE

THE BIBLE AND LITERATURE
NORMAN W. JONES

BRITISH POLITICS
BILL JONES

CAPITALISM
DAVID COATES

CHAUCER
JACQUELINE TASIOULAS

CHRISTIAN THEOLOGY
MURRAY RAE

For a full list of titles in this series, please visit www.routledge.com/The-Basics/book-series/B

FRENCH REVOLUTION

THE BASICS

Darius von Güttner

Routledge
Taylor & Francis Group
LONDON AND NEW YORK

First published as *French Revolution: The Basics* 2022
by Routledge
2 Park Square, Milton Park, Abingdon, Oxon OX14 4RN

and by Routledge
605 Third Avenue, New York, NY 10158

Routledge is an imprint of the Taylor & Francis Group, an informa business

Previously published as *The French Revolution*, Cengage Learning Australia, 2015.

British Library Cataloguing-in-Publication Data
A catalogue record for this book is available from the British Library

Library of Congress Cataloging-in-Publication Data
Names: Güttner-Sporzyński, Darius von, author.
Title: French Revolution : the basics / Darius von Güttner.
Description: London ; New York, NY : Routledge, 2022. | Series: The basics |
    "Previously published as "The French Revolution," Cengage Learning Australia,
    2015." | Includes bibliographical references and index.
Subjects: LCSH: France—History—Revolution, 1789–1799.
Classification: LCC DC148 .G88 2022 (print) | LCC DC148 (ebook) | DDC
    944.04/1—dc23
LC record available at https://lccn.loc.gov/2021028422
LC ebook record available at https://lccn.loc.gov/2021028423

ISBN: 978-0-367-74424-3 (hbk)
ISBN: 978-0-367-74423-6 (pbk)
ISBN: 978-1-003-15774-8 (ebk)

DOI: 10.4324/9781003157748

Typeset in Bembo
by Apex CoVantage, LLC

CONTENTS

PREFACE

The ideas that underpinned the French Revolution are still as relevant today as they were more than two hundred years ago. The principles enshrined in the *Declaration of the Rights of Man and the Citizen* are as valid, and perhaps even more so, in the present day and remind those who study the revolution that all human beings 'are born free and remain equal in rights'.

Since I tackled the subject of the revolution over a decade ago, some historical perspectives have changed, especially with the interest in the global impact of the events in France, the history of slavery and the role of women. These viewpoints are not overlooked in this book.

It is a pleasure to thank all those who have, in various ways, supported me in writing this book. I would especially like to acknowledge my students—their questions, curiosity and observations have shaped my teaching and provided the focus to all aspects of the text.

The staff of the University Library at the University of Melbourne very kindly enabled me to access books from the collection when the University and the library were closed due to the COVID-19 pandemic. I should also like to express my gratitude to my teachers and colleagues, Peter McPhee, Adrian Jones and David Garrioch, whose scholarship has contributed to my interpretation of the causes, progress and outcomes of the French Revolution. To Adam Zamoyski, I also owe thanks.

In preparation of this text, I have had invaluable help from Michael von Güttner-Sporzyński and Nicholas von Güttner-Sporzyński, who re-read the whole text. I'm grateful as ever.

INTRODUCTION

The obliteration of the *ancien régime* in France is one of the great turning points of the modern era. The revolution transformed France with the principle of popular sovereignty giving political representation to its entire population. France was one of the most powerful states in eighteenth-century Europe and influenced European economic, political and cultural development. French was not only spoken at the court of Versailles, but across the courts of Europe. French culture, including arts and literature, was emulated by the European elites. The ruler of France, Louis XVI, was not a despotic tyrant, but a monarch pursuing an active reform agenda. In the 1780s, the financial situation of the French monarchy was the key reason for the monarchy seeking a new national consensus with the summoning of the Estates-General. The meeting of this representative institution, the first in more than 150 years, set in motion a chain of events that challenged the very foundations of absolute monarchy. Many underlying tensions in France's institutions made a revolution, if not inevitable, at least conceivable. Louis XVI's reform agenda was overtaken by revolution, as ideas became action. The year 1789 marked the transition of France from a kingdom ruled by a divinely ordained ruler to a constitutional monarchy, and the *Declaration of the Rights of Man and the Citizen* heralded the birth of the new order. The establishment of the new society was marked by division and idealism, which turned into extremism. Religion, the position of the king and the definition of who could be considered a citizen each proved to be contentious. A series of political and economic crises forced the revolution onto the path of emergency measures and war. In 1793, terror became the 'order of the day' as France's new republican government became more authoritarian. The revolution cannot be summed up in simplistic terms as the confrontation between feudalism and capitalism, or a bourgeois clash with nobles and the monarchy. It progressed in a complex and unpredictable way, often contradicting the revolutionary ideas of universal rights of man. The process of change exacted a high human cost. The violence of the Terror and the imperial ambitions of Napoleon were examples of the compromise of the revolutionary ideals that first proclaimed 'men are born and remain free and equal in rights'. One of the most significant outcomes of the revolution is the endurance of the principles of popular sovereignty and civil equality—the foundations of modern liberal democratic societies.

THE ORIGINS OF THE REVOLUTION

In the second half of the eighteenth century, the very roots of the long-established social, political and economic foundations of French society, based on privilege, hierarchy and tradition, were being challenged. The French king, Louis XVI, faced with pressure from elite groups in his kingdom, recognised the need for reform, which in his assessment was limited to the issue of taxation. In 1781, the *Compte rendu*, the first ever statement of the Crown's finances, reflected and encouraged the growing interest by the French public in economic affairs. These challenges, together with the Crown's financial difficulties as a result of France's involvement in costly foreign wars, convinced Louis XVI and his successive finance ministers to implement a range of radical reforms to increase the income of the Crown. Although there is no consensus among historians on the causes of the revolution, there is a broad acknowledgement of the complex nature of the tensions and problems that became apparent when an unfolding political crisis brought them to the surface.

FRANCE IN EUROPE

In the early eighteenth century, France was an absolute monarchy ruled by the Bourbon dynasty, which claimed the throne by divine right. As the century progressed, France's system of government, and indeed the whole structure of society, came under increasing pressure for change. It made the crisis possible, but not unavoidable; it was not evident that France was on the brink of a revolution. The fluctuating economic activity in the 1770s and 1780s had not made

DOI: 10.4324/9781003157748-1

most peasants poorer and had not prevented the bourgeoisie from increasing its wealth. The need for change was caused mainly by the financial difficulties King Louis XVI's government faced as a result of France's involvement in foreign wars such as the War of Austrian Succession (1740–1748), the Seven Years' War (1754–1763) and the American War of Independence (1775–1783). When the Crown could no longer afford to finance the operation of the government, the king attempted to force through a reform of the fiscal system. At this critical point, the financial crisis turned into a political crisis, with various sections of French society demanding a constitution to regulate the relationship between those governing and those being governed. When the monarchy and the nobility resisted such a change in 1789, the revolution began.

For centuries, France held a dominant position in European politics. Maintaining that status caused a permanent deficit in the royal finances, in particular because of an increasingly costly rivalry with Britain. While Britain's fast-growing economy allowed it to concentrate on building its colonial empire, France's overseas expansion always came second to competition with other European states on the Continent, such as Austria and Britain's ally, Prussia. The French monarchy was badly affected by the eighteenth century's most extensive conflict, the Seven Years' War (1756–1763), perhaps indicating that the French monarchs were unable to cope with the challenges posed by the growth of Prussia and the British capture of French colonial possessions in India, Quebec and the Caribbean. Another sign of France's decreasing international influence was its inability, just prior to Louis XVI's accession in 1774, to prevent annexation of territories belonging to Poland, one of its traditional allies, by Prussia, Austria and Russia. At the beginning of Louis XVI's reign, France attempted to recover its pride from these foreign policy defeats by supporting Britain's American colonies in their war for independence. A small French contingent significantly aided the Americans, and France hosted the peace conference at which Britain conceded the colonies' independence in 1783. Britain lost their thirteen colonies, but while France won a propaganda victory over Britain, its financial losses were huge. This diplomatic success brought no tangible rewards for France and its costs added to the growing pressure for reform of France's fiscal system, which by 1789, had developed into a political crisis.

The chain of events which brought about the political crisis surprised not only the elites of the kingdom but even more so the ruler of France and his immediate family. The Bourbon dynasty, which ruled France at the time of the revolution, was one of the most ancient European royal houses. It is a branch of the dynasty founded in 987 by Hugh Capet (c. 941–996), who was elected 'King of the Franks' after the death of Louis V, the last king of the Carolingian dynasty. In 1328, when direct male descendants of Hugh Capet did not produce a surviving male heir to the French throne, the succession passed to their cousin, the head of the younger branch of the House of Capet, the Valois dynasty. Similarly, in 1589, the Valois died out and the throne passed to Henry IV (1553–1610), the first French monarch of the Bourbon dynasty. The reign of Henry's grandson, Louis XIV (1643–1715), provided the rest of Europe with an example of an absolutist style of government. During 72 years on the throne, Louis had personally ruled France for more than 50 years. This longest reign in European history was marked by the growth of France as one of the great powers of the Continent. Louis reformed the administration of justice and promoted commerce and industry, including the development of overseas colonies. As king, he established royal academies for architecture, art, literature, science and music, and built the royal palaces of the Louvre, now an art gallery, and Versailles, where he based the French court. Louis XIV outlived all of his immediate family with the exception of his grandson, Philip V of Spain, and a great-grandson, who became Louis XV when the Sun-King died in 1715. The name of Louis XIV became synonymous with greatness, power, splendour and glory.

In the course of the eighteenth century the Bourbons relied on the reflected glory of the Sun-King, yet for all the ostentatious display of power during the reign of his grandson, Louis XV, France could no longer halt the decline of its super-power status, as demonstrated in the series of military and diplomatic defeats. Shortly after the death of Holy Roman Emperor Charles VI in 1742, France in alliance with Prussia and Bavaria challenged the right of his daughter, Maria Theresa (1717–1780), to succeed to the hereditary lands of the Habsburg dynasty. In this War of Austrian Succession (1740–1748), supporting Maria Theresa's claim were Britain, the Dutch Republic, Sardinia and Saxony. France aimed at weakening Austria, her long-standing rival, through supporting various claimants to parts of the Habsburg inheritance, including election of Charles Albert of Bavaria as Holy Roman Emperor in 1742, in opposition to Maria Theresa's husband, Francis, grand duke of Tuscany. The war ended with the Treaty of Aix-la-Chapelle in 1748, which confirmed Maria Theresa's right of succession. France after some initial territorial gains was left without any material gains but Prussia acquired Silesia from Austria.

The Treaty did not resolve the French claims to hegemony in Europe and worldwide, and within a decade another major military conflict, which Winston Churchill called 'the first world war', began when the European powers sought to extend, and compete for, their influence both in Europe and overseas. The Seven Years' War (1756–1763) also became known as the 'French and Indian War', as fighting between Britain and France took place on the American and Canadian frontiers and in India. In the Treaty of Paris, which ended the war in 1763, France acknowledged the loss of all of its territory on the North American mainland and the Indian subcontinent, and Britain emerged as the dominant European colonial power. The French had been humiliated.

Under the direction of Count Vergennes (1719–1787), an influential foreign minister, French diplomacy began to pursue any means of revenge on Britain and her imperial ambitions. This opportunity arrived with a critical event, which had a major impact on Europe and the development of revolution in France. A rebellion against taxation without representation started in the British possessions on the other side of the Atlantic in 1773. The revolt turned to a revolutionary war and, on 2 July 1776, a convention of delegates from the thirteen British colonies in North America met in Philadelphia and adopted a resolution declaring the colonies' independence from Britain. Two days later, the delegates approved the Declaration of Independence in which they outlined the reasons for their renunciation of British sovereignty, providing the moral rationale for their decision and a list of grievances against King George III. The authors of the Declaration were influenced by the ideas of the Enlightenment, and in particular the theories of English thinker John Locke and French *philosophe* Jean-Jacques Rousseau. In a clear break from the past, the colonists declared 'that all men are created equal' and were 'endowed by their Creator with certain unalienable

Rights'. They declared these rights to be 'Life, Liberty and the pursuit of Happiness'. In defiance of the divine right of kings, the American colonists argued that governments derive their powers from 'the consent of the governed', who have the right to abolish them when 'any form of government becomes destructive'. The ideals proclaimed in the Declaration and the subsequent development of the Constitution of the United States of America (ratified in 1788) had a profound impact on the *ancien régimes* of Europe. The American War of Independence, which began in April 1775, ended in June 1783 with the Treaty of Paris when Britain recognised the establishment of the United States.

The court of Louis XVI celebrated the humbling of the British as a major victory. In reality, the support given by France to the American rebels stretched France's ability to finance operation of its administration beyond breaking point. Unaware of the consequences for France, Parisians were greatly interested in the revolt of the American colonies against Britain. The American agent Silas Deane (1737–1789) arrived in France in 1776 to lobby the French for aid. Deane was involved in recruiting officers and engineers and sourcing supplies to support the rebellion. The first foreign volunteers, writes historian Adam Zamoyski, were French. Officially, France maintained its neutrality, but some of the French officers, who desired glory on the battlefield or who had little chance of advancement in the French army, enlisted to help the Americans. Perhaps the best example is Marquis de Lafayette (1757–1834), who had no hope of gaining meaningful military experience as a soldier in peacetime, but his American experiences not only exposed him to the ideals of 'Liberty, Equality and the pursuit of Happiness', but also positively instilled the 'spirit of America' in his psyche. Lafayette and other returning European volunteers who had served in the American War of Independence spread the ideas of liberty and popular sovereignty.

For Zamoyski, the American revolt was seen by Europeans as a 'dramatic condemnation of the evils of Europe', and this echoes the earlier assessment of Alexis de Tocqueville, who wrote in 1835 that 'the Americans appeared to be doing no more than carrying out what our writers had conceived'. Indeed, Tocqueville suggests a direct link between the ideas of the *philosophes* and the revolutionary action. The American rebellion demonstrated to the world that there was an alternative to the *ancien régime* and, even more significantly, it was within reach.

KEY INDIVIDUAL: MARQUIS DE LAFAYETTE (1757–1834)

Lafayette was a volunteer who served on the side of the rebels during the American War of Independence. He was influenced by the ideas of the Enlightenment and was one of the liberal nobles who recognised the need for reform. During the Assembly of Notables, Lafayette supported summoning the Estates-General. He was elected as a Second Estate deputy and, due to his popularity with the Parisian crowds, was acclaimed the commander of the newly formed National Guard. His actions perhaps saved Marie Antoinette during the dramatic October Days of 1789. He supported the constitutional monarchy and lost all public support after the royal family's flight to Varennes in 1791 when he ordered the shooting of unarmed demonstrators at the Champs de Mars. He commanded an army in the war against Austria, but in 1792 he defected to Austria and was imprisoned until 1797. On Lafayette's release, Napoleon allowed him to return to live on his estates in France.

ANCIEN RÉGIME

The French system of government before the revolution is best described as an absolute monarchy and is often referred to as the *ancien régime*. The term *ancien régime* was coined in 1789 by the revolutionaries who wished to distance themselves from the world they sought to reform. The kingdom of France was ruled by the king, the head of the Bourbon dynasty. King Louis XVI, whose reign started in 1774, was an absolute monarch who ruled by divine right; his authority and the right to rule were subject to the will of God alone.

In theory, there were no legal limits to the monarch's power over his realm. In practice, however, the king was bound by the laws and customs of the land, and exercising his authority depended on the agreement of France's elite: the clergy and the nobility. The king could not on his own volition alter the rules of hereditary succession to allow his daughter to succeed him on the throne because the established law stipulated that the throne passed to a king's closest living male relative. The king resided in Versailles and from there he appointed his ministers to advise him on the government of the kingdom. The ministers did not form a collective group or a cabinet in the modern sense but were responsible to Louis XVI individually for the tasks assigned to them and their departments. The king was thus at the centre of the government, directing, if not formulating, government policy. The lack of a cabinet meant, however, that ministers and their supporters competed against each other for Louis' favour.

In the decades leading to the revolution, members of a number of institutions questioned the powers of the Crown and, in particular, the scope of the royal prerogative. The most prominent and repeated challenge for control of taxation came from the royal courts of law, known as the *parlements*. These 'last great relics of medieval French constitution'[1] played a role in promulgation of all royal edicts by performing the registration of the laws. Sometimes the *parlements* refused to register legislation pointing to a specific issue of law and petitioned the king with their *remonstrance* for an edict to be amended. This uneasy relationship between the king and the *parlements* 'produced more debate and conflict than might be expected within a theoretically absolute monarchy'.[2] During his reign, Louis XV (1715–1774) considered it necessary to remind the judges of the *parlements*, and his subjects in general, of the scope of his authority. On 3 March 1766, the Parlement of Paris, the most important of the royal courts, held a special session known as the *lit de justice*. During the *lit de justice*, a ceremony dating back to the Middle Ages, the Parlement of Paris held its session under the presidency of the king himself and in his presence the judges were compelled to register the royal edicts. During the session, Louis XV outlined his own interpretation of law. The event became known as the 'Session of the Scourging' because the king lashed out at the judges who objected to his will. Louis XV restated what he called the 'fundamental laws of the state' asserting that 'sovereign power resides' in the person of the king alone. The king, Louis XV reminded them, exercises that power through consultation and application of justice, and is guided by reason. What this necessarily meant was that the 'public order in its entirety' originates from the Crown, and it is at the Crown's mandate that the courts 'derive their existence and their authority'; the judges administer justice in the name of the Crown. The king stressed that 'undivided legislative power' belonged to him alone and the *parlements'* right of remonstrance could not in any way challenge it. Finally, addressing his subjects, Louis XV reminded them that the 'rights and interests of the nation' were the same as those of the king. During the course of his education, the king's grandson and future successor, Dauphin Louis-Auguste, reflected on these principles and wrote in his journal that 'a key foundation of the French monarchy is that all power resides with the king alone, and that no body or person can make itself independent of his authority'.[3] These tenets of the French constitution, unchallenged until the late 1780s, serve as a powerful reminder of Louis XVI's own concept of authority.[4]

THE KING AND THE QUEEN

The future Louis XVI, known before his accession as Louis-Auguste, was the eldest male heir of Louis XV, his grandfather. Before his ascent to the throne, on 10 May 1774, he was referred to as the Dauphin, which was the title of the heir to the throne of France, derived from the province of the Dauphiné and at the same time a reference to the depiction of the dolphin in the coat of arms of the province. Louis was well educated, with a particular interest in mathematics, physics and history. Although Louis was interested in technological innovations, his education and upbringing reinforced his own perception of the monarch's traditional position as an absolute ruler. From the beginning of his reign, Louis pursued a number of reformist policies, wishing to rebuild confidence in the monarchy. He often took the advice of his ministers but was not persistent when faced with firm opposition to his ideas. This inconsistency made him look indecisive and weak if not duplicitous.[5]

Abbé Jean-Louis Soulavie (1781–1813), who published his own account of the reign of Louis XVI in 1801, attributed the development of the revolution to the rigid social structure of the *ancien régime*. Abbé Soulavie pointed out that Louis XVI was unsuitable to lead his country in the time of crisis because of his indecisive personality. The king seemed unable to follow through his policy decisions and defend them when faced with firm resistance. Abbé Soulavie portrayed Louis XVI as a scrupulous and morally irreproachable monarch, who could not choose between asserting the royal authority and consenting to the demands of public opinion.[6]

In 1770, Dauphin Louis-Auguste married Marie Antoinette. The marriage was intended to show the strength of the alliance between France and Austria. The alliance was established after the conclusion of the War of Austrian Succession in 1756 and was orchestrated by the dominant faction at Louis XV's court, led by the duc de Choiseul (1719–1785). Marie Antoinette was the youngest daughter of 16 children of Maria Theresa of Austria (1717–1780) and Francis I (r. 1745–1765), Holy Roman Emperor. Her parents were an unconventional couple who married for love, shared the same bed, and raised their children in an informal family setting. Marie Antoinette was educated by a French tutor who instructed her in history, the classics, and the arts.[7]

The marriage was contracted on 19 April 1770 at a ceremony held in Vienna, and the young Marie Antoinette arrived in Versailles on 16 May. On that day, the official wedding was held in the royal chapel. The celebrations included the reception of the ambassadors, a firework display and a lavish party in the royal opera house. The day concluded with the bedding ceremony ritual: the young couple were led into the bedchamber of Marie Antoinette; the bed was blessed by the Archbishop of Reims; and the newly married couple went to bed in the presence of all the court. The marriage was not consummated until 1776, which fuelled gossip about the sexuality of both Louis and Marie Antoinette. The delay in normal sexual relations between the couple was most frequently blamed on a genital anomaly, or a strict religious education, but was likely caused by the immaturity and ignorance of the couple; they were aged 15 and 14 respectively.[8] In fact, the couple benefited from advice from the queen's brother, Emperor Joseph II, during his visit to Versailles in May 1777.[9] The couple's first child was born on 19 December 1778.

The marriage was haunted by enmity towards Marie Antoinette from all sections of the French public. Until she gave birth to a daughter and later provided a dauphin, rumours of her infidelity and infertility circulated widely, despite the king's open affection towards her in public. In the 1780s, Marie Antoinette became the subject of vilifying subversive pamphlets. These pamphlets portrayed her as immoral and self-indulgent, falsely insinuating that she had lesbian affairs, which eroded the prestige of the monarchy in the eyes of the public. The perception of her extravagance was so legendary that even when rumours were refuted, the public continued to believe the scandals.[10] The disastrous 'Affair of the Diamond Necklace' (1785–1786) exposed Marie Antoinette to further public condemnation even though she was innocent of any involvement.

The public furore caused by the 'Affair of the Diamond Necklace' contributed to discrediting the queen in the eyes of the French people, although there was no evidence that she had done anything wrong. At the centre of the scandal was Cardinal de Rohan and the necklace ordered by Louis XV for his mistress, Madame du Barry. This piece of jewellery, with an estimated cost of 2 million *livres*, never reached its intended recipient because the king died of smallpox before it could be delivered. In 1785, Cardinal de Rohan hoped to gain the favour of the queen but was duped by Jeanne de la Motte. She pretended to act as a friend of the queen and convinced the Cardinal that the queen wanted him to negotiate the purchase of the necklace and pay for it in instalments. In the end Jeanne de la Motte's husband sold the necklace's diamonds separately in London. When the payment was not received, the jeweller approached the queen directly; she rejected the suggestion that she had ordered and received the necklace. Cardinal de Rohan was taken to the Bastille in August 1785, but he was acquitted after a trial in May 1786. Jeanne de la Motte was branded on each shoulder with a V mark reserved for thieves, and imprisoned.[11] The public image of the queen was however damaged beyond repair—Marie Antoinette could do nothing right!

FRANCE BEFORE 1789

When Louis XVI ascended the throne, France was the most populous and the largest state in Europe. The territory under his control (excluding overseas territories) covered some 717,944 square kilometres and had a population of more than 28 million; a nation which was growing rapidly. The kingdom extended from the lowlands of Flanders in the north to the Pyrenees and the Mediterranean Sea in the south, and from the Atlantic Ocean in the west to the Rhine

River and the Alps in the east. France also controlled overseas colonies in Canada, the Caribbean, and the Indian subcontinent. Louis' realm was not uniform, and its constituent parts had been accumulated by his ancestors through conquest and dynastic marriages since the Middle Ages. As recently as 1766, Louis' grandfather, Louis XV, had inherited the Duchy of Lorraine from his father-in-law, the former king of Poland, Stanisław Leszczyński, and 20 years later Louis incorporated the island of Corsica into his realm. The kingdom was thus an amalgamation of provinces that were progressively added, and the kings of France tended to adapt the existing institutions of these new territories rather than develop and impose new institutions. As a result, each province had different legal and administrative systems, and taxes levied at varied rates. This made Louis XVI's France a diverse and complex realm to govern.

For administrative purposes, the kingdom was divided into 36 *généralités*, each governed by an intendant, an administrator who reported to the Controller-General of Finances. The *généralités* as administrative units were not uniform in size and their boundaries seldom coincided with the geographical boundaries of the provinces. In the exercise of the royal authority the intendants competed with the *parlements*, the 13 appellate courts of law. The premier position among these courts was held by the Parlement of Paris whose jurisdiction covered a third of the kingdom. Among the prerogatives of the *parlement* was the registration of the king's edicts before they were promulgated as binding laws and, related to it, the right to remonstrate by rising legal objections to the king's legislation. To add to this complex administrative framework, the Roman Catholic Church maintained 18 archiepiscopal provinces and 136 dioceses across the kingdom. These complex connections and interdependencies were repeated in many different ways at the town and village level.

DOCUMENT: LAMOIGNON ON THE PRINCIPLES OF THE FRENCH MONARCHY, 19 NOVEMBER 1787

This extract is from a speech delivered by Chrêtien-François de Lamoignon (1735–1789) at a sitting of the Parlement of

Paris on 19 November 1787. Lamoignon was the king's Lord Chancellor who customarily managed the system of justice.

These principles, universally acknowledged by the entire kingdom, are that the King alone must possess the sovereign power in his kingdom; that He is answerable only to God in the exercise of his power; that the tie which binds the King to the Nation is by nature indissoluble; that the interests and reciprocal obligations between the King and his subjects serve only to reassure that union; that the Nation's interest is that the powers of its head not be altered; that the King is the chief sovereign of the Nation and everything he does is with her interests in mind; and that finally the legislative power resides in the person of the King independent of and unshared with all other powers. These, sirs, are the invariable powers of the French Monarchy ... As a consequence of these principles and of our History, it is clear that the King only has the right to convoke an Estates-General; that he alone must judge if this convocation is necessary; and that he needs no other power for the administration of his kingdom.[12]

Louis XVI's subjects were all members of social groups that, except for the peasants, claimed certain special rights that set them apart from others. As such, the social structure of the *ancien régime* was rigid and built on notions of privilege and precedence. Originating in the Middle Ages, this structure divided French society into three estates or orders, known as the First, Second and Third Estates. The First Estate was made up of the clergy of the Roman Catholic Church. The Second Estate drew its membership from those who were born to a noble father or who had acquired nobility by the grace of the king. The Third Estate contained everyone else, those of common birth. Almost every group in eighteenth-century France could claim some sort of special privilege, but the most visibly privileged groups were the two so-called privileged orders, the clergy and the nobility.

The clergy of the Roman Catholic Church, which formed the First Estate, made up less than 1 per cent of the population. Numbering between 130,000 and 170,000, members of the clergy comprised monks and nuns in religious orders and priests who ministered to the spiritual needs of lay society.[13] The Church was a highly hierarchical organisation, with archbishops and bishops predominantly from the nobility in the high offices, and the priests and curates predominantly commoners. The influence enjoyed by the Church had its roots in the monopoly of public worship (97 per cent of Frenchmen were nominally Catholic) and its wealth was largely derived from extensive landholding, perhaps 6–7 per cent of the land of France, and the income from a tithe of 10 per cent imposed on farm produce at harvest. The most evident sign of the privileged status of the First Estate was its total exemption from paying taxes.[14] The Church's General Assembly made a voluntary annual grant to the king.

The nobles derived their status as members of the Second Estate by birth (the *noblesse d'épée*, nobility of the sword) or by creation or ennoblement (the *noblesse de robe*, officials raised to nobility by the king either through merit or by the virtue of the office). In terms of social mobility, the creation of more than 4,000 venal offices out of 70,000 opened the way for wealthy commoners to acquire noble status. The French nobility could be likened to a club that the wealthy among the commoners felt obliged to join. In line with the trends in other European monarchies, while not all nobles were wealthy, most of the wealthy people, eventually, ended up becoming nobles. Membership of the nobility offered standing in society that was beyond the reach of wealth alone and assisted its holders in securing prestige, positions and privileges.[15] Precisely how many nobles there were in 1789 is debatable. The estimates vary from no more than 25,000 noble families to between 140,000 and 350,000 individuals but perhaps not more than 1 per cent of the population.[16]

The nobles owned between a quarter and a third of all the land in France. Their greatest privilege was exemption from paying the *taille* and the *corvée*. The nobles as estate holders benefited from several sources of wealth and power. Notwithstanding great internal diversity of the nobility, they enjoyed the privilege of rank demonstrated by various insignia of distinction, fiscal and seigneurial privileges, and exclusive employment in a range of official positions, including the army. As members of the Second Estate, the nobles were seen as having a vested interest in an intricate hierarchical system of status from which they derived their economic, political and social privilege.[17] In their opposition to the reforms sought by King Louis XVI many nobles recognised that any significant changes in France's political institutions would most likely result in a decrease in their privileges. While some liberal nobles, influenced by the ideals of the Enlightenment, accepted the need for these reforms because they thought of themselves as the natural leaders of society, most nobles believed that reform was a threat to their position.

The Third Estate included every person who was not a member of the clergy or nobility, that is the commoners. Accounting for about 98 per cent of the French population, the Third Estate was a broadly defined group that included wealthy merchants, urban workers, peasants and beggars. The wealthiest group within the Third Estate was the bourgeoisie, or 'the citizens of a town', who represented the emerging middle classes mostly living in the towns. They accumulated their wealth through trade rather than farming. Among them were merchants, bankers, industrialists, business people, financiers, landowners, medical professionals, lawyers and civil servants. As a social group, they were growing in wealth and aspired to advance their social status in order to join the nobility. Yet, for all the aspirations to advance in terms of social status there was a growing frustration within the upper bourgeoisie, particularly those engaged in manufacturing. The causes of the dissatisfaction were deeply rooted in the structures of the *ancien régime* based on privilege. The expansion of overseas trade and the increase in the consumption of luxury goods were restricted by the rights and privileges of corporations, feudal landowners, and government. In short, the privilege of a few affected the job market, freedom of trade and thus commerce in general.[18]

Among those of the Third Estate who lived in the towns were urban workers who made their living working as servants, labourers, or industrial workers. Most of them were low skilled and survived on low wages. The burden of taxes that members of the other estates did not pay fell heavily on the Third Estate. The quality of life in the lower strata of the Third Estate depended very much on the price of food; when food prices went up, their lives got harder.

The most populous section of the Third Estate was the peasants, who constituted more than 80 per cent of the population.[19] Across the country they owned about 30 per cent of the land outright, although this varied between the provinces. They were smallholders, tenant farmers or sharecroppers; if they did not own or lease their land, they farmed at subsistence level.[20] Their low income depended on yields for grain crops and was subsidised by working on another's land or in the towns. Scarcity of food was a common feature of peasant life. Among their obligations were: feudal seigneurial dues to the lord of the manor (*seigneur*), including work on the lord's land; they had to be available for labour service on the roads (*corvée*); they paid the land tax (*taille*) and the salt tax (*gabelle*), the head tax (*capitation*), and the *vingtième* or twentieth tax as well as a tithe to the Church.

Most of the peasants survived by subsistence farming, their standard of living dependent on harvest yields and weather: crop failure and bad weather meant hunger. It is not an overstatement that the majority of peasants earned just enough to sustain their own existence. Poor harvests were a major reason for rural poverty as they reduced food supply and inflated prices. The testimony of Arthur Young, a British traveller through France in 1789, is often used to highlight the abject poverty of the rural population. Young described parts of France as backward and poverty-stricken, with farming practices not much further advanced than those of the Indigenous tribes of North America.[21] At the same time, other visitors to France reported its progress and development.

INEQUITY OF THE SOCIAL, ECONOMIC AND POLITICAL SYSTEM

Eighteenth-century France was a rural society characterised by regional diversity. Many local traditions, practices and loyalties continued to influence the lives of individuals throughout France. The growth in population and expansion of the economy was not matched by reform of the increasingly outdated feudal structures in society. By the late eighteenth century, the perception of the need for change became a source of political tension.

The nobility, although fully aware of its privilege, rank and status, was removed from active participation in the government of France by lack of any representative institution able to influence the king. The laws and privileges of the provinces prevented the creation of a uniform national market, which frustrated the growing bourgeoisie, who sought a more rational system of law, custom duties and taxes as well as a voice in the governing of the kingdom. The Third Estate was heavily taxed and increasingly resentful of the burden of feudal dues and the tithe. The growing disproportion of wealth and means was not lost on contemporary commentators. A French writer, Louis-Sébastien Mercier (1740–1814), for example, observed the increasing disparity in the standard of living between the rich and the poor, and noted that the ostentatious luxury enjoyed by some prompted bitter resentment among the underprivileged.[22] The social hierarchy based on the hereditary principle and privilege constrained the social mobility of the enterprising middle class. The predominance of nobility among the leading Church appointments and the practice of a few clerics accumulating multiple financially lucrative benefices became a frequent and bitter grievance for lower clergy denied advancement and prosperity. Expenditure was high among the nobility, who had to compete for the king's favour to maintain their position at court, and poorer nobles, in particular, resented ennoblement of rich merchants. The rich bourgeoisie was equally insulted to be ranked at the bottom of the social order as part of the Third Estate along with the peasants and labourers.

The inequity of the system was particularly striking in the fiscal arrangements: nobles paid little or no tax as the traditional defenders of the kingdom, but despite their rank they had little opportunity to influence the policies of the government. Peasants, urban workers and the bourgeoisie, who carried the fiscal burden of supporting the kingdom, had no control over how taxes were spent. It was increasingly apparent that in the absence of regular meetings of the Estates-General neither the privileged orders nor the commoners had a representative body to give them a political voice.

ESTATES-GENERAL

The Estates-General originated in 1302 when the three estates were summoned to meet by King Philip IV the Fair (1268–1314). When in session, the Estates-General formed a consultative assembly of the kingdom of France and comprised the three estates of the realm: the clergy, the nobility and the commoners. During a meeting of the Estates-General the three estates deliberated in three separate chambers independently of each other.

The Estates-General never became a legislative institution and never assumed a role like the English Parliament. Kings of France summoned the Estates-General only in times of crisis, and some did not call them at all. Deputies representing each of the three estates were elected by the members of the estate to which they belonged. Their election was accompanied by drawing up lists of grievances (*cahiers de doléances*) at meetings of adult males who elected the deputies. Traditionally, the monarchy would ask the Estates-General to approve increases in taxes and, in return, pledged to deal with the issues presented in the lists of grievances. The Estates-General of 1614 ended in fiasco and demonstrated how difficult it was to reach consensus between estates when each of them staunchly defended their rights and showed no inclination for compromise. After this experience, the Estates-General were not summoned until the fateful decision of Louis XVI to call a meeting for May 1789 to advise him on the solutions to France's financial crisis and endorse fiscal reform.

In the absence of regular sessions of the Estates-General, their advisory role was carried out by France's appellate law courts, the *parlements*. In the decades before the revolution, the *parlements* had obstructed many reforms because the right of remonstrance allowed them to hold royal authority in check by voicing their objections to legislation and seeking its review. In the final years of the fiscal crisis, the *parlements* refused to agree to the king's reform of the taxation system, arguing that only the Estates-General could consent to it on behalf of the whole nation.

When Louis XVI announced that he would summon the Estates-General, no one, including the king, knew how exactly the Estates-General were to be assembled. On 23 September 1788, the Parlement of Paris declared that the Estates-General needed to be organised as they were for the last meeting in 1614. In particular, the deputies of the three estates were to sit and vote in separate chambers. Nonetheless, Jacques Necker, the reform-minded minister of Louis XVI, persuaded the king to allow the number of deputies of the Third Estate to equal the number of the nobility and clergy combined, to permit the Third Estate to elect deputies from the privileged orders to represent the commoners, and set the number of the deputies at 1,000 at least. In an unprecedented break with tradition, the king also promised not to impose any tax without the consent of the Estates-General. These innovations ensured that the outcome of the 1789 elections would be vastly different from those of 1614.[23]

NEW IDEAS—THE ENLIGHTENMENT

As the eighteenth century progressed, a range of new ideas emerged that challenged traditional ideas about how society should be organised. These ideas were often linked to a series of interrelated economic, social and cultural changes which were undermining the institutional foundations of the European *ancien régimes* based on corporate privilege, and the authority of the Church. These new ideas, which coincided with extended, gradual economic and political change, are referred to by historians as the 'Enlightenment'.

The term 'Enlightenment' became popular and influential among educated elites, although each European nation had its own particular term to describe the phenomenon. In Germany it was called the *Aufklärung*; in France *des Lumières*; and in Italy it was known as the *Illuminismo*. All these names mean much the same as the English word 'enlightenment'. The terms were used by people at the time to describe the times in which they lived, perhaps in recognition that they were living in a time of great intellectual turmoil. Writing in 1771 Diderot declared that 'every century has its own characteristic spirit. The spirit of ours seems to be liberty.'[24]

The origins of the Enlightenment can be traced to scientific discoveries such as the publication of Sir Isaac Newton's *Principia* (1687), which outlined the law of universal gravitation and is regarded as one of the most important works in the history of science. This intellectual movement challenged established forms of society, politics and religion by insisting that the world should be understood using reason and logic rather than religion, tradition and superstition. It spread across Europe and had a particularly strong influence in France. Order, religious tolerance, rational thought, criticism and human progress became the key enlightened ideas propagated by these thinkers. These writers became known as *philosophes*. By the 1770s, Paris became the centre of the Enlightenment, but the clever, witty and often satirical and daring writings of the *philosophes* spread far and wide across Europe. The spread of their ideas was partly due to the growth of the reading public and increased affordability of printed text.

The Enlightenment as an intellectual movement was diverse and varied: the *philosophes* argued and disagreed on many questions they debated; they changed their opinions; their intellectual debate was also taken up by others, as many novelists, journalists, social thinkers, scientists and even pornographers thrived on the ideas of freedom, pushing the boundaries of what was permissible and acceptable.

The French word *philosophe* means '*philosopher*', but in the context of the Enlightenment it is used to denote intellectuals, writers and thinkers who critically scrutinised the institutions, laws and society in general, often challenging established conventions in religion and forms of behaviour. The *philosophes'* approach was empirical, that is, based on evidence and experience, and sceptical because they questioned established knowledge and examined facts, opinions and beliefs. It promoted access to human knowledge based on reason not superstition. For this reason, the writings of the *philosophes* covered many topics including agricultural techniques, printing, draining swamps, metalworking and the organisation of society.

Among the most influential French *philosophes* were Montesquieu, Voltaire and Jean-Jacques Rousseau. The writings of these key thinkers, although they disagreed on many points, created a new language to discuss and define new understandings about how society should be ruled and organised. They also shaped the values and beliefs of the revolutionaries who led the transformation of France after 1789.

MONTESQUIEU (1689–1755)

Charles-Louis de Secondat Baron de Montesquieu (1689–1755) is usually known simply as Montesquieu. In his masterwork, *The Spirit of the Laws* (1748), Montesquieu contrasted England's parliamentary system of government with France's absolutist system. By highlighting Britain's constitutional monarchy, where power was shared between the king and the parliament, Montesquieu criticised the French system, which was kept from becoming despotic only by the activity of such 'intermediate bodies' as the *parlements*. Montesquieu's ideas were subsequently reworked and simplified to promote the notion that France needed independent institutions capable of limiting the power of the king and his ministers. In *The Spirit of the Laws*, Montesquieu proposed a system of government based on the 'separation of powers', the doctrine in which a system of checks and balances is established to prevent any form of arbitrary power dominating others. Montesquieu also advocated religious tolerance and criticised the use of torture.

DOCUMENT: *THE SPIRIT OF THE LAWS*, 1748

In every government there are three sorts of power: the legislative; the executive in respect to things dependent on the law; and the judicial in regard to matters that depend on the law. By virtue of the first power, the prince enacts temporary or perpetual laws, and amends or revokes those that have been already enacted. By the second, he makes peace or war, sends or receives embassies, establishes the public security, and provides against invasions. By the third, he punishes criminals, or determines the disputes that arise between individuals ...

When the legislative and executive powers are united in the same person ... there can be no liberty; because concerns may arise that the same monarch should enact tyrannical laws, to execute them in a tyrannical manner. Again, there is no liberty, if the judiciary power is not separated from the legislative and executive. When it is joined with the legislative, the life and liberty of the subject would be exposed to arbitrary control; for the judge would be then the legislator. When it is joined to the executive power, the judge might behave with violence and oppression.[25]

VOLTAIRE (1694–1778)

Voltaire was a poet, playwright and pamphleteer. In the period when French works were read by educated people throughout Europe, Voltaire was widely regarded as the foremost literary figure in France. Like Montesquieu, he thought that the English parliamentary system had much to recommend it. He aimed his sharpest criticism at religious superstition, intolerance and fanaticism. Voltaire denounced injustice and intolerance; however, he questioned the ability of uneducated ordinary people to make sound political decisions and favoured an enlightened absolutist monarchy.

In 1763 Voltaire published the *Treatise on Tolerance* in which he drew attention to the existence in France of religions other than Roman Catholicism. The work was published in the wake of the trial and cruel execution of Jean Calas (1698–1762), a French Protestant shopkeeper from Toulouse who was accused of murdering his son Marc-Antoine because of his rumoured intention to convert to Catholicism. Voltaire argued that this most shocking example of injustice was committed because of religious prejudice and intolerance. 'Ignoring such a thing', he claimed, 'is to abandon humanity'. Voltaire's defence of the Calas family brought quashing of the court's findings by King Louis XV in 1764, dismissal of the chief judge of Toulouse, and compensation of 36,000 francs paid to the family.

ROUSSEAU (1712–1778)

Rousseau was Swiss by birth but lived much of his life in France. He wrote on a variety of topics, including music, political philosophy and literature. His ideas had great influence in France, both before and during the revolution. In *The Social Contract* (1762), Rousseau advanced the idea of 'general will' or 'common good', suggesting that all people have a right to have their opinion heard, but whatever is best for the majority of the people needs to prevail.

Rousseau formulated his political theory of 'popular sovereignty': a government represents the general will of all the people, or 'social body' (the nation), in whose name it governs. Rousseau's idea of social contract was influenced by a number of writers such as John Locke and Thomas Hobbes. *The Social Contract* was, however, relatively unknown until the outbreak of revolution in 1789. Only after 1789 was it suddenly treated as a founding text of the revolution. Certainly, Rousseau did explore his ideas in his bestselling novels and his books were banned and even publicly burned. Among the future revolutionaries who acknowledged that they were heavily influenced by Rousseau's ideas was the revolutionary leader Maximilien Robespierre.

Rousseau's ideas also had an impact outside France. In 1782 Rousseau published his political theory treatise *Considérations sur le gouvernement de Pologne* (Thoughts on the government of Poland) where he applied the ideas of the social contract to constitutional reform that he envisaged for the Polish-Lithuanian Commonwealth. Rousseau also speaks of 'three orders: the nobles, who are everything; the bourgeois, who are nothing, and the peasants, who are less than nothing'.[26] In the long term, this work is thought to have influenced the preparation of the Constitution enacted on 3 May 1791 by the parliament of Poland-Lithuania—the constitution that was only the world's second modern written constitutional act; the first in Europe.

Rousseau himself feared social upheaval, but his ideas took on a new meaning in 1789 when the French people found themselves facing the challenge of establishing a new political system. The readership of Rousseau's works increased after the revolution began and he became an icon for the revolutionary leaders, who claimed his authority for their doctrines.

DOCUMENT: *THE SOCIAL CONTRACT*

The problem is to find a form of association which will defend and protect with the whole common force the person and goods of each associate, and in which each, while uniting himself with all, may still obey himself alone, and remain as free as before ... In order then that the social contract may not be an empty formula, it implicitly includes the undertaking, which alone can give force to the rest, that whoever refuses to obey the general will shall be compelled to do so by the whole body. This means nothing less than that he will be forced to be free; for this is the condition which, by giving each citizen to his country, secures him against all personal dependence.[27]

ENCYCLOPÉDIE

The ideas of Montesquieu, Voltaire and Rousseau were to a large degree reflected in the *Encyclopédie*, a work of 17 volumes edited by Jean d'Alembert and Denis Diderot and published between 1751 and 1765. The contributors to the *Encyclopédie* presented a full range of human knowledge by applying the critical and rational approach of the Enlightenment to many aspects of society. Over the course of the second half of the eighteenth century, the *philosophes* enjoyed growing influence and acceptance. This trend was a result of the secularisation of both politics and French society. The ideas of the *philosophes* were spreading among the literate public who prided themselves on being 'enlightened'. As some of these ideas were no longer seen as radical, it meant they were entering the mainstream. The success of the *philosophes* in presenting themselves as staunch opponents of despotism persuaded many of the French revolutionaries to claim them as precursors.

THE DEBATE ABOUT THE INFLUENCE OF THE ENLIGHTENMENT

Among historians there is much debate about how far the *philosophes* and their ideas undermined the *ancien régime* and influenced the development of the revolution. The issue is not so straightforward even though the revolutionaries often referred to the *philosophes* as their precursors in the opposition to absolutism and despotism. The idea of Norman Hampson that the Enlightenment was the direct cause of the French Revolution was rejected by William Doyle who claimed that only one-third of the French were literate and thus the majority were not able to absorb the new ideas disseminated in writing.[28] On the other hand, Sarah Maza argued that it is undeniable that Voltaire's extremely witty comments on the Church, Montesquieu's cautions about the dangers of despotism, and the publication of a voluminous *Encyclopédie* containing many sacrilegious ideas, contributed to lowering respect for the institutions of the *ancien régime* among readers.[29] There is no doubt that in France there was a great demand for newspapers, magazines, dictionaries and encyclopaedias, but the French, reveals Robert

Darnton, mostly bought satirical and pornographic pamphlets targeting the royal family, which in the years preceding the revolution further destroyed the aura of divine right.[30] All these arguments are perhaps best summarised by Peter McPhee and Daniel Roche: the acceptance of the ideals of the Enlightenment was a symptom of a crisis of authority which allowed the break with tradition.[31]

For David Garrioch, the key influence of the Enlightenment was its challenge of received wisdom and effect on the eighteenth-century reading public. The writers and thinkers disseminated their ideas in plays, novels and pamphlets, and through the *Encyclopédie*, reviews and articles, reaching a wide audience even if their more theoretical works were little read.[32] Above all, the key factor in the impact of the *philosophes* was the networks they established through correspondence, which facilitated the exchange of ideas between intellectuals and educated elites. The correspondence was now full of a new language that enabled the debate of what was previously either not considered or was debated only in terms of religion. George Rudé gives examples of some of this new common political vocabulary which included such terms as 'citizen', 'general will', 'nation', 'social contract', and 'the rights of man'.[33]

The *philosophes* influenced not only the elites of France, but also the rest of the world, which was dominated at the time by Europe and North America. Economic, political, legal and social reforms were seen as necessary and often enacted by ministers and bureaucrats. The enlightened bishops acted against 'superstition' by promoting education and empowerment of individuals. Over time, these changes created a climate within which the new ideas became acceptable, and their appreciation encouraged others to consider issues that had not previously been publicly debated. In this sense the ideas of the Enlightenment undermined the ideological foundations of the *ancien régime*.

REFORM, BANKRUPTCY AND THE ARISTOCRATIC REVOLT

Throughout the second half of the eighteenth century, the king's government recognised that in order to maintain its international standing and meet its domestic obligations the king needed more revenue. The issue of changing the level of taxes, broadening their base, and the manner of their collection illustrated the institutional problems facing the monarchy. In theory, the king as an absolute monarch had no need to negotiate with any representative body before he collected traditional taxes and maintained the right to do so without going through any consultative process; he was the sole legislator as the law emanated from him as the sovereign. The process was facilitated by the limited role of the Estates-General, which successive French rulers did not convene after 1614. This prerogative of an absolute ruler had a significant weakness: there was no regular mechanism for negotiating an increase in taxes as the kingdom's needs grew. To add to this problem was the issue of an awkward and inefficient system of tax collection. Tax farmers, usually wealthy entrepreneurs, paid the treasury a set fee for the right to collect taxes in a given region, which resulted in several different tax-collection regimes that could not be coordinated or managed to deal with the royal income fluctuations.

The king's ministers made repeated efforts to increase taxes and make the French economy more productive, but they had come to realise that partial reform was inadequate and they had begun to propose sweeping reforms of the fiscal system. For example, in 1776, Jacques Turgot tried to open up France's economy by pursuing a number of free-market policies, but popular protests and opposition from the *parlement* defeated him. He realised the true state of the royal finances and warned that 'the first gunshot will drive the state to bankruptcy', arguing against France's participation in another war.

Turgot's successor, Jacques Necker, a Swiss banker, tried to save money by abolishing some 506 venal offices, with a saving of about 2.5 million *livres* a year, and improving tax collection.[34] In the spirit of the Enlightenment, Necker also introduced representative assemblies to give provincial public opinion some voice in administration and at the same time to offset the power of the *parlement*. In February 1781, Necker caused a sensation by publishing his *Compte rendu*, a summary of the government's income and expenses. This gave the public more information than it had ever had before and publicised the seemingly prosperous state of France's finances. Necker claimed that existing taxes were more than sufficient to cover normal expenditures, but he did not disclose the size of the loans that had financed the French support for the American War of Independence; by May 1781, he had raised 520 million *livres* in loans. Necker's claims were 'exactly the kind of spurious good cheer', claims Simon Schama 'that led the French monarchy down the primrose path to perdition'.[35]

Schama acknowledged, however, that Necker was not only a prudent, but a determined reformer who, like Turgot before him, recognised that France's prosperity depended on its economy developing without restraints. Necker concentrated on achieving direct savings by rationalising the administration and streamlining the revenue. Yet, the *Compte rendu* became Necker's downfall. He trusted that the public support would enable him to be promoted to the king's council from which his Protestant faith excluded him. When Louis XVI refused, Necker resigned. The effects of the *Compte rendu* were to be felt in the years to come. Whenever the king's ministers highlighted the Crown's financial difficulties, the public would distrust any proposed countermeasures, remembering that finances had been under control in Necker's time. In fact, the state of the Crown's finances became so identified with him that his resignation caused a substantial loss of public confidence.

The fact that so many reforms were undertaken exposed the fundamental problems undermining the French monarchy and pointed to the erosion of many long-established customs and institutions. With each of these attempts at reform threatening the privileges of various interest groups, those who stood to lose defended themselves by challenging the king's right to change laws and customs protected by tradition. Historians conclude that the conflicts that preceded the revolution were not simply a by-product of an outdated and inefficient structure of government. They were deeply rooted in France's complex, hierarchical social structure. When the steadily worsening financial position forced Louis XVI to allow his subjects to express their views, the king learnt that neither the nobles nor the commoners were prepared to accept changes from above without questioning them.

DOCUMENT: NECKER ON FINANCES OF THE STATE

Having devoted all my time and my strength in the service of Your Majesty ... it is important for me to give you some public explanations concerning actual state of the finances. [The publication of the annual budget] if it became permanent, would be the source of the most important improvements because it would also allow each of the people, who are part of Your Majesty's Councils, to study and follow the situation of the finances ... It could have the greatest influence on public confidence. And all the lenders who regularly know the proportion that is maintained between incomes and expenses are not troubled by suspicions and fanciful fears ... In France, the state of Finances has always been a mystery ... The sovereign of a kingdom such as France can always, when he wants, maintain the balance between ordinary expenses and incomes. The reduction of expenses, which is always the wish of the public, belongs to the King. When circumstances require, only he has the power to increase taxes. But the most dangerous is to blindly look for some temporary aid, and to borrow either through increases of income or through savings.[36]

ASSEMBLY OF NOTABLES

The man who persuaded Louis XVI of the necessity for extraordinary measures to head off bankruptcy was Charles-Alexandre de Calonne, controller-general since 1783. By 1786, the king's government faced the immediate problem of repaying a debt of 3.3 billion *livres* which required about 165.4 million *livres* per year in interest payments.[37] The money borrowed to pay the cost of France's support of the American rebels against Britain comprised about 30 per cent of the total liabilities. Again, the financial crisis faced by Louis XVI's government was directly linked to the effort to maintain France's role as a world power.

In the decision that would prove to be the first step towards the revolution, Calonne asked the king to convoke an Assembly of Notables, an advisory body to the king, which in 1787 comprised 144 notables, with no more than five who were non-noble. The purpose of this assembly was to endorse radical yet fundamental changes in the fiscal privileges of the privileged orders, the clergy and nobles, but the king's decision to summon the notables was nonetheless a sign of weakness in the monarch. It exposed Calonne's fear that the Crown lacked the authority to enforce the reforms without some appearance of consultation with the tax-payers. In February 1787, at the Assembly of Notables, Calonne proposed the ending of the existing *vingtièmes* together with all the exemptions, the reduction of the *taille* and *gabelle*, and the abolition of internal customs barriers. The abolished taxes were to be replaced by a permanent universal land tax, payable by all landowners and administered by the newly established provincial assemblies, thus giving the nobles an increased role in the management of taxation. Calonne's plan was based on proposals formulated by Turgot and Necker but he lacked the support of the notables. They recalled the optimistic accounts presented by Jacques Necker in his *Compte rendu* and contrasted it with Calonne's spending on ambitious royal projects such as the new naval harbour at Cherbourg. Between 1783 and 1786 Calonne attempted in fact to reassure the Crown's creditors by financing such major projects. The notables also realised that Calonne's proposal gave the Crown a permanent source of income without the ability of the *parlements* to intervene when the king's ministers proposed new taxes.

Calonne's proposals were rejected by the notables representing the interests of the Second Estate, who insisted that only a gathering of representatives of the three orders in the Estates-General could agree to such extensive changes in the fiscal arrangements of the kingdom. One of the notables, Marquis de Lafayette, wrote to his friend, George Washington, questioning the right of the Assembly of Notables to represent the whole of France, and remarked that he felt he could not endorse the taxation proposals unless he knew of the planned savings in the Crown's expenditure. In the months following the meeting, observers such as Arthur Young also commented that the state of the Crown's finances was such that any attempt to solve the situation was impossible without the king summoning the Estates-General; and its meeting would necessarily cause great changes in the way France was governed. Typically, when faced with opposition, the king lost interest in pursuing his reform agenda. He dismissed Calonne and gave the reins of government to the Archbishop of Toulouse, Étienne Charles de Loménie de Brienne. Brienne was also unsuccessful in convincing the notables of the need for reform, and as soon as he realised the futility of the Assembly, he dissolved its session. The Assembly of

Notables was a turning point, marking the beginning of a political crisis, which was only to be resolved by revolution.

KEY INDIVIDUAL: CHARLES-ALEXANDRE DE CALONNE (1734–1802)

Calonne was an administrator with a long career in the Crown's service, serving as the intendant of Metz (1768) and of Lille (1774). He enjoyed the reputation of a staunch supporter of the absolute royal prerogative, reinforced by the persistent gossip that he was involved in the drafting of Louis XV's speech delivered at the 'Session of the Scourging'. His skill in the management of finances and his support for an influential court faction brought him to the attention of Louis XVI, who appointed Calonne as the controller-general of finance in November 1783. Calonne's management of the Crown's financial position focused on maintaining public confidence though building projects and spending, which was mainly designed to maintain the Crown's capacity to borrow funds. His major reform proposal crystallised in 1786 and involved increasing taxation of the First and Second Estates through a proportional tax on land. The implementation of such a reform needed not only the king's approval but, in the absence of the regularly summoned Estates-General, a form of consultation with the various sections of the French population. Calonne recognised that the *parlements* were likely to reject his proposals if he submitted them as the king's edict for registration and opted instead for an endorsement by a specially convened Assembly of Notables, which began deliberating on 22 February 1787. The Assembly proved to be his downfall and Calonne was dismissed; within months he had left France for England, where he actively criticised the course of revolutionary change. Calonne returned to France shortly before his death.

DOCUMENT: THE ASSEMBLY OF NOTABLES, 1787

Calonne presented Louis XVI with a broad programme of administrative and financial reform, aiming to increase royal revenue by ending the tax privileges of the clergy and nobility. Calonne argued that the annual deficit of nearly 100 million *livres* was largely caused by servicing the Crown's debt and that a new, fairer and more efficient tax levied on wealth was needed. He presented the plan to the Assembly of Notables, seeking its endorsement.

His Majesty is convinced on establishing the principle of uniformity in the distribution of the land tax by the application of the just proportionality, of restoring the original intentions behind the tax, of raising it to its true value without increasing anyone's contribution, and of making every kind of privilege incompatible with its mode of collection. [Therefore, it is proposed] to replace the *vingtièmes* with a general land tax which, covering the whole area of the kingdom, would consist of a proportion of all produce, payable in kind where feasible, otherwise in money, and allowing no exception, even as regards his crown lands. The church lands would inevitably be included in this general assessment which, to be fair, must include all land.

Complete freedom of the grain trade with the allowance for deferring to the wishes of the provinces when any of them think it necessary temporarily to suspend export abroad ... The abolition of the *corvée* performed in person and the conversion of this excessively harsh burden to a monetary contribution and spent only for that purpose. Internal free trade, with customs houses removed to the frontiers, the establishment of a uniform tariff taking the needs of commerce into consideration, the suppression of several taxes which are harmful to industry and the alleviation of the burden of the *gabelle*.[38]

THE BIRTH OF 'PUBLIC OPINION'

The Assembly of Notables was crucial to the development of a revolutionary situation, because like the publication of Necker's *Compte rendu* the meeting publicised the state of the Crown's finances. Until the 1780s the nation's financial position had 'always been a mystery', with the Crown not held accountable to the taxpayers for the expenditure. In the face of the notables' opposition to his proposals, Calonne published his speech and the issue of the state of finances became a subject of public debate, with his proposals and pamphlets criticising him being circulated widely.

In the context of a general increase in the readership of a variety of printed works, the financial position of the Crown became another topic discussed by women and men who engaged in debate on political, social and economic issues. The phrase 'public opinion' became accepted as an acknowledgement of the growing collective body of those interested in national life. Those who read often shared their opinions with likeminded individuals in the privacy of their homes, but increasingly new forms of information exchange emerged. In cities such as Paris educated nobles and bourgeoisie met informally and often regularly in private *salons*. These gatherings became safe spaces where women, for whom public office was denied and political participation was limited, exerted a degree of influence in a social setting open to debate and opinion making. Across France, public reading rooms facilitated access to broadsheets, journals and books, thus democratising access to printed matter. Not all material read was political and economic, with a lot of poems, plays and essays, as well as pamphlets, often on subversive topics, including topics such as the state of the royal marriage and the 'Affair of the Diamond Necklace', which brought further desacralisation of the monarchy and exposed the Church's prelates to further criticism.

The increased interest in all matters affecting the life of the nation brought together groups of reform-minded intellectuals, including those of a younger generation, who grew up and were educated according to the principles of the Enlightenment. Among them individuals such as the future revolutionaries, Jacques-Pierre Brissot (1754–1793), one of the founders of an abolitionist society, the *Société des amis des Noirs* or *Amis des noirs* (Society of the Friends of the Blacks), Marquis de Lafayette (1757–1834), hero of the American War of Independence, Marquis de Condorcet (1743–1794), a philosopher, mathematician, and advocate of equal rights for women and the abolition of slavery, Henri Grégoire (1750–1831), a Catholic priest who supported the emancipation of the Jews and the end of slavery, and Honoré Gabriel Riqueti, Count Mirabeau

(1749–1791), a writer, orator and promoter of the constitutional monarchy. The growth of public opinion fed on these men's ideas for France to be governed according to a new set of constitutional arrangements in the spirit of uniformity and merit.

THE ARISTOCRATIC REVOLT

The Aristocratic Revolt started with the Assembly of Notables and lasted until the meeting of the Estates-General in May 1789. During this period, the authority of the king's government rapidly eroded. The term 'Aristocratic Revolt' was originally used by Georges Lefebvre to describe the period before 1789 when the most vocal opposition to the king's reform initiatives came from members of France's noble elite rather than from the bourgeoisie and other members of the Third Estate. Lefebvre interpreted the opposition of the reactionary landed nobles as a response to the growth of an increasingly prosperous bourgeoisie. More recently, historians, including William Doyle and Simon Schama, have questioned such an interpretation and argued that the liberals among the nobles accepted the need for change and their rejection of royal arbitrary power made them the 'first revolutionaries'. Yet, the very fact that the Assembly of Notables was dismissed in May 1787 without resolving the issue, argues Michael Fitzsimmons, created a perception that the notables were unwilling to give up their fiscal privileges to resolve the financial crisis affecting whole country.

Peter McPhee sees the refusal of the nobility to endorse the king's ambitious reform of the fiscal system as the result of the lack of their participation in the government of the kingdom and the social and economic challenge posed by the Third Estate, and in particular the wealthier bourgeoisie and an openly disaffected peasantry. The claims of the nobility of 'ministerial despotism' resonated strongly with the public, who by now lacked confidence in the government. William Doyle argues that Calonne's whole strategy misfired because he naively assumed that the notables would accept there was a crisis, and Calonne's plan was the best approach to solving it. Following Calonne's dismissal in April 1787, his successor, Loménie de Brienne, brought ever-wider circles of the population into vocal opposition to the monarchy's reform package.

Étienne-Charles de Loménie de Brienne, who replaced Calonne as minister of finance, sought to get the *parlements* to approve amended versions of Calonne's proposals. He resorted to exiling the judges of the Parlement of Paris to weaken their resistance and worked out a compromise by promising to convene the Estates-General in 1792. In exchange, he asked the *parlements* to approve an extension of tax surcharges introduced to finance the American War of Independence. This plan did not succeed because when the Parlement of Paris met on 19 November 1787 to ratify this plan, Louis XVI ordered the judges to register his edict instead of allowing a semblance of judicial independence and permitting the judges to discuss it freely. The judges refused to obey the command. With the compromise not possible, the king's government abolished the *parlements* altogether and replaced them with a single high court for the whole country. The attempt to abolish the *parlements* opened a public debate that went beyond the issues of fiscal reform. This debate raised questions about the power of the king, the king's relationship with the nation, and who ultimately had the power to make laws for the kingdom. The examples of Britain and the United States served as powerful inspiration to those who demanded a political voice in the government of France. The dismissed Assembly of Notables had already suggested a solution—calling together the Estates-General, the representatives chosen from the three estates who had the power to present grievances to the king and to consent to new fiscal arrangements.

Such thinking was expressed in the statement of the Parlement of Paris, made on 3 May 1788, which declared that France was a monarchy governed according to a number of fundamental laws that defined the rights of the monarch, on the one hand, and those of his subjects on the other, including the right of the Estates-General to give its consent to changes in taxes levied by the king, as well as the independence of judges, and the traditional laws of provinces.

By early August 1788, the treasury was virtually empty and Brienne resigned in favour of Jacques Necker. Necker's return, together with the recall of the *parlements*, produced a temporary calming effect. It was during this period that the election of deputies to the Estates-General occurred.

DOCUMENT: FUNDAMENTAL LAWS ACCORDING TO THE PARLEMENT OF PARIS, 3 MAY 1788

The court, with all the chambers assembled and the peers present, amply warned by public knowledge and notorious fact of the coup d'état which threatens the nation by striking at the magistrature ... and leaves the nation no other resource but a precise declaration by the court of the maxims it is charged with maintaining ... Declares that France is a monarchy governed by the king in accordance with the laws. That of these laws several are fundamental and that these include:

- The right of the reigning house to succeed to the throne in the male line according to primogeniture with the exclusion of females and their descendants.
- The right of the nation to grant taxation freely in an Estates General regularly convoked and of fixed composition.
- The customs and capitulations of the provinces.
- The irremovability of magistrates.
- The right of the courts in each province to verify the king's legislative volition and to proceed to its registration only in so far as it is conformable to the basic laws of the province as well as the Fundamental Laws of the state.
- The right of every citizen, whatever his offence, to appear only before his peers as defined by law.
- And the right, without which all the others are of no avail, to appear before the competent judge immediately after arrest, no matter on whose orders.

The said court protests against any future violation of the above principles.[39]

HOW DID THE FINANCIAL CRISIS BECOME A POLITICAL CRISIS?

Historians take two general approaches to the issue of the developing revolutionary situation in France before 1789. On one side, there are those who see the revolution as the outcome of the push by the bourgeoisie, urban workers and peasants for political power; on the other, those for whom the revolution was an avoidable crisis that occurred when a reform-minded monarch attempted to execute his plans. In particular, the Assembly of Notables as the key event, which led directly to the development of the revolutionary situation, was variously interpreted. For Albert Goodwin (1946), the notables were selfish defenders of fiscal privilege, countering the king's proposal of reform.[40] A different interpretation was offered by Vivian Gruder (2007), who argued that the notables were seeking compromise and were willing to give up their fiscal privileges, but demanded a measure of control over royal finances.[41] John Hardman (2010) disagreed with Gruder, arguing that the notables were defending their fiscal interests, and attributed the failure of the Assembly to the refusal of Louis XVI to share his absolute power and Calonne's miscalculation in taxing declining agriculture.[42]

Albert Soboul and George Rudé have seen the causes of the revolution in the slow rise of the bourgeois class and the decline of the nobility, which arguably represented a culture less well adapted to capitalism.[43] Albert Soboul explained that:

> The Assembly of Notables, by definition a group of aristocrats ... after criticizing the planned tax, demanded a statement of the Treasury's accounts. The paralysis of the monarchy that resulted from the quarrel between the King and the nobility led to revolution: The bourgeoisie, the leading element in the Third Estate, now took over. Its aim was revolutionary: to destroy aristocratic privilege and to establish legal and civic equality in a society that would no longer be composed of orders and constituted bodies. But the bourgeoisie intended to stay within the law. Before long, however, it was carried forward by the pressure of the masses, the real motive force behind the revolution.[44]

Similar conclusions were reached by George Rudé and Peter McPhee. Rudé wrote that: 'The Notables refused to endorse ministerial reforms because their own cherished fiscal immunities were threatened.'[45] McPhee pointed to 'The entrenched hostility of most nobles towards fiscal and social reform'.[46] He also suggested that:

> Further attempts at reform foundered on the nobility's insistence that only a gathering of representatives of the three orders as an

> Estates-General could agree to such innovation. Tension between Crown and the nobility came to a head in August 1788, with the *parlements* insisting that the measures that the King's ministry sought to impose amounted to 'royal despotism'.[47]

Simon Schama's profoundly different interpretation of the sources resulted in his claim that the privileged orders were far ahead of Calonne and were willing to sacrifice their own rights because of their

> shared sense of the historical moment that prompted their display of patriotic altruism. Allotted the role of a dumb chorus, they suddenly found that, individually and collectively, they had a powerful voice—and that France was paying attention. This abrupt self-discovery of politics was intoxicating and there are signs that though they are usually dismissed as the tail end of the old regime, with respect to political self-consciousness the Notables were the first revolutionaries.[48]

In a masterly use of allegory, Schama provided an illustrative parallel: 'It was rather as if he [Calonne] had set out to drive an obstinate mule with a very heavy wagon, only to find that the mule was a racehorse and had galloped into the distance, leaving the rider in the ditch.'[49]

Like Schama, David Andress pointed to the progressive ideas: 'much in the deliberations of the Notables suggested they, too, were finding new ways of thinking'.[50] William Doyle commented on the growth of public opinion as for the first time the Crown's financial issues were openly discussed:

> All these proceedings had formally taken place in secret. The public was agog to have news of the Assembly, rumours abounded, and a good deal of more or less accurate information leaked out. It fuelled a flurry of pamphleteering, most of it hostile to the ministers. In addition to despotism, profligacy, and incompetence, it was now alleged ... that Calonne was also guilty of shady stock-exchange dealings.[51]

CONCLUSION

The tensions within the rigid social order based on privilege and tradition and the outdated institutions of the state prevented the

French monarchy from responding to financial pressures caused by French imperial ambitions. The absolute monarchy faced demands for constitutional reform in exchange for consent to reform the fiscal system. When the attempted reforms stalled, radical solutions were sought to resolve the stalemate, with the convocation of the only body representing the population of France, the Estates-General.

NOTES

1 Alfred Cobban, 'The "Parlements" of France in the Eighteenth Century', *History* 35, no. 123/124 (1950): 64–80, here 64.

2 William Doyle, *Old Regime France* (Oxford: Oxford University Press, 2001), 157.

3 Louis Auguste, *Réflexions sur mes entretiens avec M. le duc de La Vauguyon* (Paris: J. P. Aillaud, 1851), 88.

4 Excerpts from the transcript of the 'Session of the Scourging' (3 March 1766), in Keith Michael Baker, ed., *The Old Regime and the French Revolution*, University of Chicago Readings in Western Civilization (Chicago: University of Chicago Press, 1986), 47.

5 Simon Schama, *Citizens. A Chronicle of the French Revolution* (London: Penguin, 1989), 39.

6 Jean-Louis Soulavie, *Mémoires historiques et politiques du règne de Louis XVI*, 6 vols (Paris: Treuttel et Würtz, 1801). Published in English as Jean-Louis Soulavie, *Historical and Political Memoirs of the Reign of Lewis XVI*, 6 vols (London: G. & J. Robinson, 1802).

7 Carolyn Harris, *Queenship and Revolution in Early Modern Europe. Henrietta Maria and Marie Antoinette* (New York: Palgrave Macmillan, 2016), 31–47.

8 Doyle, *Old Regime France*, 228–229.

9 Derek Beales, *Joseph II* (Cambridge: Cambridge University Press, 1987), 372–375.

10 William Doyle, *The French Revolution. A Very Short Introduction* (Oxford: Oxford University Press, 2001), 22.

11 Wendy Doniger, *The Ring of Truth and Other Myths of Sex and Jewelry* (New York: Oxford University Press, 2017), 206–227.

12 From a speech by Chrêtien-François de Lamoignon, 19 November 1787. Philip G. Dwyer and Peter McPhee, eds, *The French Revolution and Napoleon. A Sourcebook* (London: Routledge, 2002), 1–2.

13 Peter McPhee, *The French Revolution, 1789–1799* (Oxford: Oxford University Press, 2002), 13; William Doyle, *The Oxford History of the French Revolution*, 3rd edn (Oxford: Oxford University Press, 2018), 33.

14 Doyle, *The Oxford History*, 33.

15 Doyle, *The Oxford History*, 28–29.

16 McPhee, *The French Revolution*, 16; Peter M. Jones, *The French Revolution 1787–1804*, 2nd edn (Hoboken: Taylor and Francis, 2014), 4; Doyle, *The Oxford History*, 28.

17 Doyle, *The Oxford History*, 28–29.

18 McPhee, *The French Revolution*, 16.

19 Doyle, *The Oxford History*, 16; George Rudé, *The Crowd in the French Revolution* (London: Oxford University Press, 1967), 33–34.

20 Doyle, *The Oxford History*, 16–17.

21 Arthur Young, *Travels during the years 1787, 1788, and 1789* (Bury St. Edmunds: J. Rackham, 1792).

22 Anoush Fraser Terjanian, *Commerce and Its Discontents in Eighteenth-Century French Political Thought* (Cambridge: Cambridge University Press, 2013), 53. Cf. Louis-Sébastien Mercier, Christophe Cave and Christine Marcandier-Colard, *L'an 2440 rêve s'il en fut jamais*, introd. et notes par Christophe Cave et Christine Marcandier-Colard, La Découverte-poche Littérature (Paris: Éd. la Découverte, 1999).

23 McPhee, *The French Revolution*, 6.

24 Denis Diderot, *Oeuvres complètes*, 20 vols (Paris: Garnier, 1875–1877), vol. 20, p. 28. Cited in Peter McPhee, *Liberty or Death. The French Revolution* (New Haven: Yale University Press, 2016), 25.

25 Charles de Secondat, Baron de Montesquieu, *The Spirit of the Laws*, Book 11, ch. 6, 1748.

26 Jean-Jacques Rousseau, *The Plan for Perpetual Peace, On the Government of Poland, and Other Writings on History and Politics*, trans. Christopher Kelly and Judith Bush, ed. Christopher Kelly, The Collected Writings of Rousseau (Hanover: Dartmouth College Press, 2005), 184.

27 Jean-Jacques Rousseau, *The Social Contract*, Book 1, ch. 6 and Book 1, ch. 7.

28 Doyle, *The Oxford History*, 47.

29 Sarah Maza, 'Politics, Culture, and the Origins of the French Revolution', *The Journal of Modern History* 61, no. 4 (1989): 704–723.

30 Robert Darnton, *The Literary Underground of the Old Regime* (Cambridge, MA: Harvard University Press, 1982).

31 Daniel Roche, *France in the Enlightenment*, trans. Arthur Goldhammer (Cambridge, MA: Harvard University Press, 1998), 485–487; McPhee, *The French Revolution*, 31–32.

32 David Garrioch, *The Making of Revolutionary Paris* (Berkeley: University of California Press, 2002), 1–11.

33 George Rudé, *Revolutionary Europe 1783–1815* (London: Fontana, 1985), 75.

34 Schama, *Citizens*, 89.

35 Schama, *Citizens*, 89.

36 Jacques Necker, *Compte rendu au Roi*, 1781.

37 Robert D. Harris, 'French Finances and the American War, 1777–1783', *The Journal of Modern History* 48, no. 2 (1976): 233–258, here 248.

38 Calonne, speech to the Assembly of Notables, Versailles, 22 February 1787.

39 John Hardman, *The French Revolution. The Fall of the Ancien Regime to the Thermidorian Reaction, 1785–1795* (New York: St. Martin's Press, 1982), 55.

40 A. Goodwin, 'Calonne, the Assembly of French Notables of 1787 and the Origins of the "Revolte Nobiliaire"', *The English Historical Review* 61, no. 240 (1946): 202–234; A. Goodwin, 'Calonne, the Assembly of French

Notables of 1787 and the Origins of the "Revolte Nobiliaire" (Continued)', *The English Historical Review* 61, no. 241 (1946): 329–377.

41 Vivian R. Gruder, *The Notables and the Nation. The Political Schooling of the French, 1787–1788* (Cambridge, MA: Harvard University Press, 2007).

42 John Hardman, *Overture to Revolution. The 1787 Assembly of Notables and the Crisis of France's Old Regime* (Oxford: Oxford University Press, 2010).

43 Albert Soboul, *A Short History of the French Revolution, 1789–1799* (Berkeley: University of California Press, 1977); Rudé, *Revolutionary Europe*.

44 Soboul, *A Short History of the French Revolution*, 37–38.

45 George Rudé, *The French Revolution* (London: Weidenfeld and Nicolson, 1988), 8.

46 McPhee, *The French Revolution*, 35.

47 Peter McPhee, *Living the French Revolution, 1789–1799* (New York: Palgrave Macmillan, 2006), 12.

48 Schama, *Citizens*, 144–145.

49 Schama, *Citizens*, 144.

50 David Andress, *French Society in Revolution, 1789–1799* (Manchester: Manchester University Press, 1999), 37.

51 Doyle, *The Oxford History*, 72.

THE REVOLUTION OF 1789

In this chapter we will examine the events that followed the refusal of the privileged orders to approve reform of France's fiscal system and the king's decision to convoke the Estates-General with the expectation of enacting the proposed reforms. When the Estates-General, representing the three estates of the French monarchy, met in Versailles, their delegates hoped to address more than just the king's reform package and brought with them their *cahiers de doléances*, or lists of grievances, that voters had drawn up in the electoral assemblies that elected the deputies. The *cahiers* called for a range of reforms and the drawing up of the lists had created an expectation that the issues would be addressed in Versailles. In addition to these hopes, the issue of how voting was to be conducted at the meeting excited the public.

An influential pamphlet entitled *What Is the Third Estate?*, written by Abbé Sieyès, a priest who was a deputy of the Third Estate, offered a range of radical solutions. In June 1789, these solutions were adopted by the Third Estate, which claimed political power by declaring itself the National Assembly. The emancipation of the Third Estate was completed when, on 20 June, locked out of their meeting place, its deputies swore an oath not to rest until France had a new constitution—the oath passed into the annals of history as the Tennis Court Oath.

A combination of rumour and radical agitation in response to the king moving troops close to Paris, and fear of the dissolution of the National Assembly, sparked an outburst of violence against the monarchy. When, on 14 July, a crowd of thousands of Parisians captured the old royal prison, the Bastille, the monarchy's authority

DOI: 10.4324/9781003157748-2

vanished. It became the signal for a peasant uprising in the provinces and gave the National Assembly an incentive to proclaim the
abolition of the remnants of feudalism. The new society was heralded with the *Declaration of the Rights of Man and the Citizen*, proclaiming 'the sacred' rights of man. The king's refusal to accept the
declaration inspired the Parisian crowd to take action again. There
was no turning back to absolute monarchy.

THE NATIONAL CRISIS AND HOPES OF REFORM

The convening of the Estates-General was caused primarily by the
inability of the Crown to finance the operation of the government,
but throughout 1788 there were also signs that royal authority was
breaking down outside Paris, with officials unable to contain pro-
parlement demonstrations. The opposition by the members of the
parlements to the reforming edicts of Louis XVI, argued Donald
Sutherland, was seen as defending the rights of the people.[1] The
public debate concerning issues of citizenship and taxation, which
began during the Assembly of Notables, raged – in particular in
the matter of 'ministerial despotism' and 'rights'. In what David
Andress called 'explicitly social discord', the public support of the
parlements' resistance turned into a direct challenge to absolute
divine right monarchy.[2] On 7 June 1788, in Grenoble, the capital
city of Dauphiné in south-eastern France, rioters turned against
royal troops, driving them out of the city. The support for the *parlements* came from artisans and domestic servants who stood on the
roofs of their houses and dropped tiles on the soldiers below who
had come to arrest the magistrates of the *parlements* according to
the king's *lettres de cachet*; the magistrates were hailed as defenders of
the people's rights.

The Day of the Tiles was the first outbreak of the political violence that would mark the revolution. In the growing disorder,
the nobility and bourgeoisie of Dauphiné decided to convoke the
provincial estates on their own authority with the doubled representation of the Third Estate. The representatives of the estates
were to form one assembly and vote 'by head'. In the meeting of
the three estates on 21 July 1788 at Vizille near Grenoble, they
agreed to the principle of fiscal equality, thereby demonstrating that
all three estates were actively contributing to the development of

the revolutionary situation. Among the leaders who actively took part in drafting resolutions proclaiming that 'the law should be the expression of the general will' were Jean-Joseph Mounier and Antoine Barnave, who argued that the example of the Dauphiné estates offered a greater public role for the Third Estate.[3]

The helplessness of the armed forces facing continuous urban disturbances should have been a warning sign to the privileged orders that inciting riot could have unpredictable consequences, with outcomes not limited to the radicalisation of popular demands. Economic conditions added to the pressure on the king's government. By the middle of 1788, French manufacturers faced greater competition as a result of a trade treaty with Britain negotiated in 1786. In July 1788, a catastrophic hailstorm damaged grain crops across northern France. Bread prices soared in anticipation of a bad harvest and rioting engulfed Rennes and Dijon. So severe were the conditions that the Duke of Dorset, who travelled through France in the following months, was moved enough to note the misery of the poorest. These worsening economic conditions created an atmosphere of social unrest and also added a sense of urgency to the meeting of the Estates-General.

If the summoning of the Estates-General was intended to serve as a measure to calm the growing perception of national crisis, it had the opposite effect. New divisive questions were raised about the method of election of the deputies and the voting procedure. Traditionally, the Estates-General met in three separate chambers representing each of the estates. In practice, it meant that the deputies of all three chambers had to reach a compromise before the Estates-General could pass any resolution binding the king. The perception that the two privileged estates—the clergy and the nobles—could dominate the proceedings started to polarise public opinion.

THE MEETING OF THE ESTATES-GENERAL

The king's decision to formally call the Estates-General for 1 May 1789 set in motion a series of events that would not only limit his arbitrary power, but would usher in a new era in the history of France. On 25 September 1788, the restored Parlement of Paris prepared the guidelines for the Estates-General meeting.

The judges decreed that the estates of the kingdom would meet as separate orders, deliberating and voting separately, as they had done in the past. In the opinion of Bailey Stone, the Parlement of Paris simply followed an established procedure; however, Peter Jones argues the judges attempted to take over the initiative in the absence of leadership from the king's ministers.[4] The result was immediate and not favourable to the *parlements*: the public saw what they failed to notice during the struggle between the *parlements* and the king—the judges were another interest group attempting to take control of the Estates-General. The result of the *parlements'* decision changed the focus of the debate about the proceedings of the Estates-General, from the issue of the extent of royal authority to the relationship between the privileged orders and the Third Estate and the question of the political voice of commoners. In the words of the Swiss journalist Jacques Mallet du Pan, it had become a war.

That war manifested itself in the flood of hundreds of pamphlets which tackled the issues of political, social and economic reform. Some of the publications were sold, some were posted at street corners—all heightened the tension and added to the expectation of change. In the absence of clearly articulated proposals for reform coming from the king's government, the pamphlets filled the vacuum.

On 12 December 1788, the king was presented with the *Memoir of the Princes of the Blood* authored by the top-ranking reactionary representatives of the Second Estate. The Princes of the Blood called for the Third Estate to cease its attack on the rights of the first two estates, which they claimed were no less ancient than the monarchy and part of France's unchanging constitution. The signatories, including the king's youngest brother, the Count of Artois, defended the right of nobles to speak for the nation to the king through the *parlements* and the Assembly of Notables, a prerogative they refused to the commoners. The *Memoir* warned of dangers posed by radical suggestions of the Third Estate, particularly fiscal. The authors suggested that any reforms should be limited to the Third Estate's 'reduction in taxes' and that due to their 'generosity' the privileged orders would 'be able to renounce those prerogatives which have a financial dimension'.

DOCUMENT: *MEMOIR OF THE PRINCES OF THE BLOOD*, 1788

Your Majesty has stated to the Princes of the Blood that, when they wish to tell him what might be useful in his service and to the State, they may address themselves to him. The [Princes of the Blood] believe it to be their duty to respond to this invitation from Your Majesty. It is in effect the princes of the blood who by their rank are the first of your subjects, who by their position are your born counsellors, who by their rights are concerned to defend yours; above all, it is their duty to tell you the truth, and they believe it to be equally their duty to make known to you their feelings and thoughts. Sire, the State is in danger; your person is respected, the virtues of the monarch ensure the homage of the nation; but Sire, a revolution is brewing in the principles of government; it is being brought on by the ferment of opinion. Reputedly sacred institutions, which this monarchy has made to prosper for so many centuries, have become matters for debate, or are even described as injustices. The writings which appeared during the Assembly of Notables, the reports which have been delivered to the undersigned princes, the demands put forward by various provinces, towns or corporations; the objectives and the style of these demands and these reports: everything proclaims, everything reveals a system of deliberate insubordination and contempt for the laws of the State. Each author sets himself up as a legislator; eloquence or the ability to write, even when devoid of study, knowledge and experience, seems to be sufficient to determine the constitution of empires: whoever puts forward a daring proposition, whoever proposes to change the law, is sure of having readers and an audience. Such is the unhappy progress of this agitation that opinions which a short time ago might have seemed reprehensible, today appear to be reasonable and fair; and that which good people are indignant about today will in a short time perhaps pass as regular and legitimate. Who can say where the recklessness of opinions will stop? The rights of the throne have been called into question; the rights of the two orders of the State divide opinions; soon property rights will be attacked; the inequality of fortunes will be presented as an object for reform; the suppression of feudal rights has already been proposed, as the abolition of a system of oppression, the remains of barbarism ... May the Third Estate therefore cease to attack the rights of the first two orders; rights which, no less ancient than the monarchy, must be as unchanging as its constitution; that it limit itself to seeking the reduction in taxes with which it might be burdened; the first two orders, recognising in the third citizens who are dear to them, will, by the generosity of their sentiments, be able to renounce those prerogatives which have a financial dimension, and consent to bear public charges in the most perfect equality.[5]

WHAT IS THE THIRD ESTATE?

With the backdrop of ongoing debate, an influential pamphlet provocatively titled *What Is the Third Estate?* articulated a series of arguments challenging the continuing privilege of the nobles and calling for the emancipation of the French commoners. Its author, Abbé Sieyès, a clergyman, asked three radical questions, which he answered, and accused the nobles of self-interest. In his pamphlet, Sieyès contrasts the Third Estate with the nobility, which is privileged and elitist, and above all unrepresentative. The tone of Sieyès' writing is confident and incendiary, and he openly attacks the nobility as selfish. The representatives of the Third Estate, claimed Sieyès, were the rightful representatives of the will of the nation and without doubt could speak in the name of the nation. Sieyès' defiantly radical words made his readers more aware of the key issues facing the Estates–General and influenced the mood of the representatives of the Third Estate who gathered in Versailles for the opening of the Estates–General.

The most vivid popular illustration of the ideas expressed by Sieyès came in the form of the 1789 engraving carrying the caption 'We must hope that it will soon be over'. The image showed a peasant, representing the Third Estate, bent and supporting himself with his hoe and carrying the Clergy and the Nobility that reminded of the burden placed on the shoulders of the commoners.

The commoners, remarked French historian François Furet, would have a far greater affinity with the renegade Sieyès, who in the elections to the Estates-General stood for election as a deputy of the Third and not the First Estate.[6] At the end of 1788, says Furet, Sieyès raised the critical revolutionary idea—equality.[7] Indeed, Sieyès radically proposed that the Third Estate itself constituted the nation because its members performed the useful work in the country. When it was first published, no one suspected that Sieyès' words would become reality: the Third Estate 'had every right to proceed on their own, disregarding any objections of deputies from the privileged orders'.

KEY INDIVIDUAL: EMMANUEL JOSEPH SIEYÈS (1748–1836)

Sieyès had been born into a bourgeois family and was educated to be a Roman Catholic priest. After his ordination in 1773, Sieyès worked as secretary to the Bishop of Tréguier. In his pamphlet, *What Is the Third Estate?*, published in January 1789, Sieyès articulated his assessment of the problems facing France as a nation, and his vision, and offered radical solutions. These ideas, influenced by Rousseau, brought him to prominence in 1789 and he was elected as a deputy of the Third Estate to the Estates-General. He played a key role in the formation of the National Assembly and contributed to the drawing up of the Tennis Court Oath and the *Declaration of the Rights of Man and the Citizen*. As was the case with other 'men of 1789' who supported a constitutional monarchy, his influence waned when more radical ideas overtook events. Sieyès voted in 1793 for the execution of the king and survived the Terror. After Robespierre's fall in 1794 he became influential again. Sieyès retired from public life after helping clear the path for the political career of Napoleon, who seized power for himself in 1799.

DOCUMENT: ABBÉ SIEYÈS' *WHAT IS THE THIRD ESTATE?*

The plan of this work is quite simple. There are three questions that we have to ask of ourselves:

1   What is the Third Estate?—*Everything.*
2   What, until now, has it been in the existing political order?—*Nothing.*
3   What does it want to be?—*Something.*

Who then shall dare to say that the Third Estate has not within itself all that is necessary for the formation of a complete nation? It is the strong and robust man who has one arm still shackled. If the privileged order should be abolished, the nation would be nothing less, but something more. Therefore, what is the Third Estate? Everything; but an everything shackled and oppressed. What would it be without the privileged order? Everything, but an everything free and flourishing. Nothing can succeed without it, everything would be infinitely better without the others ... The noble order is not less estranged from the generality of us by its civil and political prerogatives. What is a nation? A body of associates, living under a common law, and represented by the same legislature, etc. Is it not evident that the noble order has privileges and expenditures which it dares to call its rights, but which are apart from the rights of the great body of citizens? It departs there from the common law. So its civil rights make of it an isolated people in the midst of the great nation. This is truly imperium in imperia. In regard to its political rights, these also it exercises apart. It has its special representatives, which are not charged with securing the interests of the people. The body of its deputies sit apart; and when it is assembled in the same hall with the deputies of simple citizens, it is nonetheless true that its representation is essentially distinct and separate: it is a stranger to the nation, in the first place, by its origin, since its commission is not derived from the people; then by its object, which consists of defending not the general, but the particular interest. The Third Estate embraces then all that

> which belongs to the nation; and all that which is not the Third
> Estate, cannot be regarded as being of the nation. What is the Third
> Estate? It is the whole.[8]

THE ELECTIONS TO THE ESTATES-GENERAL

During the elections to the Estates-General in early 1789, compromise between the privileged orders and the Third Estate was
still possible. The Third Estate, in the analysis of Michael Fitzsimmons, was prepared to accept social distinctions by order and to
acknowledge honorific privileges of the clergy and nobility, but
it would not agree to voting by order at the Estates-General.[9]
Necker persuaded Louis XVI to announce the 'doubling of the
Third' on 27 December 1788, overruling the objections of the
second Assembly of Notables (November–December 1788).
Louis' conciliatory gesture suggested that the Third Estate would
have more influence, but the king's edict provided no directive on
whether the approximately 600 deputies from the Third Estate
and the roughly 300 from each of the other two estates would
deliberate together as a single assembly or in separate chambers.
If in separate chambers, then the Third Estate's larger number of
deputies would have made no difference. Kenneth Margerison
and William Doyle agree that among the Third Estate and the
liberal nobles there was anticipation of all three estates uniting as
one body with the doubled representation of the Third Estate and
voting by head.[10]

The elections to the Estates-General created an expectation of
change. Across France, according to custom, men alone were called
to choose their representatives and to voice their views on the issues
the Estates-General should consider. The drawing up of *cahiers de
doléances* ('books of grievances') provides a snapshot of the concerns
of the French people on the brink of the revolution. The individuals and groups who put forward their concerns in the *cahiers* were
also hoping that the deputies would treat these as instructions on
the issues to be debated and how they should vote. The *cahiers*
were a traditional part of the preparation for the Estates-General,
upholding the established rules of respect for the Crown. The

cahiers, which were written between February and April 1789, did not simply contain a respectable address to the king; they showed that a revolutionary situation had developed.

In summary, the *cahiers* of all three estates suggested a national consensus in favour of major constitutional reforms by advocating the creation of a system of representative government, which would limit the king's powers. The privileged orders seemed ready to accept the principle of equality of taxation and were united with the Third Estate in the call for the abolition of censorship. Yet neither the nobles nor the clergy foresaw the complete abolition of their order and creation of a secular society.

CAHIERS DE DOLÉANCES—BOOKS OF GRIEVANCES

The *cahiers* of the peasants contained appeals for broad reform mixed with local concerns and issues directly affecting their economic wellbeing, but on the whole represented a serious protest again the workings of the seigneurial system and the privileges of the nobility. The Third Estate *cahiers* were revolutionary in their demands. They revealed a deep frustration with existing conditions and a widespread demand for the end of most privileges, but they did not call for the abolition of the social structure of the estates or the end of the monarchy. John Markoff argues that all levels of society were open to change in the first months of 1789, but highlights that there was little agreement as to what that change might involve.[11]

John Markoff, together with Gilbert Shapiro, analysed a large sample of *cahiers* drafted on the eve of the meeting of the Estates-General of 1789 and concluded that the majority of grievances concerned taxation in general and indirect taxes in particular.[12] Complaints about taxation characterised 66 per cent of the peasants' grievances, but only 43 per cent of the Third Estate's as a whole, and 36 per cent of the nobility's.[13] At the parish level, 43 per cent of *cahiers* complained about the *gabelle* tax. In addition to tax concerns, regular sessions of the Estates-General, the key constitutional demand, featured in 95 per cent of *cahiers* of the nobility, and in 86 per cent of the Third Estate's *cahiers*, but only 21 per cent of the parish *cahiers* made a similar demand. Moreover, the nobility were very concerned about constitutional issues, such as the organisation and authority of the Estates-General, the establishment of personal liberty, the maintenance of private property, and the financial accountability of the king's government. The Third Estate, on the other hand, was more absorbed by issues related to its place in society and its commercial activities, demanding vote by head in the Estates-General, the abolition of internal customs duties, and careers open to talent in the military. While Alfred Cobban asserted that the *cahiers* rarely condemned the seigneurial system, Gilbert Shapiro has demonstrated that 64 per cent of Third Estate *cahiers* sought the abolition of specific seigneurial institutions.[14] In contrast, according to John Markoff, 84 per cent of noble *cahiers* were silent on the matter.[15]

DOCUMENT: *CAHIERS* OF THE FIRST ESTATE OF BERRY, 1789

The following extract from the *cahiers* of the First Estate of the province of Berry in central France includes the list of grievances compiled by the Catholic clergy, who thought of themselves as the leaders of the reform of the social order. Many parish priests who rose to the rank of the First Estate from humble origins in the Third were deeply concerned about the issues that affected the daily lives of their parishioners. The list of grievances below was compiled by the Dean of the cathedral of Bourges and 31 clergy members in the cathedral chapter.

Article 1 The chapter of the metropolitan church of Bourges will ceaselessly wish for the prosperity and long reign of His Majesty ...

Article 2 May it please His Majesty to order that all those who, through their writings, seek to spread the poison of incredulity and attack religion and its mysteries, discipline and dogmas, be seen as enemies of the Church and the State and severely punished; that printers be once again forbidden to print books contrary to religion; to forbid also bookshops and pedlars to spread such books. To order that judges, accompanied by educated and enlightened clergymen, designated by the bishop, will from time to time visit printers and bookshops, and that all the books contrary to religion and good morals be seized and confiscated, and that the said offending printers and bookshops will be prosecuted according to the severity of the law.

Article 3 The apostolic and Roman Catholic religion is the only true religion ...

Article 6 The spirit of religion and of piety is being extinguished in all social orders, the divine and human laws that order the sanctity of Sundays and holidays are violated publicly and with impunity, both in the city and in the countryside. The roads are full of carriages; workshops, shops, cabarets and gaming houses are open on these holy days, even during the hours devoted to the divine service and the education of the faithful. Abuses continue despite the severity of the laws ...

Article 9 For a long time the public has been upset by and complains about this innumerable crowd of ecclesiastics and benefice holders, who from all parts of the kingdom flood towards the capital (...). Cathedral churches are especially devoted to public worship ... but the cathedrals will soon be deserted if this multitude of useless commissions and positions is not abolished in the households of the king and the princes of the blood ...

Article 14 May it please His Majesty to reduce the overly widespread jurisdiction of the *Parlements*; to reduce also the number of courts of law; to simplify further the conventions of justice, and have the code—both civil and criminal—reformed ...

Article 16 All France sees the salt tax as the most disastrous of taxes, even though it weighs most unequally on different parts of this kingdom. Berry, which is in the region of greatest salt tax (grande *gabelle*), is one of the provinces which has the most reason to complain; besides the enormous sum that the salt it consumes costs it, and which is nearly equivalent to that of the direct tax (*taille*), poll tax (capitation) and ...[16]

DOCUMENT: *CAHIERS* OF THE SECOND ESTATE OF BERRY, 1789

This *cahier* was drawn up at the gathering of 11 noble representatives in Bourges, in the province of Berry, on 28 March

1789. Their *cahier* show some similarities to the *cahiers* of other estates, but also some striking differences including the insistence on the special role for nobles.

CONSTITUTION

Article 1 The deputies will seek to discuss any other matter ... only when they will have stated in the most positive manner and in the form of fixed and unalterable law:

1   the recognition of administrative power belonging fully to the king;
2   the rights of the nation to consent to laws as well as to grants [taxes], their sharing out and collection;
3   public and individual freedom, from which derives that of the press, guaranteed according to the law;
4   the sacred and inviolable right of property, the stability of the courts, the irremovability of their officers ...
7   the periodic return of the Estates-General;
8   the establishment of provincial Estates in each province ...

TAXES

Article 1 The deputies will present to the Estates-General a picture of abuses resulting from the arbitrariness employed in assessments of the *taille*, capitation, one-twentieth levies [*vingtièmes*], contributions to roads, and will demand the abolition, modification, combination or conversion of these taxes.

Article 2 They will demand the abolition of the salt tax and the replacement of this imposition by another that is less onerous ...

NOBILITY

The deputies of the order of the nobility of Berry at the Estates-General will ask:

Article 1 That all venal nobility be abolished.

Article 2 That the provincial Estates be able to present to the king those of their fellow citizens whose services rendered put them in the position of obtaining nobility ...

Article 4 That seigneurial justice be preserved (while taking the necessary measures to improve its administration), as well as all honorific and useful rights, inherent in lands or people, excepting all the same those of pure and personal servitude, which will always be repugnant to the generous heart of the nobility.[17]

DOCUMENT: *CAHIERS* OF THE THIRD ESTATE OF BERRY, 1789

Parish *cahiers* were collated into a general *cahier* for the Third Estate at a district level. This meant that district *cahiers* tended to reflect urban middle-class grievances and aspirations, just as the deputies were almost exclusively urban men from the professions, public service or commerce.

Article 1 That the Third Estate will have in perpetuity at the Estates-General a number of voters at least equal to that of the two other orders united; that the three orders will deliberate in common ...

Article 3 That a law can be made only with the participation of the king and the Estates-General.

Article 4 That no tax be legal or be collectable unless it has been consented to by the nation in the assembly of the Estates-General; and the said Estates can consent to it only for a limited rate, and until their following meeting, so that if this subsequent meeting is not held, all taxes will cease ...

Article 10 That the press will be free, on the condition that the author will remain responsible for what is produced. Printers will equally be responsible for anonymous writings ...

Article 13 That internal customs and duties collected on entering and leaving [the provinces] be abolished, and replaced by the duties collected on entering the kingdom ...

Article 17 That taxes remaining or to be established will be borne equally and on the same roll by all orders of the State, at the rate of individual properties or capacity to pay; and the Third Estate, sensitive to the justice and the disinterest of the first two orders of the province, cannot record their wish here without offering them testimony of their gratitude ...

Article 19 That provincial Estates will be established in Berry, organised in the same manner as those newly re-established in the province of Dauphiné ...

Article 23 That positions and offices without function be abolished, or at least that the salaries that accompany them be greatly reduced.

Article 24 That all non-Catholic subjects will enjoy all the rights of the citizen, with the exercise of public worship reserved only for the Catholic religion.

Article 25 That purely personal constraints, and other supposed duties resulting from the said personal constraints, as well as toll duties, will be abolished without compensation, and that the Estates-General will advise on ways to destroy the slave trade, and to prepare for the abolition of the slavery of Negroes.

Article 26 That landed and seigneurial dues, in wheat, cash and poultry, territory, banalités [monopolies], and all other real existing servitudes, as much over holdings in the country as in the towns, will be refundable to lords and ecclesiastic and secular property owners, without prejudice to the seigneurie and the rights of directe [justice]; the said refund will be made at the rate of twenty-five times the annual worth, according to the product of the last ten years ...

Article 30 That the laws excluding the Third Estate from civil and military ranks be abolished ...

Article 37 That the reformation of civil and criminal justice will be under-taken ...

Article 44 That there be, in the future, only one sole weight and one sole measure in all of France.[18]

THE ESTATES-GENERAL AND STALEMATE

On 3 May 1789, most of the 1,200 deputies to the Estates–General assembled in Versailles. The deputies came from almost all walks of life, from parish priests, provincial noblemen and lawyers to Church and royal officials with practical experience in public affairs and government. There were, however, no deputies who were peasants or urban working people. Some of the assembled deputies represented those who called for a radical makeover of the French system of government, but the deputies did not all arrive with clearly formulated agendas.

The majority of the deputies expected Louis XVI to play a major role, and his authority as king had been bolstered by renewed popular support. There was also strong expectation that the king's chief minister, Jacques Necker, would propose a credible solution to the fiscal crisis. It became apparent that these hopes would remain unfulfilled: Louis lacked the vision to put together a radical reform agenda and lead it to completion, and Necker had few specific proposals for the deputies to debate.

The inaction of the king and Necker left the Estates-General to resolve the fundamental issue of its proceedings: whether to vote by head, with the deputies of all estates united as one body and taking decisions by majority vote; or by order, with deputies remaining in separate chambers and voting only among their own estates. The voting procedure reflected the deep divide between two visions of French society: were male French citizens to have equal rights (women from all estates did not have the same rights as men), or were they to continue to be divided into different status groups separated by differing privileges?

The ceremonial costume worn by the deputies to the Estates-General reflected the division of French society into three estates and the associated culture of deference and social rank and hierarchy. It was a visible reminder of the legal and social distinctions between the estates. It reminded everyone of the composition of the Estates-General in three chambers, deliberating separately and voting by order. Simon Schama explains that the opening of the Estates-General was treated as an extension of court ceremony, rather than like a public occasion in which rank was disregarded. Instead of being inclusive, it closed space off, reflecting an anachronistic hierarchy, not the social reality of late eighteenth-century France in which station was eroded by property and culture. The more brilliant the pomp and dress of the clergy and nobility, the more they alienated the Third Estate and provoked it against the institution altogether. While the king received the deputies of the privileged orders in the *cabinet du roi*, those of the Third filed past him in another hall 'like a crocodile of sullen schoolboys'. Schama notes that their ceremonial dress was as plain as that of the clergy and nobility was lustrous. 'In black from head to foot, they looked like crows amidst peacocks or like stage caricatures of the bourgeois: a convention of apothecaries.'[19]

FORMING THE NATIONAL ASSEMBLY

The members of the Third Estate took the initiative and refused to work as a separate chamber, demanding that all three estates meet and vote together. The impasse reached its final stage when, after weeks of unsuccessful negotiations, on 10 June 1789 Abbé Sieyès moved that the Third Estate should issue its final invitation to the nobles and the clergy to form a single assembly. Sieyès suggested that if the privileged orders declined then the Third Estate deputies would carry on without them. Within a week, a handful of deputies from the clergy joined the Third Estate and, on 17 June 1789, they proclaimed that they were speaking for the whole nation and voted to assume the new name of National Assembly. They defiantly carried out what William Doyle considered to be the founding act of the revolution—they transformed a customarily consultative body into a deliberative, representative and policy-making body and paved the way for the proclamation of sovereignty as belonging to the nation.

The Third Estate's decision to assume the role of the sole national representative body, the National Assembly, challenged the other two orders and the authority of Louis XVI. The king, who was privately grieving after the death of his eldest son, the dauphin, had initially listened to Necker's advice. Necker proposed to offer a number of significant concessions to avert the radicalism of the leaders of the Third Estate. In the end, however, according to Simon Schama, the Count of Artois and the queen persuaded the king to 'confront the Estates in a grand plenary *séance royale*, simultaneously showing his paternal benevolence in reform and his august majesty in annulling the usurpations of 17 June'.[20]

Consequently, it was announced on 20 June that a special session of all three estates would take place on 23 June and the court officials began preparations for the royal session by locking the deputies' regular meeting hall. The deputies, fearing that Louis would annul the formation of the National Assembly, moved to a nearby indoor tennis court, the only building nearby that was large enough to fit their number. There, under the presidency of the astronomer Jean-Sylvain Bailly, they swore the unifying Tennis Court Oath, insisting on their 'unshakeable resolution' to continue to act as the representatives of the nation and vowing not to allow themselves to be dispersed until they had given France a constitution.

Jacques-Louis David's sketch, for a never completed painting, immortalised the Tennis Court Oath of 20 June 1789. Within the space of a large indoor tennis court, David placed the president Bailly as standing on a table to administer the oath; among the depictions of men throwing their hats in the air and saluting, David included other prominent figures: Abbé Sieyès (sitting just beneath Bailly); Mirabeau (right foreground, in a dark coat, striding forward); Barnave (just behind Mirabeau); Robespierre (right of centre, baring his breast with his two hands); Pétion (in front of Robespierre with his back turned); Barère (sitting at left, writing); and the three men of religion: the pastor Rabaut Saint-Etienne, the priest Abbé Grégoire, and the monk Dom Gerle (centre foreground). David also included a variety of figures in the public gallery including idealised women, children and members of the Royal Guard. Commenting on Jacques-Louis David's 'pictorial account of the Tennis Court Oath', Simon Schama equated the bolt of lightning with liberty that 'cracks over Versailles as a great gust of wind blows fresh air through the crowd-filled window spaces'.[21] David exalted the ideology of the new regenerated France: patriotism, brotherhood and sacrifice.

DOCUMENT: THE TENNIS COURT OATH

The National Assembly, whereas it is called on to lay down the Constitution of the kingdom, implement the regeneration of public order, and maintain the true principles of the monarchy, can be stopped by nothing from continuing its deliberations in whatever place it may be obliged to establish itself, and that finally, anywhere its members are gathered together, that is the National Assembly. It is decided that all the members of this Assembly will now swear a solemn oath never to

> separate, and to gather together anywhere that circumstances demand, until the Constitution of the kingdom is established and consolidated on solid foundations, and that the said oath being sworn, each and every one of the members will confirm this unshakeable resolution with their signature.[22]

THE KING'S RESPONSE AND HIS CAPITULATION

In his speech at the royal session held on 23 June 1789 Louis XVI stated that the declarations made by the National Assembly on 17 June were unacceptable to him and were therefore null and void. He offered some limited reforms, but his insistence on maintaining the rights and obligations of the individual estates encouraged further defiance of his authority. The final confrontation between the king and the deputies might have been averted if Louis had followed the more accommodating approach advised by Necker. Louis, however, did not count on the courage of the deputies, who three days earlier had sworn the Tennis Court Oath; he dismissed the act as empty posturing. When, after the king's speech, the Grand Master of Ceremonies ordered the deputies to leave the hall, Count Mirabeau, a nobleman from Provence elected to represent the Third Estate, demonstrated the resilience of those who had sworn the oath three days earlier and rebelliously declared that they were there 'by the will of the people, and we will only be dispersed by the force of bayonets'.[23] This retort forever etched upon the popular imagination the image of the triumph of liberty over a despotic monarchy.

Through Mirabeau, the National Assembly stated plainly that their right to deliberate unhindered was based on the will of the nation and not hereditary or divine right. Sovereignty was no longer vested in the Crown but in the representatives of the nation. In the days that followed, 'patriotic clergy' joined the National Assembly, and on 25 June, 47 of the liberal nobility did the same. The stubbornness of the Third Estate deputies met with little resistance from the king, who abandoned the decisions outlined in his speech, and on 27 June Louis XVI wrote to the deputies of the two privileged orders asking them to unite. Thus the Estates-General came to an end by the hand of the king who had commanded it be assembled. Arthur Young, an English traveller who was in Versailles on the day Louis XVI capitulated, observed that 'The whole business now seems over, and the revolution complete'.[24] In the background, however, the government had begun to assemble troops near the capital; an indication that some factions at the court had not abandoned the possibility of using force to subdue radicalised deputies.

Historians offer opposite views about the potential use of military force to disband the deputies of the newly proclaimed National Assembly. The deputies were convinced that the king was prepared to use force against the National Assembly and had 'betrayed their trust and thrown in his lot with the nobility'.[25] Yet, writes John Hardman, evidence suggests that Louis XVI acted to protect the seat of the government and the royal family at Versailles rather than to use his army offensively. Barry Shapiro disagrees and sides with the position held for a long time by most historians that the king's intention was to dissolve the Assembly.[26]

On 7 July 1789, the deputies gave another strong indication of their intention to provide France with a new constitution, by changing the name of the National Assembly to the National Constituent Assembly. They also decided that from that day onwards the only binding mandate of the deputies was to serve the best interests of the nation as a whole. In this way, argues William Doyle, all distinctions between deputies of different orders would vanish forever. They were no longer bound by the *cahiers*.[27]

While the court considered its next move, the people of France had already begun to take their country's future into their own hands. The growing expectation of change that accompanied the 1789 elections to the Estates-General produced an environment in which popular unrest stemming from worsening economic conditions encouraged local revolts across France. In March, riots shook Marseille, and on 27 and 28 April Parisian workers sacked the house and factory of the wallpaper manufacturer Réveillon, accusing the owner of forcing lower wages on his employees. The Réveillon riot saw several houses and businesses pillaged and left several rioters dead after troops intervened firing into the crowd. In Paris, the public awaited news from Versailles, which was about 20 kilometres away. Crowds gathered in public places to share the reports from the National Assembly and listen to speeches by excited political orators. The public overwhelmingly supported the actions of the Third Estate and were suspicious of the intentions of the privileged orders.

While public excitement ran high, the king was persuaded by his courtiers to remove Necker, whom they held responsible for the emancipation of the Third Estate despite his lack of leadership during the first month of the Estates-General. The dismissal of Necker, who still maintained the aura of reformer, on 11 July 1789 brought the people of Paris out onto the streets. In the days that followed, Parisians surrounded royal arsenals in the city, demanding weapons and expressing their fears that troops would be used to disperse the National Assembly. In Simon Schama's view, after the rioting, Paris was lost to the monarchy; military intervention was no longer possible.[28] The king's army commanders warned the government that they could not rely on their men to fight against the Parisians. To William Doyle, the moment when the king could no longer enforce his will signified the end of royal authority.[29]

THE FALL OF THE BASTILLE

The warning about the loyalty of the royal troops proved prophetic on 14 July 1789. Faced with the soaring bread prices, Parisian women, returning home from their daily errand of securing food for their families, 'made their husbands go out and urged them on, telling them, "Get going, coward, get going"'.[30] On Paris's left bank the crowd that surrounded the buildings of the Invalides had successfully seized muskets from its stores after soldiers refused to fire on them. Later that day, some soldiers from the Paris regiments joined a crowd of up to 8,000 who were demanding gunpowder and weapons from Marquis Bernard René Jourdan de Launay, the governor of the Bastille, an imposing fortress which served as a prison. The fortress had no strategic military significance, but for Parisians it represented despotic royal authority; on that day only seven prisoners and a hundred troops were there. No one knows who fired first but to those surrounding the fortress it seemed that the soldiers who were defending the prison fired on the crowd, killing almost 100 and wounding many more. The Parisians, incensed by their inability to access the gunpowder and weapons stored at the Bastille, stormed and captured the prison, immediately making it the symbol of the newly born popular revolutionary movement.

An account of the fall of the fortress published in a Parisian newspaper, *Les Révolutions de Paris*, on 14 July 1789 describes the advance of the French Guards and armed bourgeois after the governor's flag of peace was raised. The newspaper reports that approximately 600 of the revolutionaries who entered the Bastille before the drawbridge was raised were trapped inside and were fired upon. The text describes the eagerness of the rallied militia as it besieged the fortress, commenting on the bravery of those who advanced beneath ceaseless rounds of fire. It continues to the celebration of the conquest, the massacre of the officers and ends with the statement that the 'glorious day must amaze our enemies, and finally usher in for us the triumph of justice and liberty'. The fall of the Bastille became the symbol of victory of liberty over despotism, and in the eyes of Parisians they saved the National Assembly from the danger of counter-revolution.[31] When, in 1790, the 954 officially recognised 'conquerors of the Bastille' were honoured, their number included one woman, the laundress Marie Charpentier, with the oldest of the revolutionary heroes aged 72, and the youngest a boy of 8.[32] Among the 'conquerors of the Bastille' all classes of society were represented, wrote Georges Lefebvre, with a particularly large number of artisans from the faubourg Saint-Antoine.[33]

The scenes of the people returning victorious from the Bastille were immortalised in the painting 'The Conquerors of the Bastille in front of the City Hall 14 July 1789' by Paul Delaroche, who was commissioned in 1839 to celebrate the heroes of the day. In vivid colours the image glorifies the arrival of the victorious crowds at the City Hall. There, soldiers, artisans, women and children carry the spoils of the battle in a triumphal procession: a man carried on other's shoulders holds the keys to the fallen fortress, a wounded woman supports herself on the arm of a man holding a rifle, a child carries broken chains, and the royal standard is dragged carelessly on the ground.

In the wake of the fall of the royal fortress, on 15 July 1789, Louis XVI recalled his troops and reappointed Necker. In Versailles, the king, flanked only by his brothers, the Count of Provence and the Count of Artois, addressed the deputies, denying that there were any plans to use the troops to disband the Assembly. Two days later, the king travelled to Paris where he accepted a tricolour cockade from Sylvain Bailly, the new mayor, and addressed the crowd from the balcony of the Hôtel de Ville, telling them that they could always count on his love. The symbolism of the event was apparent to the bystanders: the monarch and his people were reconciled once more. For Louis, once an absolute ruler, the recognition of the will of the people was an admission of his own defeat as much as an acknowledgement of reality.

A contemporary etching captioned 'Awakening the Third Estate' captures the essence of popular feeling in July 1789. On the ground, the figure representing the Third Estate awakens from the nightmare of the *ancien régime*, breaks the chains of servitude and reaches for weapons. The figures representing the clergy and nobility are shocked and seem to panic. In the background, the Bastille is being demolished, and decapitated heads of those lynched on the day are paraded on pikes. The image reverberates with earth-shattering change: a new order is emerging secured by the ability of the Third Estate to fight for its rights.

The actions of the Parisian crowd gave the reform-minded deputies of the National Assembly a much needed show of public support and endorsement, legitimising the shift in power. The violence unleashed during the storming of the fortress was brutal—the fortress's governor, the Marquis de Launay, was lynched by the crowd and his head, sawn off by a butcher, placed on a pike and marched through the street—and it demonstrated how quickly popular action could turn to punitive violence.

The seizure of the Bastille had several other implications for the development of the revolutionary situation. It gave the control of Paris to members of the Third Estate under a new municipal government led by the astronomer Sylvain Bailly, the mayor, and a bourgeois citizens' militia, the National Guard, commanded by the hero of the American War of Independence, Lafayette. Across France the royalists were forced to recognise the improvised municipal councils led by men loyal to the National Assembly who derived their authority from the support of the local population. Louis XVI was now finally forced to accept that the Estates-General he had summoned for advice had been replaced by a new body claiming representation of the whole nation. The National Assembly was constituted not of orders but of deputies with the mission to create a constitution.

Now united in purpose and insistence on their responsibility to the nation, the deputies who proclaimed themselves the National Assembly challenged absolutism and privilege. The bloody capture of the Bastille, writes Peter McPhee, indicated that the Parisian working people claimed the cause of the National Assembly as theirs too, and it 'sent shock waves both across the kingdom and all of Europe'. The deputies personified the people's will, which it was the Assembly's duty to interpret and implement.[34]

THE GREAT FEAR

In the weeks that followed the fall of the Bastille the social order of the *ancien régime* was challenged by the wave of peasant insurrections, which demonstrated that the peasants wanted the end of the seigneurial rights. During the period that came to be known as the 'Great Fear', peasants attacked the households of the local nobles in many rural regions, occasionally killing their owners and burning their chateaux, but more often forcing their *seigneurs* to release the charters which stipulated peasants' special obligations to the local *seigneurs*. Simon Schama notes that despite the myth of the lynching of *seigneurs*, the fatalities were remarkably few. Yet, this flood of disobedience completed the breakdown of royal authority. The popular violence in the countryside, argues Schama, reflected the population's desire for security. If true that the intent behind the disturbances was not revolutionary, their impact definitely was.[35] The situation presented the National Assembly with an opportunity to enact significant reforms. At the same time, the deputies of the National Assembly faced the task of restoring order in Paris and across France. The country faced a power vacuum, with royal authority diminishing day by day.

THE ABOLITION OF FEUDALISM

The storming of the Bastille by the Parisian crowd provided the National Assembly in Versailles with an extraordinary measure of popular support. But the outburst of violence in Paris on 14 July and the peasant revolts in the country demonstrated to the deputies that the revolutionary violence could not be easily controlled. Within two months of the fall of the Bastille, the deputies defined the principles on which the new society would be based. On the night of 4 August 1789, encouraged by the reports of rural revolts, the deputies from the privileged orders embarked on the most revolutionary legislative programme since 17 June: representatives of the clergy moved to abolish tithes; deputies from the provinces gave up their exemptions from taxes and customs fees. Church, government and military positions were made open to all citizens, regardless of rank or birth. On a wave of patriotic enthusiasm the deputies announced their desire to 'abolish the feudal regime entirely', which, while inspirational, was also open to interpretation. The great importance of the August Decrees, according to Peter McPhee, was also that it signified the age of privilege was over, as the French would now all enjoy the same rights and be subject to the same laws.[36]

THE AUGUST DECREES

Enacted between 4 and 11 August 1789, the August Decrees were an expression of the wish to abolish the feudal regime in France. The deputies, however, clarified that two key parts of the feudal system needed to be separated: that of the individual ('personal servitude') and that of property ('seigneurial dues'). Consequently, all of the feudal institutions and practices considered to be 'personal servitude' (such as serfdom, *corvées*, seigneurial courts, hunting rights) were abolished with immediate effect, but peasants would only stop paying property rights (such as dues payable on harvests) when they could compensate the lords for their losses. Similarly, the Assembly announced the end of the tithe and some taxes but insisted that they continue to be paid. Citizens could hold any military, ecclesiastical or civilian job. The symbolism of the August Decrees, like that of the fall of the Bastille, was resounding, if ambiguous because of the unresolved issue of the last vestiges of feudalism. The *ancien régime* was no more. France ceased to be a class society. The French were no longer subjects. France was now a nation of citizens equal in rights before the law, a historic fact never to be reversed. Within the month, the National Assembly enacted the blueprint for the new society with the *Declaration of the Rights of Man and the Citizen* (26 August 1789). The 17 articles of the declaration defined the fundamental principles of a new society based on equality, individual rights and a representative government.

DOCUMENT: THE AUGUST DECREES ON FEUDALISM, 4–5 AUGUST 1789

Article 1 The National Assembly destroys the feudal regime completely. It decrees that both feudal and censuel [that is, levied on crops] rights and dues which stem from real or personal servitude or mortmain [a lord's inalienable hold over some land], and those who represent them, are abolished without compensation; all the others are declared redeemable, and the price and the manner of the redemption will be set by the National Assembly. Those of the said rights that are not abolished by this decree will continue nonetheless to be collected until redemption has been made.

Article 2 The exclusive right to bird shelters and dovecotes is abolished. Pigeons will be confined for periods determined by communities; during this time, they will be regarded as game, and each man will have the right to kill them on his land.

Article 3 The exclusive right to hunting and open rabbit warrens is equally abolished, and any property owner has the right to destroy and have destroyed, on his own property alone, any type of game, except in conformity with police regulations that may be made in relation to public safety. All *capitaineries* [hunting jurisdictions], even royal ones, and all hunting preserves, under whatever denomination, are equally abolished; and the preservation of the personal pleasures of the king will be provided for in a manner compatible with the respect due to property and liberty. The President will be given the responsibility of requesting from the king the freeing of galley slaves and those banished for the simple fact of hunting, the release of prisoners currently detained, and the abolition of the existing procedures in this respect.

Article 4 All seigneurial courts are abolished without compensation, but nonetheless the officers of these laws will continue their duties until the National Assembly has provided for the establishment of a new judicial order.

Article 5 Tithes of any nature, and taxes that take their place, under whatever denomination that they be known and collected ... are abolished ... Other tithes, whatever they are, can be bought back ...

Article 6 All perpetual loans ... can be bought back. Any kind of harvest share can also be bought back.

Article 7 Venality of judicial fees and municipal offices is abolished. Justice will be dispensed at no cost. And nevertheless officers holding these offices shall fulfil their duties and be paid until the assembly finds a way to reimburse them.

Article 8 County priests' casual offerings are abolished and the priests will not be paid anymore.

Article 9 Financial, personal, or real privileges are abolished forever. Every citizen will pay the same taxes on everything.

Article 10 Every specific privilege of provinces, principalities, regions, districts, cities and communities of inhabitants, either in the form of money or otherwise, are abolished.

Article 11 Every citizen, whatever their origins are, can hold any ecclesiastic, civilian, or military job.[37]

THE DEBATE ON THE DECLARATION OF RIGHTS

On 11 July 1789, just days before the storming of the Bastille, Marquis de Lafayette, a liberal noble, proposed in the National Assembly the idea of providing France with a written declaration of the rights of its citizens. A hero of the American War of Independence, Lafayette was influenced by the *American Declaration of Independence* of 1776.

The debate started by Lafayette continued for some time and a number of deputies rose to speak on his motion. Lafayette said that the declaration would contain the key principles of the constitution and could therefore be often referred to by the deputies. He argued that these principles would 'recall the sentiments that nature has engraved on the heart of every individual' and 'express these eternal truths from which all institutions should be derived'. In short, Lafayette stated the declaration would become for deputies 'a loyal guide that always leads them back to the source of natural and social right'.[38]

On 1 August 1789, another deputy, nobleman Mathieu de Montmorency, who together with his father served on the side of the rebels in the American War of Independence, rose to express his support for the proclamation of the declaration as a preamble to the constitution. 'One does not draw conclusions without having posed principles', Montmorency warned, and concluded that 'it is important to declare the rights of man before the constitution, because the constitution is only the continuation, the conclusion of this declaration'. He argued that 'the rights of man in society are eternal; no sanction is needed to recognise them'. 'The rights of man are invariable like justice, eternal like reason; they apply to all times and all countries'. Above all he stressed that 'the declaration be clear, simple, and precise; that it be within the reach of those who would be least able to comprehend it'.[39]

On the same day Mathieu de Montmorency spoke, deputy Pierre Malouet disagreed with the notion that American models could be adapted to suit France with her traditions and larger population. He called for 'more action and reflection than speechifying', because the nation was awaiting 'order, peace, and protective laws'. He contrasted the 'American society, newly formed … composed in its totality of landowners already accustomed to equality, foreigners to luxury as well as to poverty, barely acquainted with the yoke of taxes' and 'no trace of feudalism', with France with her 'immense multitude of men without property who expect above all their subsistence from an assured labour, right regulation, and continual protection' who 'become angry sometimes, not without just cause, at the spectacle of luxury and opulence'. He stressed that he did not believe that 'this class of citizens does not have an equal right to liberty' but he argued that 'the rights of man in society should be developed and guaranteed by' a constitution, to which the declaration 'should be the introduction'.[40]

DECLARATION OF THE RIGHTS OF MAN AND THE CITIZEN

The National Assembly's idealistic hope that the new society the French were embarking upon would be totally different from that of the past was expressed in the declaration's stirring preamble. Influenced by the ideals of the Enlightenment, the *American Declaration of Independence* and the English *Bill of Rights* (1689), the deputies claimed that 'ignorance, neglect, and scorn of the rights of man are the sole causes of public misfortunes'. The articles of the declaration rejected the principles underlying absolute monarchy and its hierarchical social system with entrenched privilege, but despite the arguments of Nicolas de Condorcet, the declaration did not extend the equality of rights to women. Article 1 stated powerfully that 'men are born and remain free and equal in rights'.

Article 2 defined the purpose of government as guarantor of the rights of individuals to 'liberty, property, security, and resistance to oppression'. Article 3 declared that the supreme authority in France belongs to its citizens and not the king alone. Consequently Article 6 states that 'law is the expression of the general will', echoing Rousseau's *Social Contract*, implying that all citizens have a right to participate in the legislative process either by themselves or through their representatives. Article 4 gave a very broad definition of liberty as 'anything that does not harm another person'. This new liberty was linked with that of security in other articles of the declaration, and with prohibition of arbitrary arrest (the infamous *lettres de cachet*), announcement of religious tolerance (Article 10) and freedom of expression (Article 11), although the declaration also stated that those fundamental rights could be limited by law. Article 12 called for a 'public force' to uphold the law 'for the advantage of all', and the following article provided for taxes 'shared equally among the citizens' to finance the operation of government functions. Article 14 asserted the principle that there should be no taxation without representation. Article 15 affirmed government accountability with the citizens possessing 'the right to require every public official to account for his administration'. Article 16 proclaimed that any society which does not guarantee the rights of citizens, or where the separation of powers does not provide for the system of checks and balances of government, has effectively no constitution, implying that absolutist regimes lacked legitimacy. This article, which required the sovereign power to be accountable, was a principal revolutionary element of the French Revolution. The declaration's seventeenth and final article indicates that the deputies were uneasy about attacks on rural estates, with a specific reference to the nature of property as 'inviolable and sacred'.

The declaration heralded the birth of a new society, with citizens enjoying extensive rights and protected by a system of government. The authors of the declaration at the same time spoke to the world at large and—as Norman Hampson argued—triumphantly proclaimed their faith in men's ability to govern their affairs by the light of reason.[41] The declaration established universal concepts valid not only for France, but also for all nations.[42]

The fundamental nature of the *Declaration of the Rights of Man and the Citizen* is reflected in its imagery as it has been published and 'posted on the walls in all public places and even in the homes of peasants; it has been used to teach children to read'.[43] Popular symbolic representations of the *Declaration* are often full of allegorical elements with the articles of the *Declaration* written on two tablets resembling the tablets with the ten commandments of Moses; the eye of wisdom overlooks the scene; a crowned female figure representing France holds the broken chains; the fasces (a bundle of rods containing an axe, which was an emblem of power for the magistrates of ancient Rome) topped with the cap of liberty represent unity and strength; the snake biting its tail signifies infinity; and the angel with the sceptre denotes authority.

By the time of the completion and enactment of the Constitution in 1791, the *Declaration* had acquired 'a sacred and religious character', wrote one of the deputies, Jacques-Guillaume Thouret, 'It has become the creed of all the French'.[44]

DOCUMENT: *DECLARATION OF THE RIGHTS OF MAN AND THE CITIZEN*, 26 AUGUST 1789

The representatives of the French people, constituted as a National Assembly, considering that ignorance, forgetfulness or disregard for the rights of man are the sole causes of public misfortunes and of the corruption of governments, have resolved to set out, in a solemn declaration, the natural, inalienable and sacred rights of man, so that this declaration, constantly present for all the members of the social body, may ceaselessly remind them of their rights and their duties; so that the acts of the legislative body and those of the executive body, being comparable with the goal of all political institutions, be the more respected for it; and so that the demands of citizens, based henceforth on simple and incontestable principles, may be always directed towards the maintenance of the Constitution and the happiness of all men. Consequently, the National Assembly, in the presence and under the auspices of the Supreme Being, recognises and declares the following rights of man and of the citizen:

1   Men are born and remain free and equal in rights. Social distinctions may only be based on common usefulness.
2   The goal of every political association is the preservation of man's natural and imprescriptible rights. These rights are liberty, property, security, and resistance to oppression.
3   The principle of all sovereignty resides essentially in the nation. No body or individual may exercise authority that does not expressly emanate from it.
4   Liberty consists in being able to do anything that is not harmful to others. Thus, the only limits to the exercise of the natural rights of each man are those that ensure the enjoyment of the same rights for other members of society. Only the law may determine these limits.
5   The law has the right only to forbid acts that are harmful to society. Anything that is not forbidden by the law may not be prevented, and no one may be constrained to do what it does not command.
6   The law is the expression of the general will. All citizens, or their representatives, have the right to work solemnly towards its formulation. It must be the same for all, whether it protects or punishes. All citizens, being equal in its eyes, are equally admissible to all public dignities, posts and employment, according to their abilities, and without any distinction other than that of their virtues and their talents.
7   No man may be accused, arrested or detained, other than in those cases determined by the law, and according to the conventions it has prescribed. Those who solicit, expedite or execute arbitrary orders, or have arbitrary orders executed, must be

punished; but any citizen who is summoned or apprehended by virtue of the law, must obey immediately; he makes himself guilty through resistance.

8   The law may only establish punishments that are strictly and clearly necessary, and a man may be punished only by virtue of a law that is established and promulgated prior to the crime, and legally enforced.

9   All men being presumed innocent until they have been declared guilty, if it is deemed indispensable to arrest a man, any severity that is not necessary in the apprehension of his person must be severely repressed by the law.

10   No man may be harassed for his opinions, even religious ones, as long as their manifestation does not trouble the public order established by the law.

11   The free communication of thoughts and opinions is one of the most precious rights of man; thus any citizen may speak, write and print freely, on condition that he will have to answer for the abuse of this freedom in those cases set down by the law.

12   Guaranteeing the rights of man and the citizen necessitates a public force: thus this force is instituted for the benefit of all, and not for the individual use of those to whom it is entrusted.

13   To maintain the public force, and for administrative costs, a common tax is indispensable; it must be equally divided among all citizens, on the basis of their property.

14   All citizens have the right to observe for themselves, or through their representatives, the need for public taxation, to consent to it freely, to scrutinise its use, and to determine the quota, the basis on which it is assessed, its payment and duration.

15   Society has the right to request an account of his administration from any public agent.

16   Any society in which the guarantee of rights is not ensured, nor the separation of powers established, has no constitution.

17   Property being an inviolable and sacred right, no man may be deprived of it, unless in cases where public necessity, legally recorded, clearly demands it, and on condition of just and prior compensation.[45]

THE OCTOBER DAYS—HUNGER AND ANGER

Louis XVI's position as the sovereign and absolute ruler of France was effectively eroded by the decrees proclaimed by the National Assembly. In the months following the fall of the Bastille, the king did not openly oppose any of the fundamental reforms that restructured government and altered the cornerstones of society. On 10 September the National Assembly voted on one of the first constitutional principles of the new society, deciding that the French parliament, the National Assembly, would be unicameral. The next day it was decided that the king would have the power of 'suspensive veto'. This power would allow the king to postpone but not to cancel legislation proposed by the National Assembly. On 19 September, the king declared his qualified acceptance of the August Decrees and the *Declaration of the Rights of Man and the Citizen* in writing.

The many reservations included in the king's statement read much more like a rejection than an acceptance. In the end, Louis did not give royal assent to the Assembly's legislation and the deputies who wanted his cooperation became increasingly uneasy about the king's attitude towards these two documents heralding the principles of the revolution. Some of the deputies began questioning Louis' sincerity towards the new society the National Assembly was eager to establish and their cautious distrust further raised public suspicions about the king's intentions. These suspicions were reinforced when the public learnt about an army regiment being deployed to Versailles, ostensibly to protect the court at Versailles; and in particular when the exaggerated details of the lavish welcoming reception for the regiment were published on 2 October. The story that caused an uproar in Paris was the report that the patriotic tricolour cockade had been trampled underfoot by the soldiers. The circulating rumours coincided with the sharp increase in bread prices in Paris. Bread was the staple food and its purchase could take as much as half of a worker's wages. George Lefebvre estimates that in 1789 a Paris worker earned on average some 30 to 40 sous a day and if bread prices rose above 2 sous a pound the worker's family faced the possibility of starvation. In the first half of July 1789 the price of bread was twice this figure;

in October the price rose again.[46] The worsening food crisis highlighted the public's perception that the king and the court were
contemptuous of the reforms of the National Assembly. The discontent was focused on the king and, for the second time in 1789,
Parisians intervened to defend a revolution they themselves identified with. This time it was the women of the markets in particular
who associated the daily struggle to secure food for their families
with lack of support from the king for both the August Decrees
and the declaration.

On 5 October, a large crowd of women, including a large number of market women, assembled at the Hôtel de Ville (Town Hall),
demanding the mayor of Paris take action to protect the revolution. They ransacked the place and took rifles, muskets and cannons
before setting out to march to Versailles, dragging cannons and
followed by the National Guard under the command of Lafayette,
who like a prisoner of his own troops had no option but to join
in. The marchers reached the royal palace late at night and clashed
with the king's guards. Shocked by the violence, Louis capitulated
and agreed to their demands: he and his immediate family would
from now on reside in Paris. The deputies of the National Assembly
decided to follow the example of the king and moved their seat to
the capital city as well.

On 6 October 1789, the marchers, carrying the severed heads
of the royal guards on pikes, led the convoy carrying the royal
family to Paris. They shouted that they were bringing 'the baker,
the baker's wife and the baker's boy' (the king, queen and their
son) back to the city. The events had a similar effect to the storming of the Bastille on 14 July. These two days, known later as the
'October Days', set a precedent; they were, in Peter McPhee's
view, another key moment in the revolution of 1789; they showed
that violence perpetrated by the crowd could influence the course
of national politics as it exerted pressure on both the king and the
Assembly.[47]

Edmund Burke, who abhorred the frenzy of the revolutionary crowd of the October Days, ascribed unearthly features to
revolutionary women. He called them 'the unutterable abomina-
tions of the furies of hell, in the abused shape of the vilest of
women' who followed 'the royal captives' 'amidst the horrid yells,

and shrilling screams, and frantic dances'.[48] 'Probably you mean', responded Mary Wollstonecraft, 'women who gained a livelihood by selling vegetables or fish, who never had had any advantages of education'.[49]

Popular engravings of the October Days focused on the actions of women, often showing the victorious market women hauling cannons, armed with lances, pitchforks, swords, pistols, and muskets. Some depictions exposed class differences with market women attempting to persuade bourgeois women to join them. Others gave prominence to the figure of Anne-Josèphe Théroigne de Méricourt, depicting her in a red jacket on a white charger leading the advance of the Guard of Women on 5 October 1789 and thus perpetuating the myth of her involvement in the October Days. Her character would in time became the target of attacks in Parisian pamphlets and the press as she campaigned, unsuccessfully, for women's rights.

JOURNAL DE PARIS—A PARISIAN NEWSPAPER ON THE OCTOBER DAYS

The *Journal de Paris* was founded in 1777 as the first French daily for the educated middle class. On 8 October 1789 the newspaper's commentary on the 'recent upheavals' reported on the 'anxiety which has been felt for some time about the capital's food supply' caused by 'the difficulty encountered for some days in getting bread'. This 'popular discontent' 'gained new force' with the details of 'a military banquet given last week by the Royal Guardsmen at Versailles' during which 'attitudes quite contrary to the public spirit and the national interest' were displayed. The article acknowledged that 'these incidents have perhaps been exaggerated' but argued that they gave 'rise to legitimate cause for concern, and to reawaken the suspicions and fears that were only just beginning to calm down' after the events of July and August. Lafayette was credited with calming the situation on 4 October but on the following morning 'a large group of women' arrived at the Town Hall shouting 'bread, bread!'

> They made their entry *en masse*, and soon they were followed by a crowd of men, armed for the most part with pikes and sticks.

They broke down the doors, seized weapons and ammunition, and spread out from there to the various quarters of Paris ... The general tumult soon set in motion a hundred detachments of armed citizens. No longer did they speak of bread; it was only a question of going to Versailles, but for reasons which were as vague as they were varied.[50]

A SHIFT IN THE BALANCE OF POWER

The action of the Parisian women, which forced the royal household and the Assembly to transfer to Paris, significantly altered the balance of power. With the royal family and the National Assembly based in Paris, both became hostages of the people of Paris, whose capacity for violence was now undeniable. The Assembly recognised the danger to public order and to themselves of unrestrained demonstrations. On 21 October 1789, the deputies enacted the *Decree on Martial Law*, which stipulated that any demonstrations that were not approved by the authorities of Paris would be treated as a criminal act and the National Guard could be used to restore order. Different paths to revolution were emerging. The Assembly wanted to concentrate on writing a constitution for France and to maintain law and order. The crowd were now convinced that direct action could achieve their goals because they were the defenders of the revolution. This self-perception was further reinforced by their belief that the revolution was theirs, as sovereignty resided with 'the people'.

JUSTICE IS ON THE STRONGER SIDE

An image entitled 'This time Justice is on the stronger side' illustrates the changes that occurred during the course of 1789 in the relative positions of the three estates. The fall of the Bastille and the October Days changed the balance of power in France to the benefit of the Third Estate. In this allegorical depiction, the artist draws on Justice's traditional representation as a woman with the attributes of a blindfold, scales, and a sword. In the etching, Justice is transformed into evolutionary Justice. The scales, one of the attributes of Justice, are replaced by a seesaw. The artist used a seesaw as a visual representation of the idea of a change in the balance of power. The figure of Justice gives authority to this new power relationship and actively establishes it by placing her foot on the seesaw to rebalance it. She does not wear a blindfold, yet she is still armed with a sword. The image can be understood as a commentary on the events of 1789 during which the Third Estate's significance evolved. The chronology of events establishes the growing importance and political power of the commons: the declaration of a National Assembly (17 June), followed by the Tennis Court Oath (20 June), the refusal to disperse (23 June), and the uniting of the orders (27 June). In addition, in the image the Third Estate now holds a rifle, a reference to its newly acquired strength: the capture of the Bastille (14 July), which forced the king to withdraw the troops, to recognise Bailly as mayor of Paris and to confirm the formation of the National Guard commanded by Lafayette. The meaning is simple: in this new regenerated France the Third Estate had assumed more importance and now outweighed the once dominant privileged orders.

HISTORIANS AND THE REVOLUTION OF 1789

Historians' interpretations of the revolution of 1789 are not uniform, but at the same time not totally conflicting. Broadly, the differing views are a reflection of the historians' position on the nature of the revolutionary struggle. Was it the emerging social classes in a bid for political power, social empowerment and wealth, or was it an extension of the inability of the monarchy to control the reforms it initiated and the increasing appetite of the Third Estate for a real voice in the government of France?

In his discussion of the composition of the Estates-General, William Doyle highlights the fact that Necker, who expressed the opinion that 'government interference in the elections would do more harm than good', himself manipulated the electoral rules to ensure that 'the electoral assemblies of the first estate were dominated by parish priests rather than members of the ecclesiastical corporations who had hitherto monopolized the government of the Church'.[51] Moreover, Necker 'excluded from the second-estate assemblies all new nobles whose status had not yet become fully hereditary, and swamped formerly dominant groups, such as courtiers and sovereign court magistrates, with petty nobles of long lineage, slender means, and little public experience'. Significantly, 'the indirect system adopted for the third estate effectively eliminated peasants, artisans, and everybody without abundant leisure from the stage at which deputies were chosen, while allowing the possibility of electing members of the other two orders'.[52] Peter McPhee agrees with Doyle and gives figures that confirm Doyle's assertions. For the First Estate: '208 of the 303 chosen were lower clergy; only 51 of the 176 bishops were delegates'. But 'most of the 282 noble deputies were from the highest ranks of the aristocracy and were not inclined 'to accept the importance of surrendering at least fiscal privileges'.[53] No historian objected to Georges Lefebvre's assessment that 'Necker's dismissal was a torch set to a powder keg'.[54]

Moreover, both Doyle and McPhee agree that the storming of the Bastille was a triumph of the people of Paris who were now 'convinced that they alone had saved the National Assembly'[55] and 'would see themselves as guardians of the liberty won that day'.[56] McPhee, however, notes that while 'The Revolution of the bourgeois deputies had only been secured by the active intervention of the working people of Paris', the deputies were fearful of the influence the popular movement would exert on the revolution.[57] The increasing importance of the common people and their lack of hesitation in resorting to violence became the key element which propelled the revolution, for Simon Schama, who argues, 'From the very beginning ... violence was the motor of the revolution'.[58]

Michael Fitzsimmons sums up the consensus of historians as to the night of 4 August 1789, seen as 'a striking series of relinquishments ... driven by emotion, competition, and even a sense of theatre'.[59] But it is François Furet who offers the most enduring assessment:

> The decrees of August 4–11 number among the founding texts of modern France. They destroyed aristocratic society from top to bottom, along with its structure of dependencies and privileges. For this structure, they substituted the modern autonomous individual, free to do whatever was not forbidden by law.[60]

The destruction of privilege on 4 August set the principles of 1789: a new model for society based on freedom, equality and mutuality of the whole nation. The principles which were enshrined in the *Declaration of the Rights of Man and the Citizen* represented the 'most profound expression of the nature of the French Revolution'.[61]

The essence of 1789, wrote Robert Darnton, was the 'energy—a will to build a new world from the ruins of the regime that fell apart in the summer of 1789'.[62] Again, Fitzsimmons agreed:

> The principles of 1789 proclaimed the right of a people to break with its past and to create a constitution, laws, and institutions that it believed best met its needs, an assertion that permanently transformed the nature of revolution by henceforth making it a process of change and improvement.[63]

François Furet summed up the experience of 1789 in terms of the most profound changes:

> Until May, the old mode of political sociability, centred on the king of France at the summit of the social order, more or less held up—as the *cahiers* indicate—for the area of power he had in fact relinquished had not yet been discovered. But all that changed with the events of May, June and July. The victory of the Third Estate over the king, the capitulation of the First and Second Estates, the taking of the Bastille, and the vast popular excitement that preceded and followed it clearly went beyond the framework of the old legitimacy ... the king was no longer the king, the nobility was no longer the nobility, the Church was no longer the Church.[64]

The revolutionary events of 1789 saw the emergence of a new political force. 'The idea that women's actions had forced a decisive reversal of the relations between the king and the people', wrote Jeremy Popkin, 'underlined the degree to which the Revolution was putting fundamental aspects of French society into question'. The history of the revolution of 1789 would have been incomplete without acknowledging the role of women, even if men 'could not bring themselves to accept that women could intervene so force-fully in politics'.[65]

CONCLUSION

The king's decision to call the Estates-General for the first time in over a century provided France with a chance to solve the financial crisis, but the consequences of this act were far-reaching. Within two months of the inauguration of the Estates-General, the deputies of the Third Estate had challenged the power of the Crown by claiming representation of the whole nation and adopting the name the National Assembly. The chain of events that followed demonstrated the immeasurable force of the combination of ideas, conviction, and violence in achieving visionary goals. Before the end of 1789, the revolution had achieved the establishment of a representative legislature and the destruction of the last vestiges of feudalism, and proclaimed to the world that all men are born and remain free and equal in rights. France was changed, yet the revolution had not yet run its course.

NOTES

1 Donald Sutherland, *The French Revolution and Empire. The Quest for a Civic Order* (Oxford: Blackwell, 2003), 10, 19–20.
2 Andress, *French Society in Revolution, 1789–1799*, 42.
3 Jean-Joseph Mounier, *Délibération de la ville de Grenoble, du samedi 14 juin 1788* (Grenoble: [s.n.], 1788).
4 Bailey Stone, *Reinterpreting the French Revolution. A Global-Historical Perspective* (Cambridge: Cambridge University Press, 2002), 89–90; Jones, *The French Revolution 1787–1804*, 26.
5 Archives parlementaires, 12 December 1788, Series 1, vol. 1, pp. 487–489, in Dwyer and McPhee, *The French Revolution and Napoleon*, 2–3.
6 François Furet, *The French Revolution, 1770–1814*, trans. Antonia Nevill (Oxford: Blackwell, 1996), 45.
7 Furet, *The French Revolution, 1770–1814*, 45–51.
8 Emmanuel Joseph Sieyès, *What Is the Third Estate?*, 1789.
9 Michael Fitzsimmons, *The Remaking of France. The National Assembly and the Constitution of 1791* (Cambridge: Cambridge University Press, 1994), 143–144.

10 Kenneth Margerison, *Pamphlets and Public Opinion. The Campaign for a Union of Orders in the Early French Revolution* (West Lafayette: Purdue University Press, 1998), 178–181; William Doyle, *Aristocracy and Its Enemies in the Age of Revolution* (Oxford: Oxford University Press, 2009).

11 John Markoff, *The Abolition of Feudalism: Peasants, Lords, and Legislators in the French Revolution* (University Park: Pennsylvania State University Press, 1996).

12 Gilbert Shapiro and John Markoff, *Revolutionary Demands. A Content Analysis of the Cahiers de Doléances of 1789* (Stanford: Stanford University Press, 1998).

13 John Markoff, 'The Claims of Lord, Church, and State in the Cahiers de Doléances of 1789', *Comparative Studies in Society and History* 32, no. 3 (1990): 413–454, here 451.

14 Alfred Cobban, *The Social Interpretation of the French Revolution*, 2nd edn (Cambridge: Cambridge University Press, 1999), 25–35.

15 Markoff, *The Abolition of Feudalism*.

16 Archives parlementaires, États Généraux 1789, Cahiers, Province du Berry, 509–512.

17 Archives parlementaires, États Généraux 1789, Cahiers, Province du Berry, 319–322.

18 Archives parlementaires, États Généraux 1789, Cahiers, Province du Berry, 323–325.

19 Schama, *Citizens*, 339.

20 Schama, *Citizens*, 357.

21 Schama, *Citizens*, 34–35.

22 Tennis Court Oath, *Gazette nationale ou le Moniteur universel*, no. 10, 20–24 June 1789, vol. 1, p. 89, in Dwyer and McPhee, *The French Revolution and Napoleon*, 16–18.

23 Honoré Gabriel Riquetti, *Speeches of M. de Mirabeau the Elder*, trans. James White (London: J. Debrett, 1792), I:67.

24 Young, *Travels*, 123.

25 John Hardman, 'The Real and Imagined Conspiracies of Louis XVI', in *Conspiracy in the French Revolution*, ed. Peter Robert Campbell, Thomas E. Kaiser and Marisa Linton (Manchester: Manchester University Press, 2007), 63–84, here 65–67.

26 Barry M. Shapiro, *Traumatic Politics. The Deputies and the King in the Early French Revolution* (University Park: Pennsylvania State University Press, 2009), 83.

27 Doyle, *The Oxford History*, 118.

28 Schama, *Citizens*, 328.

29 Doyle, *The Oxford History*, 118.

30 Citations in Jeremy D. Popkin, *A New World Begins. The History of the French Revolution* (New York: Basic Books, 2019), 136.

31 *Les Révolutions de Paris*, no. 1, 12–18 July 1789.

32 Popkin, *A New World Begins*, 138.

33 Georges Lefebvre, *The French Revolution*, trans. Elizabeth Moss Evanson (London: Routledge, 2005), 119.

34 Peter McPhee, *Robespierre. A Revolutionary Life* (New Haven: Yale University Press, 2012), 65–68.

35 Schama, *Citizens*, 366–368.

36 McPhee, *The French Revolution*, 60.

37 *Gazette nationale ou le Moniteur universel*, no. 40, 11–14 August 1789, vol. 1, pp. 332–333.

38 Speech by Marquis de Lafayette, National Assembly, 11 July 1789. Lynn Hunt, *The French Revolution and Human Rights. A Brief Documentary History* (Boston: Bedford Books of St. Martin's Press, 1996), 71–73.

39 Speech by Mathieu de Montmorency, National Assembly, 1 August 1789. Hunt, *The French Revolution and Human Rights*, 73–74.

40 Speech by Pierre Malouet, National Assembly, 1 August 1789. Hunt, *The French Revolution and Human Rights*, 75–76.

41 Norman Hampson, *A Social History of the French Revolution* (London: Routledge, 1966), 116–118.

42 *Gazette nationale ou le Moniteur universel*, no. 44, 20 August 1789, vol. 2, pp. 362–363.

43 Cited in Popkin, *A New World Begins*, 167–168.

44 Cited in Popkin, *A New World Begins*, 167.

45 *Gazette nationale ou le Moniteur universel*, no. 44, August 1789, vol. 2, pp. 362–363.

46 Georges Lefebvre, *The Coming of the French Revolution*, trans. Robert R. Palmer (New York: Vintage Books, 1947), 93.

47 McPhee, *The French Revolution*, 149.

48 Edmund Burke, *Revolutionary Writings. Reflections on the Revolution in France and the First Letter on a Regicide Peace*, ed. Iain Hampsher-Monk (New York: Cambridge University Press, 2014), 73.

49 Mary Wollstonecraft, *A vindication of the Rights of Men. A Vindication of the Rights of Woman. An Historical and Moral View of the French Revolution*, ed. Janet Todd (Oxford: Oxford University Press, 2008), 29.

50 *Journal de Paris*, 8 October 1789.

51 Doyle, *The Oxford History*, 97.

52 Doyle, *The Oxford History*, 97.

53 McPhee, *The French Revolution*, 51.

54 Georges Lefebvre, *The French Revolution* (London: Routledge, 1962), 118.

55 Doyle, *The Oxford History*, 111.

56 McPhee, *The French Revolution*, 62.

57 McPhee, *The French Revolution*, 62.

58 Schama, *Citizens*, 859.

59 Michael Fitzsimmons, 'The Principles of 1789', in *A Companion to the French Revolution*, ed. Peter McPhee (Chichester: Wiley-Blackwell, 2013), 75–90, here 84.

60 François Furet and Mona Ozouf, eds, *A Critical Dictionary of the French Revolution* (Cambridge, MA: Belknap Press, 1989), 112.

61 Furet and Ozouf, *A Critical Dictionary of the French Revolution*, xiii.
62 Robert Darnton, *What Was Revolutionary about the French Revolution?* (Waco: Baylor University Press, 1990), 5.
63 Fitzsimmons, 'The Principles of 1789', 87.
64 François Furet, *Interpreting the French Revolution*, trans. Elborg Forster (Cambridge: Cambridge University Press, 1981), 45–46.
65 Popkin, *A New World Begins*.

3

THE REFORM AND RESTRUCTURING OF FRANCE, 1789–1792

In this chapter, we will examine the years of reform during which the National Assembly continued to deliberate on the shape of France's constitutional set-up while attempting to deal with the worsening financial crisis and the king's growing apprehension in the face of dismantling of the *ancien régime*. The initial success of the revolution was put to the test with the confiscation of land properties belonging to the Church, in order to help settle France's national debt. The subsequent enacting of the *Civil Constitution of the Clergy* further divided the French over the revolution, with public election of the clergy and the mandatory oath of loyalty. The wide-ranging reforms, including redrawing the administrative divisions of France, culminated in the new Constitution of 1791. This constitution provided the separation of powers, with the National Assembly as the legislative body, the king and his ministers at the head of the executive branch, and the judiciary independent of the other two branches.

The enthusiasm for the new France was not shared by Louis XVI, who, with his family, attempted to flee France in June 1791 to seek safety and foreign protection so he could rally those opposed to the revolution. All crowned heads of Europe were gravely concerned about the affairs of France and the impact the revolutionary ideas might have on the rest of Europe. Louis' escape was unsuccessful, and the king became a virtual prisoner of the revolution. The image of the monarchy was shattered forever even though Louis reluctantly accepted the new Constitution in September 1791, the enactment of which was quickly followed by elections to the new Legislative Assembly. After the king's flight, the course of the

DOI: 10.4324/9781003157748-3

revolution changed, and the general mistrust of the king over his support for the revolution undermined any attempts to continue with a constitutional monarchy. It was a combination of factors that caused the revolution to become steadily more radical, but Louis XVI's uncompromising rejection of the new system played a key role.

REFORMS OF THE NATIONAL ASSEMBLY

The 18 months following the events of the October Days were a time of reform. With heightened political tensions in Paris, the deputies of the National Assembly focused on extensive political reforms, including the first constitution of France. During this period of the revolution, the foundations of a society based on the principles of individual liberty were laid. These principles generally benefited the bourgeois middle class.

In the first year of its existence, the National Assembly had progressively abolished the privileges of the nobility and the clergy. The deputies of the National Assembly, most of whom were property owners, presented a constitutional framework in which only men of property could fully exercise the rights of citizen. Recognition of this dominant theme of this liberal phase of the revolution is important to our understanding of the later stages.

The National Assembly, as the representative body of the nation, reflected a broad range of views, from radical and progressive, to moderate and conservative. Within the first year of its existence, like-minded deputies grouped themselves around leaders, forming factions or informal parties. No overall leader emerged in this 1,200-strong body, although there were many excellent orators who often dominated proceedings. Among these orators was Count Mirabeau, a powerful speaker representing those who favoured a British-style representative government. Sieyès, who influenced the early days of the Estates-General, disappointed his fellow deputies in his defence of the Church. Lafayette, a well-known fighter in the American War of Independence, was now associated with the protection of public order as the commander of the National Guard. There were some new voices in the Assembly. The deputy Maximilien Robespierre, a small-town lawyer, became a leading advocate of the common people's interests.

A striking feature of these days of the National Assembly was that it reached its decisions collectively, though debate and compromise. 'The union existing among the three orders', commented the deputy Antoine-François Delandine, was 'held together by a compromise of ideas and a unity of purpose'.[1] Many contemporary depictions of the work of the deputies reflected optimism for the future. One of the etchings, with the caption 'Quick, quick, quick, beat it while it's hot', shows a literal 'hammering out the constitution', in clear reference to the three orders, united in the National Assembly, forging the new revolutionary constitution. The image depicts members of the First, Second and Third Estates holding hammers and hitting them down on a book that bears the title 'Constitution'. On the left is a member of the Second Estate in uniform with a sword. In the centre is a member of the Third Estate depicted as a blacksmith, wearing an apron, and holding tongs. To the right of the image is a clergyman. He wears a purple jacket, black cloak, and a skull cap. This idealised picture of national unity demonstrates the hope that France can look to a future built together by all members of its national community irrespective of their former estate.

The Assembly deliberated on how to improve the government of France; what the powers of the king should be as constitutional monarch; how the ministers should be selected; and what would be the relationship between the Crown and the Assembly. The prestige of the Crown was diminishing as Louis XVI resisted the changes implemented by the Assembly. In Louis' view, the reforms limited royal authority and the role of the Church in public life, but he offered no alternative. The public image of the monarchy was further undermined by rumours that the queen, Marie Antoinette, was working behind the scenes to secure foreign intervention in support of Louis XVI.

KEY INDIVIDUAL: COUNT MIRABEAU (1749–1791)

Honoré Gabriel Riqueti, Count Mirabeau (1749–1791), was one of the influential leaders in the early stages of the French Revolution (1789–1791). He was a noble, but stood and was elected to the Estates-General as a representative of the Third Estate, hoping to be recognised as the voice of the people. He was a popular orator and the leader of the moderate faction in the National Assembly, which favoured a constitutional monarchy built on the British model. Necker called Mirabeau 'an aristocrat by inclination, a tribune by calculation'. Shortly before his death, as the radical movement in the revolution became stronger, public support for Mirabeau's ideas began to slip away. The discovery later that Mirabeau was secretly advising Louis XVI tarnished his image as a revolutionary leader. Some accorded him hero status; others saw him as lacking political and moral integrity. When he died of natural causes, Mirabeau's remains were interred in the Panthéon, a secular mausoleum containing the remains of eminent French citizens, which was established in the church of Saint Geneviève in Paris by the National Assembly in the wake of Mirabeau's death.

POWERS OF THE KING

In this climate of uncertainty and suspicion over the king's true intentions, the Assembly had started to debate the issue of the king's constitutional powers. The monarchists, a moderate group of the deputies, led by several reform-minded nobles, proposed a constitution modelled on the British constitution. Under such a constitution, the king retained a range of executive powers, including the right to reject legislation passed by the National Assembly. The French parliament, according to the monarchists' proposals, was to have two legislative chambers representing separately, as in Britain, the commoners and the nobles.

This monarchist vision was not shared by more radical deputies, who were afraid that the king would use his constitutional powers to override the will of the people, and felt that a bicameral legislature would enable the nobles to exercise too much control over the affairs of the state. In the end, the compromise reached in the Assembly provided the king with limited constitutional powers as the head of the executive branch of the government, and his authority was checked by an elected unicameral legislature representing the people. The king retained the right to delay legislation for up to three two-year sessions of the legislature, a mechanism referred to as the power of 'suspensive veto'.

DOCUMENT: THE DEBATE ON THE CONSTITUTIONAL POWERS OF THE KING

As early as 1789, the National Assembly considered the issue of the extent of royal power. The debate split the deputies into two main groups: those who wished to give the king the power of an absolute veto and those who were suspicious of any extensive powers in the hands of the executive. Some deputies, such as Sieyès and Robespierre, opposed giving the king any right to suspend or reject legislation. Robert Blackman argues that there was fear that an 'absolute' veto might be used by the king or his ministers to hinder national sovereignty as if in an 'absolute' monarchy.[2]

THE VOICE OF COUNT MIRABEAU, NATIONAL ASSEMBLY,
1 SEPTEMBER 1789

It is not, therefore, for his particular advantage that the monarch interferes in legislation, but for the interest of the people; and in this sense it is, that we can and ought to say, that the royal sanction is not the prerogative of the monarch, but the property, the domain of the nation.

THE VOICE OF JEAN-JOSEPH MOUNIER, NATIONAL ASSEMBLY,
5 SEPTEMBER 1789

Democracy is a foolish dream in a large state. If the throne loses authority only to give way to the degrading yoke of aristocracy; and feudal tyranny was established in France by the successive invasions of those who composed the general assemblies under the first and second dynasties of our kings; thus defence of the crown's independence is defence of the people's liberty.

THE VOICE OF ABBÉ HENRI GRÉGOIRE, NATIONAL ASSEMBLY,
4 SEPTEMBER 1789

Unfortunately, kings are men. Flattered by courtesans, and often escorted by lies, truth reaches their thrones only with difficulty ...

One of the most deeply rooted in the human heart, one of the most ardent, is the thirst for power and the penchant for extending its empire. A king capable of dominating by the ascendancy of his genius ... and who will always put himself before his people; by virtue of an absolute veto, such a king will rapidly encroach upon legislative power by the facility of wielding the lever of executive power alone.

THE VOICE OF ELYSÉE LOUSTALLOT, EDITOR OF
RÉVOLUTIONS DE PARIS, *RÉVOLUTIONS DE PARIS*,
NO. 11, 19–25 SEPTEMBER 1789

The suspensive veto, which has been presented to the people as a good measure, and which we could not avoid granting to the king, will put the nation in chains on account of the intended length of its operation, for one would have to be blind or a fool to doubt ... that the suspension is valid for three legislatures, that is to say, for six years, without doubt long enough for [a king] to recover a despotic authority. Considering the influence of the ministerial party in the Assembly, that is, the nobles, the clergy and some deputies of the commons who have feudal property, or who aspire to the favours of the Court, we cannot in any way expect to gain a constitution for the nation.

THE VOICE OF JEAN-PAUL MARAT, EDITOR OF *L'AMI DU PEUPLE*,
L'AMI DU PEUPLE, 20 SEPTEMBER 1789

There is the prince [Louis XVI], who has become once more the supreme arbiter of the law, seeking to oppose the Constitution even before it is finished. Then there are the ministers [whom the king still appoints] so ridiculously exalted, whose only thought is to return to the hands of the monarch the chains of despotism that the nation has taken from him. Here then is the nation itself enchained by its representatives and delivered defenceless to an imperious master, who, forgetful of his powerlessness, violates his promises and oaths.

DOCUMENT: PHILIP MAZZEI ON THE CHANGING ATTITUDES TOWARDS THE REVOLUTION

Philip Mazzei (1730–1816) was an Italian physician and a friend of Thomas Jefferson. Jefferson was a leading figure in the American War of Independence and he and Mazzei shared an interest in politics. In 1779–1783, Mazzei acted as the agent for the state of Virginia in Europe, and in 1788–1795 as the representative in Paris for King Stanisław August of Poland. The idea that 'all men are created equal', which is incorporated into the *American Declaration of Independence* (1776) and the *Declaration of the Rights of Man and the Citizen* (1789), was paraphrased from the writings of Philip Mazzei several years prior to the writing of the *Declaration of Independence*.

In his written report to the King of Poland (8 January 1790), Mazzei quotes from a letter sent to his friend by a resident of St Omer, in Artois:

We are being flooded here with incendiary pamphlets monks and aristocrats distribute to stir up the people against the National Assembly; and to judge by the inclination I notice in the minds, the people of Artois, Flanders, and Hainaut, could well be won over to the views of the firebrands if matters continue to drag on for still some time, and if the National Assembly does not see to it that an eye is kept on them. The final decision for the sale of church property and the announcement that was made regarding a quarter of every citizen's income, could well ignite the fuse.

Mazzei comments on the situation:

The former privileged classes, with the exception of a few good and honourable individuals, show more and more that they prefer the total destruction of the structure to the correction of the abuses. They yearn for civil war; but more probably they will get a massacre at their own expense. In that case, the worst evil would be the impossibility of distinguishing the innocent from the wicked.

The report to the King of Poland, 22 March 1790, stated:

There is a sufficiently clear account of the intentions to oppose the completion of the Constitution, intentions shared by all the aristocrats and a small number of alleged democrats, who, while pretending to be the most zealous defenders of the rights of the people, try to bring everything to excessive disorder, whereby they hope to give rise to a new state of affairs favourable to their views. The wickedness of these fellows surpasses that of the advocates of former abuses; but since both base their hopes on widespread disorder, they often travel the same roads. I hope, however, that both will be equally disappointed, for the party of reason is forging ahead every day.[3]

REVOLUTIONARY REFORM

In the sweeping rationalisation of the country in February 1790, the Assembly divided France into new administrative districts. These units, called *départements*, were approximately equal in size. With this radical redrawing of the map of France, all internal customs, tolls and dues were abolished, and the boundaries of the Catholic Church dioceses and the jurisdiction of courts were changed. The aim, influenced by the principles of the Enlightenment, was to simplify and rationalise administration to one uniform state. This idealistic vision of the government, which decentralised the collection of taxes, and the administration of justice and law enforcement, depended, however, on effective cooperation between local elected officials and the central government; this later proved difficult in the times of national emergency.

In 1790, the popular Parisian ensign, the Tricolour, became the national flag. In March and June 1790, the Assembly abolished all remaining personal privileges and honorary distinctions, which had previously divided people of the *ancien régime*, including all titles of nobility and all clerical titles. The French were now to use their family name and were addressed as citizen or citizeness because they were all now equal.

Before 1789, France was divided administratively into provinces, which reflected the growth of the kingdom since the Middle Ages.

The historic provinces had their own law codes and separate systems of taxation, often impeding the growth of commerce. The National Assembly was determined to institute uniform administration and laws for the entire country. The debate over the administrative reforms began in October 1789 and these reforms became law in February 1790 when the Assembly voted to divide France into 83 *départements*, with names based on their geographical characteristics, for example, Basses-Pyrénées for the Pyrénées mountains, Haute-Marne for the upper Marne River.

In May 1790, the Assembly heard a preliminary report into a common system of weights and measures based on the principles of logic. The new system defining units of measure for the whole of France was one of the demands of the *cahiers* and culminated in enactment of the *Decree Introducing Uniform Weights and Measures* in August 1793, introducing the system across France. Uniformity of weights and measures was seen as essential for economic growth and thus the prosperity of the nation. The deputies favoured the use of a system of units that was logical and offered units easily understood and interrelated; above all ordered on a decimal basis. The new system of measurement, the decimal system, became one of the enduring legacies of the revolution and has been widely adopted throughout the world.

The new measure of length, metre, was defined as one ten-millionth of the distance between the North Pole and the Equator along the meridian crossing through Paris. The *are* (100 square metres) was devised to measure area of land, and the litre (1 cubic decimetre) for liquid volume. The gram, measuring mass, was defined as the mass of one cubic centimetre of water. Decimal multiples of these units were defined by Greek prefixes: *kilo* (1,000), *hecta* (100), *deka* (10); submultiples by Latin prefixes—*deci* (the tenth), *centi* (hundredth) and *milli* (thousandth). The term 'centigrade' was adopted for the measurement of temperature, interchangeable with the term 'degree Celsius'.

Among other reforms, the National Assembly provided for religious freedom and the separation of the state from the Church, extending full civil rights to French Protestants and French Jews by 1791. Arbitrary arrest and detention without trial were abolished. Censorship was no longer imposed and the press remained free.

In August 1790, the new system of administration of the law was decreed, providing for election of judges for a six-year term from among lawyers with at least five years' professional experience. A new office of Justice of the Peace was introduced to arbitrate in matters not requiring a trial. The Assembly also introduced the office of Public Prosecutor appointed for life, and trial by jury in criminal cases. Torture was abolished and capital punishment, which applied to far fewer crimes than before, could only be carried out by decapitation with the guillotine.

The principle of equity was also introduced in public service and military appointments. Their ranks were opened to men on the basis of ability, not birth, thus accelerating inclusion of the middle classes in the professions previously unattainable by their members. In spite of its revolutionary nature, the National Assembly did not open the way for a full democratisation of French politics. Rather, the right to vote was now opened to all male citizens aged over 25 who were in possession of personal wealth on which they paid taxes equivalent to three days of an ordinary labourer's wage; estimated to be 4.3 million men.[4] This restriction, in the opinion of the deputies, was supposed to give the 'active' citizens necessary independence to make reasoned choices for the benefit of the whole nation, that is, elect their representatives. The citizens who did not possess the required wealth status were classified as 'passive' citizens with no right to vote.

Among the deputies who spoke against such a distinction were Abbé Grégoire and Maximilien Robespierre, who argued that it was inconsistent with the provisions of Article 6 of the *Declaration of the Rights of Man and the Citizen*, which defined law as 'an expression of the general will'. While restrictive, this provision gave the right to vote in national elections to over half of adult Frenchmen. The Assembly's decision was, argued Peter McPhee, the result of the ambiguous definition of citizenship in the *Declaration of the Rights of Man and the Citizen*, which also excluded women as well as 'passive' male citizens.[5]

The change in the electoral laws was nonetheless groundbreaking, in particular when compared with the French experience under absolute monarchy and other European monarchies. At that time, only about 3 per cent of the total population of approximately 8 million in England and Wales could vote, and in Scotland the electorate was limited to 4,500 men out of a population of more than 2.6 million people. The new French electoral law also changed the eligibility for those who aspired to stand for election as a deputy, with a requirement of landownership and a tax payment of at least a 'silver mark', the equivalent of 54 days of labour. This effectively meant that between 700,000 and 800,000 men were eligible to be elected as deputies.[6]

Camille Desmoulins pointed to the contradiction in this treatment of French citizens in his newspaper by reminding his readership that 'the active citizens are the ones who took the Bastille'.[7] Many revolutionary cartoons ridiculed the distinction between active and passive citizens, depicting active citizens as those who actually contributed to the wealth of the nation with the work of their hands. Satirists highlighted that the distinction between who could and could not vote created a legal division between those in France who had property and those without, and it was seen as another form of privilege that prevented the true liberty of all citizens.

Such an apparent elitist approach to the issue of franchise did not, however, mean that the deputies were neglecting social problems faced by the lower classes. For example, the Assembly considered medical care as a basic human right and legislated for its free provision for the poor, orphans and the elderly. The Assembly also aspired to make basic education available to all citizens, although the subsequent economic crises meant basic education for all was never implemented. In May 1791, the Assembly granted full citizenship to non-white males born to free parents in the colonies after a lengthy debate that failed to abolish slavery. Among the voices in the debate was Julien Raimond (1744–1801), an indigo planter in the French colony of Saint-Domingue (present-day Haiti). He was the first man of African descent to address members of a Western legislature.[8]

In October 1790, the whole range of internal customs, duties and royal monopolies that had been a feature of the *ancien régime* were replaced with a single, uniform tariff on imports and exports, with no exemptions. These economic reforms aimed to destroy the last vestiges of the corporate society by targeting monopolies, privileges, and specific economic rights. In 1791, the National Assembly legislated to remove what it perceived as obstacles to a free labour market, and abolished guilds (March 1791) and other forms of association for both employers and employees (June 1791). One of the most significant of these economic reforms was the *Le Chapelier Law*, passed on 14 June 1791, named after the lawyer Le Chapelier, a radical Breton deputy and founder of the Jacobin Club. Some of the economic reforms, and the *Le Chapelier Law* specifically, argues Peter McPhee, were a sign of the Assembly's commitment to liberalisation of the labour market because 'economic liberalism' was seen as part of liberty in general.[9] However, they did not result in increased wages and improved work conditions. The *Le Chapelier Law* banned any form of workers' association and the right to strike, which left workers at the mercy of their employers.[10]

REFORM OF THE CHURCH

The National Assembly's attempt to reform the Catholic Church in France became the most divisive issue of the revolution. The reform was initiated with the abolition of tithes in the August Decrees (4–11 August 1789) and the guarantee of religious freedom in the *Declaration of the Rights of Man and the Citizen* (26 August 1789). On 2 November 1789, the Assembly voted to nationalise the Church's property. The proceeds from the sale of the lands accumulated over centuries by the Church were to be subsequently used to support the introduction of the public education system, to provide aid for the poor and salaries to parish priests, as well as to repay the massive national debt. The Church owned as much as 8 per cent of the land in France and the deputies' decision to put it 'at the disposal of the Nation' deprived the Church of much of its economic independence and influence.[11]

The appropriation of the Church's property came at a time when the Assembly faced the challenge of ensuring the financial stability of the government and at the same time feared that the wholesale of the property of the Church would drive the values of land down. The deputies decided to issue a new financial instrument, called the *assignat*, intended as a bond, with its value secured against the estimated value of church lands. The *assignats* were certificates that could be redeemed for church property when it was available for sale. As the Assembly was unable to pay its suppliers in cash, they received *assignats*, which soon evolved into a commonly accepted paper currency. The economic value of *assignats*, however, decreased as the government issued more of them.

In reforming the Church, the deputies did not stop at expropriating Church property. In February 1790, the National Assembly abolished monastic religious orders, except for those devoted to teaching and charitable activities. Theoretically, monks and nuns were now free of their vows because they were ordinary citizens. Contemporary etchings, sympathetic to the decision of the deputies, depicted jubilation of the clergy, with monks and nuns enjoying their newly granted freedom, embracing and kissing. The dissolution of the monastic religious orders was followed by the comprehensive reform of the Church.

On 12 July 1790, the National Assembly enacted the *Civil Constitution of the Clergy* (*Constitution civile du clergé*). The law restructured the Church's administration in France and in line with the introduction of the *départements* as the basis of local government resulted in the Assembly redrawing the boundaries of Catholic dioceses to correspond to the boundaries of the *départements*. The number of archdioceses and dioceses was reduced; accordingly, the number of bishops was cut from 130 to 83. All ecclesiastical titles other than bishop and priest (*curé*) were abolished. Each diocese was to have a bishop and parish clergy, to be called vicars, and a single seminary for the training of priests. The pope's right to appoint bishops was replaced by a system of popular election, making their nomination a civil matter rather than a religious one.

The National Assembly did not consult with Church leaders about the reforms because the majority of deputies saw it as civil reform only and did not plan to interfere with the spiritual set-up of the Church. The deputies assumed that, like the Crown before, the Assembly had the right to change the Church's organisational structure. In their eyes, the legislation was a continuation of the Assembly's wholesale reform of the *ancien régime*. Peter McPhee notes that the deputies had not considered separating Church and state because most of the public functions of the Church were part of people's daily life.[12] 'Nobody', wrote William Doyle about the deputies' attitude, 'disputed the Pope's authority in matters spiritual or doctrinal; but how the French Nation chose to organize the practice of religion within its own frontiers was none of his business'.[13]

Such an extensive intervention of the National Assembly into the operation of the Church meant the legislation became divisive even before it received royal assent. In the long term it alienated devout Catholics, including the king, even though Louis XVI initially endorsed it. Not surprisingly, the decision to have departmental electoral assemblies elect parish priests and bishops was rejected by the faithful and the clergy of the Catholic Church because it interfered with the Church's own established practices. For Catholics, the governance of the Church was centred on the pope's supreme and universal authority as the Vicar of Christ, and his sovereign jurisdiction over appointment of bishops. The election of parish priests and bishops made it possible for French citizens who were not Catholics, such as Protestants, Jews and atheists, to participate in the appointment process.

The National Assembly effectively disregarded a written protest of 30 bishops who argued that the Assembly had no jurisdiction to reform the Church's administration in France.[14] The objections of the French bishops and their supporters, noted Alfred Cobban, were not shared by the majority of the deputies, who were keen to modernise the institution.[15] They saw the Catholic Church as outdated, but unknowingly added religion to the litany of causes of political and social unrest. In order to assure the allegiance of the bishops and priests to the reforms of the *Civil Constitution of the Clergy*, further legislation was enacted on 27 November 1790 requiring the clergy to swear an oath of fidelity to uphold the law. The king found himself under pressure to assent to this legislation and, when he did, only 81 out of 263 clerical deputies in the National Assembly took the oath. Across France almost half of the parish clergy refused to take the oath and only seven bishops swore their allegiance to the law.

The swearing of the oath became a public declaration of patriotism and support for the revolution, and a refusal not only meant the loss of a clerical post but branded the 'refuser' a recalcitrant; in time it became the mark of a counter-revolutionary. The terms 'refractory' and 'non-juring' entered the public vocabulary to denote clerics who would not take the clerical oath. The resulting dismissal of the refusers often led to violent local resistance from the parishioners because, according to Timothy Tackett, the actions of the National Assembly challenged community life, and the parish was important both socially and religiously.[16] The opposition to the reforms raised a fundamental question for the Assembly: how far they were prepared to go to impose their ideas on their fellow citizens who refused to accept them.

On 13 April 1791, the head of the Catholic Church, Pope Pius VI, addressed all Catholics in France in the encyclical *Charitas quae docente Paulo*. In the encyclical, the pope condemned the *Civil Constitution of the Clergy* for being heretical because it challenged his authority in matters of the Church, and for causing a schism as it separated the Church in France from the universal Church by making it a constitutional church, subordinate to a national government. Pius VI gave 40 days to those who had sworn the oath required by the law of 27 November 1790, to retract it. He reminded the bishops that their religion 'is the one and the true religion' and asked them to reject 'the insidious voices of this secular sect, whose voices furnish death'. The pope called for unity of the Church by reiterating that 'no-one can be in the Church of Christ unless he is unified with the visible head of the Church itself'.[17]

A Parisian newspaper, *Révolutions de Paris*, promoted an altogether different view of the reforms of the Church. It proudly declared that 'the reign of the priests has passed'. Its editor predicted that the more the clergy opposed, the sooner organised religion would collapse in France. The justification of the reforms was found, the newspaper argued, in the fact that the clergy were more 'concerned with their past glory and wealth' and their display of wealth was 'both insolent and absolutely opposed to the principles and spirit of the Gospel'. The clergy, it concluded, should not resist 'the lawful will of the nation'.[18]

Political satire of the time leaves no doubt about the revolutionaries' feelings about the *Civil Constitution of the Clergy* and the subsequent papal condemnation. A mocking French engraving from 1790 presents the 'great heartbreak of monsignor'. The member of the higher clergy, identifiable by the robes of a prelate and the mitre placed on the side table, is portrayed as ill and vomiting receipts of tithe and taxes. The man standing next to him, presumably of the Third Estate, is checking the prelate's temperature. 'Be brave

Monsignor', he encourages, 'you are going to purge yourself and this will make you feel better'.

Another illustration in the same vein shows a supporter of the reforms, with a cockade on his hat and a big smile, using the papal encyclical to clean himself after defecating on some papers on the ground. In the background, an effigy of Pope Pius VI is being burned on a pyre, and the symbols of the papacy, a tiara and the keys of Saint Peter, are being paraded around on a donkey as a sign of humiliation. The derisive tone of the illustration suggests that the papal objections to the Church reform were received with contempt by the radicalised French public. The evidence from across France, nevertheless, suggests that refractory clergy received support from a broad section of the population, including predominantly women, who organised networks of assistance for those of the clergy who stayed faithful to Rome.

BRITISH RESPONSES TO THE REVOLUTION IN FRANCE

In Britain, the early stages of the revolution were met with widespread enthusiasm. The predominant understanding of the events was that the French were rejecting absolutism and were on the path towards a liberal constitution based on the British model. Interest in the French reform was mostly among those who argued for domestic electoral and suffrage reforms. 'Behold all the friends of freedom', exclaimed Richard Price (1723–1791) in November 1789, in a sermon commemorating England's Glorious Revolution of 1688,

> behold the light you have struck out, after setting America free, reflected to France and there kindled into a blaze that lays despotism in ashes and warms and illuminates Europe. I see the ardour for liberty catching and spreading ... the dominion of kings changed for the dominion of laws, and the dominion of priests giving way to the dominion of reason and conscience.

But later, the revolution also met with criticism.

In November 1790, Edmund Burke (1729–1797), a member of the British House of Commons, published his *Reflections on the Revolution in France*. Burke's pamphlet contained a criticism of the revolution and was an immediate bestseller in Britain. Burke observed that political tradition was a better foundation for reform of the political system than the abstract ideas espoused by the National Assembly. 'You began ill', he warned the French, 'because you began by despising everything that belonged to you. You set up your trade without a capital.' Burke, now recognised as the philosophical founder of conservatism, argued that limiting the king's power would ultimately result in abolition of the monarchy and he anticipated that the nationalisation of the property of the Church would lead to a wholesale change in the property structures in France.

Among many satirical works that commented on Burke's ideas was the cartoon by James Gillray, 'Smelling out a Rat', published in 1790. This caricature depicts Richard Price writing a fictional work, 'On the Benefits of Anarchy, Regicide, Atheism', beneath a picture of the execution of Charles I of England. King Charles I was executed in 1649 and England was declared a republic, which lasted until 1660. Richard Price, a Presbyterian preacher, saw the revolution in France as fulfilment of a divine plan for humanity in his 1789 sermon about the benefits of progressive ideas. Edmund Burke responded to Price's ideas and attempted to rebut them, igniting the pamphlet war known as the Revolution Controversy.

THE *FÊTE DE LA FÉDÉRATION*, 14 JULY 1790

On the first anniversary of the storming of the Bastille, Parisians held the great *Fête de la Fédération* on the Champ de Mars, presided over by the king and attended by an estimated crowd of 300,000 people. Similar festivities, demonstrating the unity of all France, were held in towns and villages all over the country to highlight the success of the revolution. In Paris, the solemn celebrations involved the National Assembly. During the *Fête de la Fédération*, Talleyrand, the Bishop of Autun, with a tricolour sash tied around his ecclesiastical vestments, celebrated Mass. At the altar erected in the middle of the field Lafayette pledged to remain faithful to the Nation, Law and King, to defend the Constitution, and to stay united to 'all Frenchmen by the indissoluble ties of fraternity'. The actual Constitution, which was to be promulgated in September 1791, had not yet been written. Louis XVI was acclaimed as king of the French, his title demonstrating the bond between the monarch and the people. Simon Schama commented that the public cries of 'Long live the King!' that followed signified that the French people still respected their citizen-king.[19]

THE FLIGHT TO VARENNES AND THE CRISIS OF 1791

The imposition of the *Civil Constitution of the Clergy* resulted in growing tensions outside Paris, with mainly localised opposition. The most significant outcome of the schism was the increasing alienation of Louis XVI, who was shaken by the pope's strong rejection of the *Civil Constitution of the Clergy* and grew ever more uncompromising. The king did not give in to the pressure to decree stronger measures against the émigrés who had fled abroad after July 1789. Louis initially appealed to the nobles and members of the royal family who found refuge in the Rhineland to return to France, but his calls were ignored. The émigrés were later to be seen as a dangerous counter-revolutionary group seeking to form an army to invade France.

Why Louis and his family considered themselves prisoners of the revolution was sharply demonstrated when, on 18 April 1791, acting on the rumour that the king planned to take communion from a non-juring priest, the Parisian crowd prevented the royal family from leaving the Tuileries Palace to attend an Easter church service in the nearby town of Saint-Cloud. Thus, the religious conflict directly undermined the process of building a new society in France and struck at the heart of the emerging constitutional system because its key player, Louis XVI, refused to compromise in a matter of conscience and would not accept the religious rites of the new constitutional church.

The caricature *Le Roi Janus, ou l'homme à deux visages* ('The King Janus, or the man with two faces'), produced in 1791, depicting Louis XVI, demonstrated the public perception of the king. The king is portrayed as the Roman god Janus, an individual with two faces. With one of his faces, Louis agrees to support the *Civil Constitution of the Clergy*; with the other, he is doing the exact opposite, promising its repeal as demanded by the pope.

On 20 June 1791, the king and his family attempted to flee from Paris to the safety offered by the loyalist army at the fortress of Montmédy, near the border with the Austrian Netherlands, in north-eastern France. Their escape was initially successful and while the National Assembly ordered immediate pursuit of the fugitives, the deputies announced publicly that the king had been kidnapped. The escape plan was foiled in part by Louis' chronic indecisiveness. The royal party's large coach was delayed, which prevented them from meeting at the agreed time the troops who had pledged to protect the king. In the end, the fugitives were recognised and detained in the small northern town of Varennes by the local authorities and escorted back to Paris under guard.

DOCUMENT: THE KING'S PROCLAMATION ON HIS FLIGHT FROM PARIS, 20 JUNE 1791

When Louis XVI fled Paris on 20 June 1791, he left behind a lengthy document outlining his objections to the course of the revolution. In the text he outlined his hopes that 'the order and happiness of the kingdom' would be restored by the National Assembly. The king was deeply concerned that the revolution had resulted in 'all authority ignored, personal property violated, people's safety everywhere in danger'. He explained that his powers were limited to such an extent that he could not 'repair even one of the evils that afflict the kingdom'. Louis alleged that the National Assembly had been overtaken by the 'spirit that reigns in the clubs' which brings anarchy and new despotism. He went on to ask whether his people wished him, their king, to be showered with insults and deprived of his liberty, when his only goal had been to firmly establish theirs. He called on the French people to 'come back to' their king because he would always be their father.

As long as the king was able to hope to see the order and happiness of the kingdom revived through the methods employed by the National Assembly, and through his residence close to this

Assembly in the capital of the kingdom, no personal sacrifice has aggrieved him; [...] but today, when the only recompense for so many sacrifices is to witness the destruction of the kingdom, to see all authority ignored, personal property violated, people's safety everywhere in danger, crimes remaining unpunished, and a complete anarchy established above the law, without the appearance of authority that the new Constitution grants him being sufficient to repair even one of the evils that afflict the kingdom: the king, having solemnly protested against all the decrees that were issued by him during his captivity, believes it to be his duty to put a picture of his behaviour and that of the government that has been established in the kingdom under the eyes of the French and of all the universe ...

From the spirit that reigns in the clubs, and the way in which they seize control of the new primary assemblies, what can be expected from them is apparent; and if they show any sign of some tendency to go back over something, it is in order to destroy what is left of royalty, and to establish some metaphysical and philosophical government which can never be achieved in reality. People of France, is that what you intended when you sent your representatives to the National Assembly? Did you wish for the anarchy and despotism of the clubs to replace the monarchical government under which the nation prospered for 1,400 years? Did you wish to see your king showered with insults, and deprived of his liberty, while his only goal was to establish yours? ... People of France, and especially you Parisians, inhabitants of a city that the ancestors of His Majesty delighted in calling 'the good city of Paris', be wary of the suggestions and lies of your false friends; come back to your king; he will always be your father, your best friend. What pleasure will he not have in forgetting all his personal wrongs, and to see himself once again in your midst, when a Constitution that he has freely accepted ensures that our holy religion will be respected, that the government will be established on a stable footing, and will be useful through its actions, that each man's goods and position will no longer be disturbed, that laws will no longer be infringed with impunity, and that, finally, liberty will be placed on a firm and unshakeable base.[20]

DOCUMENT: THOMAS PAINE ON THE KING'S FLIGHT

Thomas Paine (1737–1809) was the author of influential pamphlets that contributed to the development of the American rebellion against Britain. He visited France during the 1790s and became a strong supporter of the revolution and the establishment of a republic in France. Following the capture of the royal family at Varennes, Paine made the following appeal to the National Assembly.

The nation can never give back its confidence to a man who, false to his trust, perjured to his oath, conspires a clandestine flight, obtains a fraudulent passport, conceals a King of France under the disguise of a valet, directs his course towards a frontier covered with traitors and deserters, and evidently meditates a return into our country, with a force capable of imposing his own despotic laws.[21]

DOCUMENT: PARISIAN NEWSPAPER *LE PÈRE DUCHESNE*, JUNE 1791

The attempted escape of the king influenced the tone and direction of many newspapers including *Le Père Duchesne*. Jacques René Hébert's newspaper was often written in crude and foul language, and demonstrated a perpetual anger towards the enemies of the revolution.

You my king. You are no longer my king, no longer my king! You are nothing but a cowardly deserter; a king should be the father of the people, not its executioner. Now that the nation has resumed its rights it will not be so bloody stupid as to take back a coward like you. You king? You are not even a citizen. You will be lucky to avoid leaving your head on a scaffold for having sought the slaughter of so many men. Ah, I don't doubt that once again you are going to pretend to be honest and that, supported by those scoundrels on the constitutional committee [Feuillants], you are going to promise miracles.

They still want to stick the crown on the head of a stag; but no, damn it, that will not happen! From one end of France to the other, there is only an outcry against you, your debauched Messalina, and your whole bastard race.[22]

KEY INDIVIDUAL: ANTOINE BARNAVE (1761–1793)

Barnave was a lawyer from a prosperous family in Grenoble and an excellent speaker. He was one of the co-founders of the Jacobin Club. From late 1789 to the summer of 1791, together with Alexandre Lameth and Adrien Duport, Barnave dominated Jacobin politics. With the split within the Jacobins, Barnave became one of the founders of the Feuillants. After his return to Grenoble at the beginning of 1792, he was denounced as a traitor on 15 August 1792 and arrested. On 28 November 1793, Barnave was tried by the Revolutionary Tribunal and sentenced to death for treason. He was guillotined the next day.

AFTER THE KING'S FLIGHT

France's reforms and its new, about to be finalised, Constitution faced the challenge of legitimacy when it was discovered that Louis had left behind a statement denouncing the revolution. It gave those who suspected the king of counter-revolutionary sympathies the opportunity to openly demand a change in France's system of government from a monarchy to a republic. The French people saw Louis as a liar, who had broken the oath he made in 1790 to support the Constitution. The Cordeliers Club directed its republican appeals to the National Assembly, but the majority of the deputies were convinced that the monarchy should continue in spite of Louis' dubious position. In the Assembly on 15 July 1791, such eloquent speakers as Antoine Barnave argued that the removal of the king from office would trigger other, more radical demands, including changes to the nature of the private ownership of property. Barnave's views were a reflection of the fears of the moderates for whom declaration of the Republic would allow the radicals to demand the redistribution of wealth and property. The majority of the deputies, including Abbé Sieyès, Jean-Sylvain Bailly and Lafayette, now voted to preserve the monarchy with the expectation of the king's full cooperation, but suspended the king's ability to exercise executive power until he had sworn an oath to the Constitution. But in a similar way to the *Civil Constitution of the Clergy* the decision to keep France a monarchy split the revolutionary movement. The most popular of the political clubs, the Jacobins, was deserted by the majority of the deputies, who founded a rival club of moderates and constitutional monarchists, the Feuillants. The remnant of the members of the Jacobins sided with the Cordeliers Club, demanding the formal deposition of the king and drafting a petition for a referendum on the matter.

KEY GROUPS: JACOBINS

The Jacobins originated as the Society of the Friends of the Constitution and became the most prominent political club of the French Revolution, with almost 7,000 branches across France and a membership estimated at half a million. The club leaders were among the radical group of revolutionaries. After the king's flight to Varennes (20 June 1791), the radical faction of the Jacobins demanded removal of Louis XVI and the club split along factional lines over the issue, which led to the massacre at Champ de Mars. The Jacobins influenced the revolutionary government from June 1793 to July 1794, instituting such emergency measures as the Terror. After the fall of Robespierre the club was closed and many of its leaders were executed.

KEY GROUPS: FEUILLANTS

The Feuillants (the name derived from their meeting place at the former convent of the Feuillant monks in Paris) were a political club that emerged in July 1791 after the split of the Jacobin Club between moderates and radicals. The moderates established the Feuillants

Club and sought to preserve the constitutional monarchy, with the king at the helm of the executive branch of government. The group was led by Antoine Barnave, Alexandre de Lameth and Adrien Duport.

KEY INDIVIDUAL: JEAN-PAUL MARAT (1743–1793)

Jean-Paul Marat was a radical journalist who advocated ferociously on behalf of the lower classes of society. His uncompromising and often inflammatory views were published in pamphlets and newspapers. He edited the newspaper *L'Ami du peuple*, which became the tribune for radicals such as the Jacobins and Cordeliers Club. As the vigorous defender of the *sans-culottes*, Marat was one of the most ardent voices of the French Revolution. Marat became one of the 'revolutionary martyrs' after he was assassinated by Charlotte Corday, and was immortalised in Jacques-Louis David's famous painting of his death in a bath.

CHAMP DE MARS MASSACRE, 1791

On 17 July 1791, the radicals organised a mass demonstration at Champ de Mars in protest against the Assembly's decision to reinstate the king, and presented a petition demanding Louis' dethronement and trial for treason. Bailly as the mayor of Paris had declared martial law and the demonstrators were confronted by the National Guard sent to restore order by their commander, Lafayette. The demonstrators did not disperse despite Lafayette addressing them in person, and he ordered the troops to fire on the crowd. In the worst outburst of violence since the fall of the Bastille, the actions of the National Guard resulted in the death and injury of over 60 Parisians. In the immediate aftermath, radicals such as Desmoulins and leading members of the Cordeliers Club were arrested, Danton fled to England, and Marat's newspaper was shut down. Among the long-term effects of the massacre was the decline in influence of both Bailly and Lafayette and the rise of radical leaders such as Danton and Robespierre. The event marked a parting of the ways for the moderates and radicals in the Assembly, asserts David Andress, and the polarisation of the political spectrum between those who drew their power from the growing strength of the popular movement, the *sans-culottes*, and those who, fearing a social revolution, if not anarchy, attempted to restrain them.[23]

David Andress's position stands in contrast to George Rudé's. Rudé argued that the revolutionary crowd represented a cross-section of the lower classes for whom hunger was the primary consideration. He also stressed that while the crowd was influenced by political ideas, in the end they acted spontaneously.[24] For Gary Kates, on the other hand, the massacre was a by-product of the ideological conflict between the policies of Bailly and Lafayette and the 'direct democracy' demanded by the more radical of the *sections* of Paris.[25] The clash between different paths to achieving revolution was thus inevitable.

The *Révolutions de Paris* newspaper portrays the confusion in the immediate aftermath of the massacre as 'so far all the writers [had] presented garbled versions'. The paper portrays two versions of events, on the one hand that the massacre was of brigands paid for by the representatives of foreign powers, who had stirred up conflict, and on the other that the victims were citizens with their wives and children. It concludes that either had the possibility of being the herald of counter-revolution but that it was 'for the public to form its judgement' and to do so would need 'full knowledge of the facts', which at the time were not available.

DOCUMENT: ACCOUNTS OF THE CHAMP DE MARS MASSACRE IN THE PARISIAN NEWSPAPER *RÉVOLUTIONS DE PARIS*

Blood has just flowed on the field of the federation [the Champ de Mars]; the altar of the fatherland is stained by it; men and women have been murdered; the citizens are in a state of consternation. What will become of liberty? Some say that it is finished, that the counter-revolution is complete; others are certain that liberty has been avenged, that the Revolution has been consolidated in an unshakable manner. Let us examine impartially two such strangely differing views. The majority of the National Assembly, the *département* [of the Seine], the Paris municipality [commune], and many of the writers say that the capital is inundated by brigands; that these brigands are paid by the representatives of foreign courts ... However, if the victims of Champ de Mars were not brigands; if these victims were peaceful citizens with their wives and children; if that terrible scene is but the effect of a formidable coalition against the progress of the Revolution, then liberty is truly in danger, and the execution of martial law is a horrible crime, and the sure precursor of counter-revolution. For the public to form its judgement it will need full knowledge of the facts. So far all the writers have presented garbled versions.[26]

DOCUMENT: ACCOUNTS OF THE CHAMP DE MARS MASSACRE BY PHILIP MAZZEI

For some time now the *Société fraternelle* ... has appeared to be following in the footsteps of the Cordeliers Club, in which the most moderate are not outdone by extremist Jacobins. In that Société and in that Club meet mainly the disturbers of public peace. Everything has been tried to intimidate the Assembly, which has evinced intrepidity and shown supreme contempt for the numberless incendiary writings hawked throughout the city, spread through the kingdom, and even posted on street corners and all public places. That Société and that Club even dared to make audacious and insolent petitions ... The Assembly cannot refuse a petition signed by 50 active citizens. Saturday they submitted one signed by 100. The Assembly had it tabled, not wishing to interrupt its discussions. It was read Friday morning ... As it was known that the Assembly wished to settle the matter before adjourning, even if it had to sit all night, the troublemakers did not give up. They met at the Champ de Mars and about noon came to the Assembly with a second petition they said had been signed by 15,000. There were about 500 of them, but only six were allowed to enter as delegates to deliver the petition, not in the hall, but in the corridor and to an usher sent by the Assembly to receive it. They refused to give it to him and took it back to their fellow members, whose insolence the cavalry was about to repress by dint of sabre blows when the city officials that always kept close to the Assembly intervened ...

There can be no doubt that the hope of impunity was bound to attract to this capital ruffians from all countries and for a double reason render them stronger and more daring ... The above occurrence, and even more the great concourse of people to the Champ de Mars in the afternoon, besides the none too good intentions that were well known, induced the Marquis de Lafayette to go himself at the head of a large detachment and followed by some pieces of ordinance. There were municipal officials with a red flag to indicate that martial law had been declared. The rabble had the audacity to try to prevent the troops from entering the Champ de Mars. One of the many stones cast wounded an officer standing beside the Marquis de Lafayette. The troops finally fired, and last night people were saying that there were 10 or 12 casualties between killed and wounded. The cavalry seized 40 or 50, some of whom will no doubt be hanged.[27]

CONSTITUTION OF 1791

The Champ de Mars Massacre subdued the radical voices within the revolution. The National Assembly decided to revise its draft of the Constitution in August and September 1791. The new French Constitution, unveiled in September 1791, enshrined the individual liberty of citizens and equality of all male citizens. In the preface to the Constitution the deputies decided to include a list of fundamental freedoms enjoyed by the citizens of France.

Peter McPhee points to the bourgeois values enshrined in the Constitution, the inviolability of property and the distinction between 'active' and 'passive' citizens. Private property could only be expropriated for the public good and acquired at a just and true price reflecting its value. Sovereignty was vested in the whole of the nation and was defined as 'indivisible, inalienable, and imprescriptible' and exercised by the representatives of the nation.[28] The deputies' uncertainty about the true position of Louis XVI was reflected in the clauses that specifically stated the circumstances under which the king may have been 'deemed to have abdicated the throne': if the king failed to take the oath of office; if he assumed command of an army in a war against the Assembly; and if he left France and did not return when requested within two months. With the Constitution of 1791, the transition to constitutional monarchy was now complete. On 30 September 1791, the president of the Assembly declared that its mission was fulfilled, and its sessions were over.

Because the Constitution of 1791 enshrined the individual liberties, security and equality of all male citizens, explicitly excluding women, Olympe de Gouges, an outspoken advocate of the rights of women, published her *Declaration of the Rights of Woman and the Female Citizen* (1791), in which she argued for women to be given the same political and legal rights afforded to men by the Constitution.[29] When the 'Report on Public Instruction' tabled in the National Assembly recommended that women's education should be structured to enable them to support the revolution as spouses and mothers, Mary Wollstonecraft denounced educational double standards in *A Vindication of the Rights of Woman* (1792) and argued for women's education to correspond to their fundamental role in society.[30]

DOCUMENT: OLYMPE DE GOUGES, *DECLARATION OF THE RIGHTS OF WOMAN AND THE FEMALE CITIZEN*

Olympe de Gouges (1748–1793) was a political activist and an outspoken advocate for the rights of women. In her *Declaration of the Rights of Woman and the Female Citizen* (1791), she argued for women to be given the same political rights as men. She was executed during the Terror, charged with being a counter-revolutionary.

Mothers, daughters, sisters, female representatives of the nation, ask to be formed into a National Assembly. Considering that ignorance, forgetfulness or disdain for the rights of women are the only causes of public unhappiness and government corruption, [they] have resolved to set out in a solemn declaration the natural, inalienable and sacred rights of women, so that this declaration, constantly before all members of the social body, will remind them ceaselessly of their rights and duties, so that the power of women, and the power of men being at any moment comparable with the goal of any political institution, be better respected, so that the complaints of female citizens, founded henceforth on simple and incontestable principles, always focus on the maintenance of the Constitution, of good morals, and the happiness of all people.

Consequently, the sex that is superior in beauty as it is in courage in maternal suffering, recognises and declares in the presence and under the auspices of the Supreme Being, the following rights of woman and of the citizeness.

Article 1. Woman is born free and remains equal to man in rights. Social distinctions can only be founded on common utility.

Article 2. The goal of any political association is the preservation of the natural and imprescriptible rights of Woman and Man: these rights are liberty, property, safety and most especially resistance to oppression.

Article 3. The principle of all sovereignty resides essentially in the nation, which is merely the bringing together of woman and man: no body, no individual, can exercise authority that does not expressly emanate from it.

Article 4. Freedom and justice consist in recognising all that belongs to others; thus the practice of woman's natural rights has no limits other than the perpetual tyranny which man opposes to her; these limits must be reformed by the laws of nature and reason.

Article 5. The laws of nature and reason forbid all actions harmful to society: all that is not forbidden by these wise and divine laws cannot be prevented, and no-one can be compelled to do what they do not order.

Article 6. The law must be the expression of the general will; all female and male citizens must assist personally, or through their representatives, in its formation; it must be the same for all: all female and all male citizens, being equal in its eyes, must also be eligible for all public dignities, positions and employments according to their abilities, and without any distinction other than that of their virtues and their talents.

Article 7. No woman is excepted; she is accused, arrested and detained in cases determined by the law. Women obey this strict law as do men.

Article 8. The law must only establish strictly obvious and necessary punishments, and no-one may be punished unless it is by virtue of a law established and promulgated before the crime and legally applied to women.

Article 9. Any woman being declared guilty will be judged according to the letter of the law.

Article 10. No-one may be troubled for their own personal opinions; woman has the right to climb the scaffold, she must equally have that to come forward and speak, as long as her protestations do not affect the public order established by the law.

Article 11. Free communication of thought and opinions is one of the most precious rights of woman, since this freedom ensures the legitimacy of fathers towards their children. Any citizeness can thus say freely, *I am the mother of a child that belongs to you*, without a barbaric prejudice forcing her to hide the truth, except to respond to the abuse of this freedom in cases determined by the law.

Article 12. The guarantee of the rights of woman and of the citizeness requires a public force; this guarantee must be introduced for the benefit of all and not for the special use of those women to whom it is entrusted.

Article 13. For the maintenance of the public force, and the expenses of administration, the contributions of woman and man are equal; she has a part in all the drudgery, in all the painful tasks; she must therefore have an equal part in the distribution of positions, employment, offices, dignities and industry.

Article 14. Female and male citizens have the right to judge for themselves, or through their representatives, the need for public contributions. Citizenesses can only adhere to it through the admission of equal shares, not only in fortune, but also in public administration, and to determine the quota, the basis, the levying and the duration of them.

Article 15. The mass of women, united with men as tax payers, has the right to demand an account of their administration from any public agent.

Article 16. Any society in which the guarantee of rights is not assured, nor the separation of powers determined, has no Constitution; the Constitution is null if the majority of individuals who make up the nation have not cooperated in its drafting.

Article 17. Properties belong to both sexes, united or separate; they are for both an inviolable and sacred right; no-one can be deprived of them as a true inheritance of nature, unless it is when public necessity, legally recorded, clearly requires it, and under condition of a just and prerequisite compensation.[31]

THE LEGISLATIVE ASSEMBLY

In the 1791 elections, less than a quarter of the 'active' citizens entitled to vote exercised that right and elected the Assembly of 745 deputies. The new deputies had no parliamentary experience because the electoral law enacted in May 1791 prevented deputies originally elected to the Estates-General from standing in the election to the new legislature.

The first session of the new French parliament, now called the Legislative Assembly, opened on 1 October 1791. The deputies were predominantly of bourgeois origin and many of them had held local government offices established by the reforms of the National Assembly. Their focus was firmly set on protecting public order, enforcing the reforms of the revolution and safeguarding the rights of property. Initially, a large proportion of the deputies supported the moderate Feuillant Club, which advocated the new constitutional system, while the radicals sided with the Jacobins, who no longer had faith in the monarchy. A paradoxical situation developed, however, with the political debate conducted outside the Legislative Assembly becoming more influential on public opinion because the former National Assembly deputies who were now out of office continued to be vocal in matters of national importance; political speeches delivered at political clubs were publicised by the partisan newspapers. Groups of radicals advocating the involvement of the common people in national politics became members of political clubs such as the Cordeliers Club.

CONTINUATION OF THE REFORM AND THE RADICALISATION OF DEMANDS

The deputies of the Legislative Assembly pursued the reform agenda set by their predecessors, focusing on creating a new society. However, the failure of harvests in 1791 resulted in rural hardship and the deputies had to deal with the growing rural unrest that followed. In Paris some outbreaks of violence were seen as incidents inspired if not organised by members of the former privileged orders. Among the emergency measures that limited the rights of those blamed for counter-revolutionary activities was the law requiring émigré nobles to return to France by the end of 1791 or suffer the severe penalties of the loss of their property and execution; Louis XVI vetoed this law. The king's actions again reinforced the perception that Louis was insincere in his support of the revolution.

NEW SOCIETY, NEW POLITICAL CULTURE

The 1791 electoral laws restricted participation in politics to wealthier Frenchmen, thereby influencing the nature of the legislature; yet the new society, void of censorship, enjoyed discussion, debate and controversy in other ways. Among the most influential institutions of this new political culture were publications, political clubs and public patriotic festivities—newspapers circulated among the reading public who exchanged the news and gossip; anyone could participate in or just listen to debates in the political club meetings and everyone in the general public could attend festivals, such as the *Fête de la Fédération*, which celebrated the storming of the Bastille.

Since the calling of the Estates-General, newspapers had disseminated political news, including the proceedings of the deputies' debates. New journals, perhaps as many as 150 new titles before the end of 1789, were circulating throughout France, spreading the news and commentary of the events affecting all citizens. The press gave voice to those who had not been successful in attaining a political mandate in the Assembly. Revolutionaries such as Camille

Desmoulins and Jean-Paul Marat became popular if not populist voices and, in their publications, argued, challenged and commented on the actions of the deputies with conflicting opinions. The public's participation in politics, given the 1791 electoral restrictions for the Legislative Assembly, was conducted unrestrained through organised debating clubs. In Paris there were numerous political clubs. The first clubs grew out of informal debating gatherings as early as 1788, often meeting in public places such as coffeehouses. During 1789, and especially after the events of the October Days, which transferred the Assembly to Paris, a number of deputies formed a group that met frequently to discuss their actions in the Assembly. The group soon became a political club with expanded membership that included other interested citizens. Its members named themselves the Society of Friends of the Constitution, but over time it became known as the Jacobin Club, because its members met in a church formerly owned by Jacobin monks. The club and its provincial branches became the most influential political network supporting the revolution, in particular during its radical phase of 1793–1794. The club members got together to learn the latest news from the Assembly, talk over the issues of the day, and often prepare local political strategy. When in 1791 the Jacobin Club's admission fee was lowered, its membership changed dramatically and the club embraced increasingly radical policies.

The more radical ideas were actively pursued by the Cordeliers Club, which attracted revolutionaries such as Desmoulins, Marat and Danton. The club's membership was opened to 'passive' citizens, who gave its debates a militant fervour against the Assembly's laws favouring the middle classes. Women, who like 'passive' citizens were excluded from participation in the electoral process, took part in a variety of the clubs and founded their own clubs across France.

CONCLUSION

The course of the revolutionary reforms from the October Days until the elections of the Legislative Assembly in 1791 demonstrated the complex nature of the progress of the revolution. The enthusiasm of the deputies of the National Assembly for the revitalisation of France resulted in a number of decisions that, in their divisive nature, forced the French people to make choices. The most striking example was King Louis XVI who decided that he could no longer endorse the Assembly's religious reforms; this led to the schism of the Church in France from the universal Church. Louis and his family attempted to escape to seek personal safety and political freedom. The repercussions of their capture *en route* in Varennes were far-reaching and included the French people's loss of faith in the monarchy. Louis' acceptance of the new Constitution in September 1791 and the elections to the new Legislative Assembly ushered in a period of increasing division between the radicals, some of whom wanted France to become a republic, and the moderates, who remained confident in the constitutional monarchy.

NOTES

1 Mémorial historique des États généraux, pendant le mois de mai 1789 par un député du troisième ordre, Antoine-François Delandine, Veuve Desaint, 1789.

2 Robert Blackman, 'What Was "Absolute" about the "Absolute Veto"? Ideas of National Sovereignty and Royal Power in September 1789', *Journal of the Western Society for French History* 32 (2004): 123–139.

3 Margherita Marchione, Stanley J. Idzerda and S. Eugene Scalia, eds, *Philip Mazzei. Selected Writings and Correspondence*, 2 vols (Prato: Edizioni del Palazzo, 1983), 255, 303–304.

4 Doyle, *The Oxford History*, 124.

5 McPhee, *The French Revolution*, 87.

6 Doyle, *The Oxford History*, 124.

7 Doyle, *The Oxford History*, 124.

8 Popkin, *A New World Begins*, 233–234.

9 McPhee, *Liberty or Death*, 107.

10 McPhee, *Liberty or Death*, 134.

11 McPhee, *Liberty or Death*, 92.

12 McPhee, *Liberty or Death*, 119.

13 Doyle, *The Oxford History*, 139.

14 Doyle, *The Oxford History*, 143.

15 Alfred Cobban, *A History of Modern France: The Old Regime and the Revolution, 1715–1799*, 2 vols, vol. 1 (Harmondsworth: Penguin, 1957), 173.

16 Timothy Tackett, *The Coming of the Terror in the French Revolution* (Cambridge, MA: Belknap Press, 2015), 107–110.

17 Pope Pius VI Encyclical Charitas, 13 April 1791, in Dwyer and McPhee, *The French Revolution and Napoleon*, 49–50.

18 Elysée Loustalot, editor, *Révolutions de Paris*, no. 73, 27 November–4 December 1790, 390–394. Bibliothèque nationale de France.

19 Schama, *Citizens*, 434–435.

20 Dwyer and McPhee, *The French Revolution and Napoleon*, 51–52.

21 Thomas Paine, *The Political and Miscellaneous Works of Thomas Paine*, 2 vols (London: R. Carlile, 1819), 395.

22 *Le Père Duchesne*, no. 61, June 1791. John T. Gilchrist and William J. Murray, eds, *The Press in the French Revolution; a Selection of Documents Taken from the Press of the Revolution for the Years 1789–1794* (Melbourne: Cheshire, 1971), 132–133.

23 David Andress, *Massacre at the Champ de Mars. Popular Dissent and Political Culture in the French Revolution* (Rochester: Boydell Press, 2001), 1–18.

24 Rudé, *The Crowd in the French Revolution*, 228–232.

25 Gary Kates, *The Cercle Social, the Girondins, and the French Revolution* (Princeton: Princeton University Press, 2014).

26 *Révolutions de Paris*, no. 11, 19–25 September 1789.

27 Marchione, Idzerda and Scalia, *Philip Mazzei*, 597–602.

28 McPhee, *The French Revolution*, 91.

29 Dwyer and McPhee, *The French Revolution and Napoleon*, 39–42.

30 Wollstonecraft, *A Vindication of the Rights of Men. A Vindication of the Rights of Woman*.

31 Dwyer and McPhee, *The French Revolution and Napoleon*, 39–42.

4

THE REPUBLIC AND BEYOND

With the elections of the Legislative Assembly, it was hoped the constitutional monarchy would bring stability to France. Yet the revolutionaries still didn't believe Louis XVI supported the reforms, and the growing resentment of the 'passive' citizens over their exclusion from political participation continued to undermine the normalisation of French politics. The king was given a second chance to prove his loyalty to the nation, but the events examined in this chapter will demonstrate that the days of the monarchy in France were numbered. France's declaration of war against Austria in April 1792 and Prussia in June further contributed to the sense of fear of internal and external threats. With France facing the prospect of being invaded and with Paris itself in danger, the fear became anger, which was directed at the monarchy. When the Tuileries Palace was stormed by anti-royalist insurgents on 10 August, the king was deposed and the Constitution of 1791 was destroyed. Before the end of September 1792, France was declared a republic and the introduction of a new republican calendar ushered in a new era of French history with what was known as Year I. The war emergency forced France's new legislature, the National Convention, to assume the powers of executive government in order to face the challenges of the country's defence and create a new republican constitutional framework. The main principles on which the new France was to be established were debated between different factions in the Convention. The disputes, disagreements, opposition and dissent pushed the revolution onto the radical path that included the Terror and war.

DOI: 10.4324/9781003157748-4

TO WAR

The Constitution of 1791 brought with it the hope of a fresh start for France as a constitutional monarchy and a return to some form of normality. On 20 April 1792, the Legislative Assembly voted to declare war against Austria, acting in desperation to remove the threat of intervention by the émigrés. This decision went against the previous idealistic declarations of the revolutionaries: in 1790, the deputies proclaimed that wars of conquest were the result of ambitious rulers seeking glory and that the French would never undertake any war or use their armies against the 'liberty of any people'. At the same time, the decree of 22 May 1790 removed the power to declare war and make peace from the hands of the king and made it the sole prerogative of the Assembly.

The dismantling of the *ancien régime* in France had an immediate impact on other European monarchies. The *Declaration of the Rights of Man and the Citizen* challenged the very foundations of absolute monarchy by denouncing all forms of privilege. The ideals of the rights of man, and of equality in particular, challenged the established European order, which was based on the divine right of kings and rigid social structures. The news from France also caused alarm when, in addition to the wholesale reform of France's institutions, the Assembly decided to annex various territories located within France that were the possessions of various foreign rulers. The most significant of these annexations was the seizure of Avignon in September 1791, which had been governed by the pope. European monarchs followed closely the events unfolding in France, perhaps anticipating that France's preoccupation with internal matters would reduce its influence abroad. In central Europe, Prussia and Russia became alarmed about the influence of the *Declaration of the Rights of Man and the Citizen* and the spread of the revolutionary ideals when Poland introduced a new liberal constitution. Prussia and Russia, convinced of the need for action to destroy the 'Jacobin menace' spreading across Europe, acted to prevent implementation of reform in Poland by further partitioning its territory in 1793.

AUSTRIA AND PRUSSIA THREATEN INTERVENTION

On 27 August 1791, Marie Antoinette's brother, Leopold II, and Frederick William II of Prussia met in Pillnitz and issued a declaration in which they expressed their concern about the situation in France and in particular about the safety of Louis XVI and his family. They did not, however, take any military action to aid Louis and his family. In reality, in spite of the appeals of the growing numbers of French nobles who had left France, no European monarch came to the rescue of Louis XVI. Across the channel, Britain held its neutral stance, and on the continent, Prussia, Austria and Russia were preoccupied with their interests in Turkey and Poland. In May 1791, Leopold's half-hearted efforts resulted in the Mantua Conference where the King of France's safety was discussed. On 5 July 1791, Leopold issued the 'Padua Circular', calling for common action to limit the spread of the dangerous ideas of the French Revolution. This expression of concern on behalf of the European sovereigns fuelled the revolutionaries' fear of foreign intervention against the revolution. In addition, the French émigrés, who opposed the revolution and had left France and joined the counter-revolutionary forces abroad, resided near the French borders; this gave the revolutionaries another reason to act against foreign hostility. In 1791, the numbers of French people choosing to leave the country increased. For example, 6,000 officers left France, which had a great impact on morale in the army, leading to a breakdown of discipline and mutinies. With this stream of emigration and with both the younger brothers of Louis XVI now abroad, deputies of the Legislative Assembly fell under the spell of eloquent deputy Jacques-Pierre Brissot, who argued that the revolution was in danger from its external enemies and their conspiracies.

KEY INDIVIDUAL: JACQUES PIERRE BRISSOT (1754–1793)

Brissot was a leading member of the Girondist faction during the French Revolution. He was a supporter of the declaration of war with Austria (1792), but argued against the direct democracy advocated by radical Jacobins and the *sans-culottes*, and called for the maintenance of the constitutional monarchy established by the Constitution of 1791. In June 1793, Brissot and other Girondin deputies in the National Convention were arrested by the Convention under threat from the *sans-culottes*. They were charged with espionage and counter-revolution and sentenced to death by guillotine on 31 October.

DOCUMENT: ROBESPIERRE ON WAR, DECEMBER 1791

It seems that those who desired to provoke war adopted this view only because they did not pay sufficient attention to the nature of the war ... and to the circumstances in which we today find ourselves ... [W]hat kind of war can threaten us; will this be a war of one nation against other nations? Will it be a war of a king against other kings? No, it will be a war of all the enemies of the French Constitution against the French Revolution. These enemies, who are they? They are of two kinds: the enemies within and the enemies without. [These] external enemies, the French rebels, and those who could be counted among their supporters, claim that they are only the defenders of the court of France and of the French nobility ... Can we fear to find the internal enemies of the French Revolution, and to find among these enemies the court and the agents of the executive power? If you reply in the affirmative, I shall say to you: To whom will you entrust the conduct of this war? To the agents of the executive power? By this act you will abandon the security of the empire to those who wish to destroy you. It follows from all this that what we have most to fear is war ... War gives opportunity for terror, danger, retaliation, treason and finally loss. The people grow weary. Is it necessary, they will say, to sacrifice the public treasury for empty titles? ... The parties come together; they slander the National Assembly ... they blame it for the misfortunes of the war.[1]

DOCUMENT: BRISSOT ON WAR, DECEMBER 1791

The question under discussion is to know whether we should attack the German princes, who support the émigrés, or whether we should await their invasion ... It is by force of reason and fact that I am persuaded that a people that has conquered liberty after ten centuries of slavery has need of war. It needs war to consolidate its victory, it needs it to purge itself of the vices of despotism, it needs it to dispel from its bosom the men who could corrupt it. Thank heaven for the way it has favoured you and for the fact that it has given you time to settle your Constitution. You have to chastise the rebels, you have the force to do it; be resolved then to do it ... For two years, France has exhausted all the peaceful means to bring back the rebels into its bosom; all the attempts, all the requests have been fruitless; they persist in their revolt; foreign princes persist in supporting them; can we hesitate to attack them? Our honour, our public credit, the need to moralise and to consolidate our revolution, everything makes it imperative; for would not France be dishonoured if the Constitution being finished, it tolerated a handful of dissidents who insulted its constituted authorities; would it not be dishonoured if it endured outrages that a despot would not have put up with for a fortnight? Louis XIV declared war on Spain, because his ambassador had been insulted by that of Spain; and we who are free would hesitate for a moment![2]

DECLARATION OF WAR ON AUSTRIA

The increasing hostility towards the émigrés was based on the idea that all dissidents were supporters of counter-revolution. On 31 October 1791, the Assembly cautioned the king's brother, the Count of Provence, to return to France within three months, and in November all émigrés were warned that their possessions would be expropriated and that they would be denounced as supporters of counter-revolution if they remained outside France after 1 January 1792. These measures were vetoed by the king. Nonetheless, towards the end of 1791, support for war came from both extremes of the political spectrum in an Assembly that had become polarised. The most prominent pro-war faction came from the Jacobin Club. Many of its members were deputies from the *département* of Gironde, and they later became known collectively as the Girondins. In the Assembly their ideas were eloquently and forcefully presented by Jacques-Pierre Brissot, who also drew support from the debates and the circle of supporters who met in the salon of Madame Roland, the energetic wife of another leading deputy.

Brissot and like-minded deputies argued that a war against Austria offered the prospect of settling the émigré issue. In their view, the war would finally reveal the stance of the king, as Louis would be forced to take a side. Moreover, the war as 'a crusade for universal liberty' offered the opportunity to promote the ideals of the revolution to other European nations because the French soldiers would be received as 'missionaries'. Brissot also maintained that a war would stimulate the French economy, which had been suffering since the poor harvest in 1791 and as a result of unemployment and inflation. All Brissot's calculations appeared to rest on the assumption that war would be fought on foreign territory and would result in a victory for the armies of the revolution. Among the Jacobins, Robespierre alone took a cautious stand and argued that war would give Louis XVI a chance to recover his authority. The excitement at the prospect of war seemingly united the goals of the Jacobin war party with those of deputies who supported the stronger role of the king. The war, the court party deputies argued, as a national emergency would restore extensive powers to the monarch and they hedged both ways: a successful war would strengthen Louis' position and a French defeat would allow foreign intervention to destroy the revolution. That possibility was evident to Robespierre as well. In December 1791 and January 1792, he spoke openly against war, questioning its benefits to the revolution and its impact on the new constitutional system of France. He warned that war, as history shows, gives opportunity to influential generals to assume power. He might have referred to Lafayette who took command of the army on the eastern border after resigning his post as commander of the National Guard. In any event, both moderate deputies grouped in the faction of Feuillants and Robespierre found themselves in a minority of public opinion. In the Assembly, the deputies, seeking to leave their mark on history, put their faith in war and its unpredictable outcomes.

Simon Schama suggested that Louis XVI could have been convinced that he had hardly anything to lose.[3] The war seemed to the king and Marie Antoinette to be the way to involve European powers in the affairs of France. In the end, Louis sided with the war party by appointing a new ministry drawn from the pro-war Girondin group. On 10 March 1792, Jean-Marie Roland was appointed minister of home affairs and Charles-François Dumouriez minister of foreign affairs. The new ministry signalled the decline of the influence of the Feuillants. The Assembly demanded that Austria expel the French émigrés from its territories. When this ultimatum was rejected, Louis XVI addressed the Assembly with the formal request to declare war on 20 April 1792. The vote in favour of the declaration of war was almost unanimous; the overwhelming support came from Brissot's faction, the court party, the Feuillants and most of the non-aligned deputies. Only a handful of deputies voted against war. The declaration of war on Austria started a series of revolutionary wars that would last for the better part of the next two decades.

KEY GROUP: GIRONDINS

The group known as the Girondins took its name from the *département* in south-west France that included Bordeaux. Initially, they were known by a number of names, including the Brissotins, as Brissot was one of the group's leaders. It was not an organised political party, but when Robespierre named the group the 'faction from the Gironde', linking the individuals with the *département*, the name stuck. Among its prominent members were the influential orator the lawyer Pierre Vergniaud, the constitutional bishop Claude Fauchet, a deputy from south-east France, Maximin Isnard, and the Rolands. The Girondins were committed supporters of the revolution and were also committed to the provincial elites and free trade. Unlike Robespierre, they did not want the crowd dictating the direction of the new society. Among their leadership was Madame Roland whose influence was paramount. Olympe de Gouges, author of *The Declaration of the Rights of Woman and the Female Citizen*, was another of the women revolutionaries who were close to the Girondins. In her writings, Gouges called for a greater role for women in the political process and full rights of citizenship. Her ideas were supported by the philosopher Condorcet, also a member of the Girondins.

THE IMPACT OF WAR ON FRANCE

The declaration of war resulted in a further division in the revolution and changed the way the political debate in France was conducted. For self-proclaimed patriots, those who supported radicalisation of the revolution, anyone criticising, questioning or opposing the revolution was unpatriotic or a traitor who deserved the severest possible punishment. The war, as a national emergency, required the involvement of all classes of Frenchmen. With the reforms of the army undertaken by the Assembly, the ranks of the officers were now open to men of any social background, like every other French institution. In addition to old regiments, new ones were established with fresh pro-revolutionary volunteers or from the recruits of the National Guard. The perception of divided loyalties among the officers recruited from the nobility influenced their relationship with the newly appointed corps which was often strained. Army morale was low at the beginning of the war and the troops blamed the defeats of the French on their commanders. Many of the volunteers lacked military training and discipline. Suspicion about the sympathies of the commanding officers culminated in the murder of General Théobald Dillon by his own soldiers on 29 April 1792, following their loss in their battle with Austrian troops near Lille. The soldiers accused Dillon of being a 'traitor and aristocrat', believing that their defeat by the Austrians was the result of a conspiracy in which Dillon took part. In other regiments soldiers were disobeying orders, often voting against the commanders. In May, an entire cavalry unit defected to the Austrians. The disarray in the French armies enabled the Austrian and Prussian armies to march into France, and before the end of June 1792, Paris itself was under threat. The public opinion in the capital turned against the king. The constitutional monarchy faced a fatal crisis.

THE *SANS-CULOTTES*

Sans-culottes, literally 'those without knee breeches', were so called because the long trousers workers wore distinguished them from the wealthy, who wore elegant knee breeches, or culottes. Their ranks included local businessmen, master artisans, shopkeepers, journeymen, white-collar workers and peasants; thus *sans-culottes* were neither exclusively middle-class, nor working-class. They dominated local and grassroots politics because they were influential in the *sections*' assemblies and in revolutionary committees. They promoted anti-noble, egalitarian and populist policies. Many *sans-culottes* were well-known figures in their communities and commanded their neighbours' respect because they often advocated on behalf of their communities. They could mobilise their communities for action when necessary, becoming the influential force.

DOCUMENT: WHO WERE THE *SANS-CULOTTES*?

When asked to give an explanation of the origins and definition of the *sans-culottes*, the radical newspaper *Les Révolutions de Paris* took the opportunity to explain that 'every citizen who is neither royalist, nor aristocrat, nor idle rich, nor selfish, nor moderate, deserves to be saluted by the honourable title of sans-culotte'. Then it asked the rhetorical question, 'Do you know what a sans-culotte is?', and provided the answer:

He is not the equivocating type, the person without character who lets himself go with the tide of events; who, as it is said, howls with the wolves in order not to be devoured by them. Nor is he the smug egoist who has no other country than the inside of his house, and who, like the snail, withdraws into its shell while the tempest blows, and who swims near the surface ... The true sans-culotte is a man of nature, or one who has preserved all his energy in the heart of civil society, regenerated by the Revolution. He is a patriot strong in mind and body, who has always shown himself openly and taken a step ahead, consequently he has not waited for the country to summon him to her. It is this artisan, this head of the family, endowed with good sense, who, far from giving to the service of the republic the spare part of his time, regarded himself, from 12 July 1789, as permanently requisitioned, both in his person and in his abilities. A true sans-culotte is what one used to call the man of the people, open, cordial, sometimes rough and ready but always humane, even in those revolutionary moments when a veil is thrown over the statue of humanity. The true sans-culotte desired the death of the despot and of all the conspirators; he is seen where traitors pass on their way to execution; he is seen even pressing about their scaffold, because his humanity does not exclude justice.

He carries the sense and love of justice to a point that distressed the moderates, the undecided, the temporisers, all those who compromise with their principles. The true sans-culotte loves to get to the heart of the matter, even if he has to forgo his interests, provided it is in the public interest; thus no sans-culotte becomes or remains a rich man. Rich and sans-culotte! The two terms never go together ... he is hard-working, economical, but at the same time he is the opposite to selfish and dislikes those who are such. Selfishness is the curse of patriotic virtues and generous sentiments ... Love of work and frugality justifies, more than enough, the *sans-culottes* slandered; the share they take in the affairs of their country makes them deaf to the comforts of life that they could get for themselves, like so many others. They are neither less active nor less intelligent; but they are less selfish.[4]

THE OVERTHROW OF THE MONARCHY

With the start of the hostilities against the Austrians in April 1792, the French political system based on the Constitution of 1791 was suffering its most serious test. The reforms of the Assembly opened almost every sphere of civic life to the lower classes, but its decision to exclude 'passive' citizens from full political participation was increasingly difficult to justify. Particularly in Paris, after the storming of the Bastille and the Women's March to Versailles, the crowd who saved the revolution never accepted their exclusion from politics. Economic difficulties added to the growing fear of defeat, and with riots erupting in January 1792, grocers were forced to sell staple foods at 'fair prices'. Combined with the devaluation of the *assignats*, the food shortage created a climate of paranoia, focusing on the 'enemy within' who they believed were sabotaging the revolutionary effort. Political activists such as the journalist Jean-Paul Marat in his newspaper *L'Ami du peuple* and the members of the Cordeliers Club agitated against the 'traitors', openly accusing the king and the court of betraying the cause. The conflict also began to take on a social dimension, with the property-owning bourgeoisie accused of hoarding food. The radical priest Jacques Roux took an active role in promoting the ideals of direct democracy and a classless society, radicalising the lower classes including labourers and shopkeepers. This newly emerging group became known collectively as the *sans-culottes*, those who wore the worker's long trousers and not the elegant knee breeches, or culottes, of the middle classes and aristocracy. Jacques Hébert, the founder and editor of the extreme radical newspaper *Le Père Duchesne*, supported the action of the *sans-culottes* against the government, labelling the crowd's violence 'patriotism'. Newspapers such as those of Marat and Hébert influenced public opinion and reinforced the *sans-culottes*' perception that they were a political force.

With the defeats of the revolutionary armies in the war, the *sans-culottes* became increasingly radicalised by anti-royalist and anti-government agitation, organising street demonstrations and protests. They were convinced that both the king and the Assembly were unconcerned by the Austro-Prussian army's advance into France. Before June 1792, the activists, claiming representation of this growing popular movement, became influential in many of the 48 *sections* of Paris.

THE KING'S VETO CRISIS

In May and June 1792, Parisians' fear of attack by the advancing foreign army forced the Assembly to pass a number of emergency laws to deal with apparent counter-revolutionary activities. The Assembly decided that all foreigners in Paris were to be placed under surveillance, refractory priests were to be deported, and all remaining regular troops stationed near Paris were to be sent to the front. On 8 June 1792, the Assembly decided that the National Guard defending Paris was to be strengthened with additional recruits from the countryside. The decree called for 20,000 volunteer troops to be stationed within the districts of the capital. This move was meant to seal the bonds of fraternity between the National Guards from other *départements* and those of Paris. In reality, it transformed the army into a new revolutionary force. Louis XVI recognised that the decree placed him in a dangerous position and used his veto to delay the legislation. Louis' move was criticised by the Assembly, and in particular by the Girondin ministers; in response, the king dismissed them on 13 June, replacing them with the Feuillants. The events of the week that followed showed the widening division between the moderate deputies, who were afraid of a popular insurrection, and the radicals, who demanded the purging of traitors and counter-revolutionaries.

ATTACK ON TUILERIES PALACE, 20 JUNE 1792

The date 20 June 1792 marked the anniversaries of the Tennis Court Oath and the flight to Varennes. The *sans-culottes* crowd, armed with pikes and pitchforks, presented petitions to the Assembly against the king's veto and demanded the reinstatement of the Girondin ministers. The leaders of the demonstration were encouraged by the Cordeliers Club and represented a wide cross-section of 'passive' citizens. After delivering their petitions the demonstrators invaded the Tuileries Palace, facing very little resistance from the National Guard. The demonstrators made their way to the royal apartments and surrounded the king. He put on the red cap of liberty, indicating that he was one of the people, and made a toast to the nation; Louis remained calm and refused their demands to withdraw his veto. No authorities came to the king's rescue. Jérôme Pétion, the mayor of Paris, and the deputies of the Assembly did not intervene, perhaps because some of them shared the Cordeliers Club's conviction that Louis was deliberately delaying the war effort to give the Austrian and Prussian armies ample time to get to Paris. The king's courage won him and his family only a temporary reprieve. In the days that followed, a sense of outrage at the threats against the king and his family was expressed by sections of the public across France, and the Assembly was criticised for its failure to protect him. In any event, Louis was now at the mercy of the Parisian crowd.

AFTER THE INVASION OF THE TUILERIES PALACE

The Parisian tabloid press reported the invasion of the Tuileries Palace as a confrontation between the king and the *sans-culottes* and a torrent of pamphlets depicting the scene flooded the capital. Most of the symbolic graphics focused on Louis himself presented in a full-length portrait, wearing the Phrygian cap of liberty and raising a bottle of wine in a toast to the nation. The gesture on the part of Louis might have been meant to signify a new contract between the king and the people, but it was turned into the opposite in other representations, with a new caption:

> Louis XVI had donned the red cap of liberty, he had cried Long live the nation! He had drunk the health of the *sans-culottes*. The same Louis XVI waited courageously until his fellow citizens had gone back home to wage a covert war against them and to exact his revenge.

In order to emphasise the incompatibility of the king and the red cap, Louis had been given the Order of Saint Louis on his chest. When, on 10 August 1792, the royal family fled the Tuileries Palace and took refuge in the Assembly, from where they were finally interned in the Temple, the pamphlets portrayed the deposed king as drunk and wearing the green cap of bankruptcy.

THE 'HOMELAND IN DANGER' DECREE, 11 JULY 1792

The continuing French losses in the war had a profound impact on the development of the revolutionary situation in Paris. The radicalisation of public opinion in the face of external danger was fed by the uncompromising anti-royalist propaganda of the clubs and newspapers. The centrality of Paris to the revolution cannot be overestimated; yet at the same time, from February until at least June 1792, rural France was in a state of rebellion, on a scale not seen since the middle of 1789. The tensions caused by the continuing existence of seigneurial laws and the fear that French defeat would bring a return to the *ancien régime* brought on a wave of anti-feudal violence, known as the *guerre aux châteaux*. With the rural society's heightened anxieties and with Paris threatened directly by the invading armies, the Assembly passed the decree *La Patrie en Danger* on 11 July, which declared that 'the homeland is in danger' and called on all citizens to share in the defence of the revolution. In the Assembly, Brissot accused the king of being the reason why French forces were paralysed. He went further and suggested that the revolution had to defeat the enemies within before it could face the foreign armies. In the decree *La Patrie en Danger* the Assembly stated that:

> A league of kings has been formed in order to destroy [the Revolution], their battalions are advancing, they are numerous, subject to rigorous discipline and trained long ago in the art of war ... Our armies are barely yet brought to completion, an imprudent sense of security moderated the spirit of patriotism too early; and the recruitment which was ordered did not have as much success as your representatives had hoped. Interior agitation increases the difficulty of our position ... Make haste, citizens, save liberty and avenge your glory.[5]

In such a charged atmosphere, just before the anniversary of 14 July, the new armed battalions of *fédérés*, volunteer units from all over the country, were arriving in Paris. The unit from Marseille entered the capital singing a new marching song. It called on all 'children of the Fatherland' to take up arms and let the blood of their enemies water the furrows of France. This 'song of the Marseillais' became a rallying cry for the assault on the monarchy. The Assembly deputies' inaction once again gave a perception that the *sans-culottes* were the defenders of the revolution—the defenders ready to act!

DOCUMENT: 'LA MARSEILLAISE'—WAR SONG FOR THE ARMY OF THE RHINE

Claude-Joseph Rouget de Lisle (1760–1836) was the French army officer who composed what was to become the French national anthem. The song was written in April 1792 in Strasbourg to 'rally our soldiers from all over to defend their homeland that is under threat'. The song was initially titled 'The War Song of the Army of the Rhine' and it became known as 'La Marseillaise' when a battalion of volunteers from Marseille reached Paris in July 1792. It was quickly adopted as the anthem of the revolution.

> Come, o ye children of the Fatherland,
> The day of glory has arrived!
> Against us tyranny's
> Bloodstained standard is raised! (repeat)
> Now listen, all over the land
> The roar of the ferocious soldiers,
> They are coming right into our arms,
> To slaughter our sons and wives.
> To arms, citizens!
> Form your battalions!
> Let's march! Let's march!
> Let impure blood
> Water our furrows! (repeat)
> What means this slavish horde before us
> Of traitors, and conspiring kings?
> For whom are these dreadful fetters,
> Those chains so long since prepared? (repeat)
> Frenchmen, for us, what an outrage!
> What feelings must it provoke!
> It is us they dare to contemplate
> Making slaves as in the days of old!

THE FALL OF LOUIS XVI

On 25 July 1792, the proclamation of the commander of the Austro-Prussian forces, the Duke of Brunswick, was published. The declaration threatened summary justice for the inhabitants of Paris if any harm was to come to Louis XVI and his family. The right-wing press in Paris had been publishing vivid images of streets red with the blood of *sans-culottes* and Jacobins, as well as the lists of supposed targets.[6] If the aim of the proclamation was to subdue anti-royalist feeling, it had the opposite effect—Paris became more radical.

Coupled with the news that the Austrian and Prussian armies had marched onto French soil, the Brunswick manifesto galvanised the *sans-culottes* into action against the king, seen firmly as complicit in the defeats suffered by the French armies. On 3 August, a petition for the abolition of the monarchy was presented to the Legislative Assembly on behalf of the *sections* of Paris, but the deputies refused to remove the king. On 6 August, a public meeting organised at the Champ de Mars also demanded the king's abdication. The Assembly's refusal to act on these demands led the 48 *sections* of Paris to take over the municipal government in Paris and form a new insurrectionary Commune of Paris on 9 August 1792, with leaders Georges Danton, Camille Desmoulins and Jacques Hébert at its helm.

On the morning of 10 August 1792 the tocsin awoke Parisians to action. Under the auspices of the new Paris Commune, the Cordeliers Club, the *fédérés* and the *sans-culottes* joined in the assault on the Tuileries Palace, the residence of the king, which had been attacked only a few weeks earlier. Unlike the spontaneous *journées* of July and October 1789, the overthrow of the monarchy was a planned assault with the troops summoned during the previous night, the arrest of the mayor Jérôme, and the murder of the commander of the National Guard. The king was initially persuaded to stay at the palace, defended by the Swiss Guard supported by National Guards, but when the latter deserted their posts, he changed his mind. Perhaps he wished to remain true to the course of action he adopted in 1789 and hoped to prevent bloodshed; in any case, Louis and his family took refuge at the building of the Legislative Assembly. During the day, despite the king's orders for the Swiss Guard not to fire on demonstrators, fighting broke out between the defenders of the Tuileries and insurgents, and a wholesale massacre of the guards by the crowd followed. The number of insurgents killed or wounded was 376, including 83 *fédérés*, of which 42 were Marseillais; on the other side, 900 defenders, including 600 Swiss Guards, were killed or wounded. The day Louis XVI was deposed by the popular insurrection was thus the bloodiest of the *journées* to that date. The terrible carnage in Paris, notes Donald Sutherland, had horrible equivalents in the provinces where the Assembly's declaration of *La Patrie en Danger* was taken to mean that public safety overrode other laws.[7] Napoleon Bonaparte, who walked through the Tuileries in the aftermath of the attack, wrote later that 'no other battlefield made such an impression on him as this one'.[8] 'This rediscovered penchant for violence should not surprise us', argued Micah Alpaugh, because 'radicals actively planned the overthrow of the monarchical government'.[9] For the nobility, remarked Norman Hampson, the *ancien régime* ended on 10 August 1792, rather than 14 July 1789.

The *Dix Août* (Tenth of August) was also among the most decisive *journées* politically.[10] It represented, for William Doyle, a long-awaited trial of strength between two different visions of the revolution: the bourgeoisie's, shared by the majority of the Assembly; and the *sans-culottes'* as espoused by the *sections* of Paris, the Jacobins and the Cordeliers—of which Louis was the chief victim.[11]

The Assembly, faced with the violence of a popular insurrection, had very limited choices. In reality, the Assembly did not hold power in Paris and was at the mercy of the newly formed insurrectionary Paris Commune. An uneasy compromise was reached, with the deputies recognising the authority of the Commune, while the Commune accepted the mandate of the Assembly to legislate for the whole of France. In the background, leaders such as Maximilien Robespierre, argues Peter McPhee, understood the insurrection of 10 August as an expression of the people's will.[12] Robespierre called for a new legislative body, a democratic National Convention elected through universal male suffrage. The Legislative Assembly suspended Louis XVI from his functions and thereby annulled the Constitution of 1791. On 11 August 1792, the deputies voted to end the division between 'active' and 'passive' citizens and called elections in which all adult males were eligible to vote for a new parliament, the National Convention, that would determine the fate of the monarchy—the revolution entered its radical phase.

EMERGENCY MEASURES AND THE SEPTEMBER MASSACRES

With the suspension of the Constitution of 1791 after the uprising of 10 August 1792, the first period of revolutionary government began. During this time, political, social and economic life was subordinated to the task of defending the revolution. With Louis XVI and his family imprisoned in the Parisian Temple prison, control of the capital was shared awkwardly by the remnant of the Legislative

Assembly and the Paris Commune, led by the *sans-culottes* and Jacobin radical leaders. Most of the deputies who had supported the constitutional monarchy no longer participated in the proceedings of the Assembly because of fear of reprisals. This left only about 300 active deputies, dominated by the Girondins.

One of the radical leaders of the Cordeliers Club, Georges Danton, also came to prominence. Danton, whose ability to communicate with ordinary people allowed him to influence the *sections* of Paris before the deposition of the king, was now minister of justice. When on 15 August Robespierre called for the establishment of a tribunal with jurors chosen from each *section* to judge counter-revolutionaries, his radical ideas mobilised the deputies. The Assembly set up a Revolutionary Tribunal on 17 August. The new revolutionary justice enacted in the decrees approved by the Assembly in the days following provided for: no appeal from the tribunal's sentences; execution by a new mechanical decapitation device, the guillotine; the deportation of refractory priests; confiscation and sale of the property of émigré nobles; abolition of almost all reimbursement payments to former *seigneurs*; as well as bringing the provinces in line with Paris by dispatching its representatives to rural France. Among the statutes enacted by the Legislative Assembly was the law providing for the civil registration of births, deaths and marriages, which also gave the right to initiate divorce to husbands and wives equally. Marriage was thus defined as a voluntary agreement between two consenting adults, further separating the revolution from traditions rooted in observation of religious customs. The redefinition of marriage as a secular matter was followed by decriminalisation of same-sex sexual acts.

Within the Assembly, the Feuillants' faction became synonymous with support of the monarchy. On 19 August, its leaders, including Barnave, were arrested and later executed. Lafayette was spared the same fate because he commanded the army at the battlefront; he defected to Austria and was imprisoned there for the next five years. Demands for immediate action to defeat the counter-revolution increased when, on 2 September 1792, *sans-culottes* learnt that the major fortress of Verdun was about to surrender. *Sans-culottes* invaded the main prisons in Paris, setting up improvised tribunals. The massacres continued for several days, with at least 1,300 people killed. There was no attempt by the Legislative Assembly and the Paris Commune to stop the bloodshed in the capital or in other cities. The revolutionaries, notably Danton and Marat, excused the killings.

In their interpretation of these events, François Furet, Norman Hampson and, most prominently, Simon Schama attribute the violence of September 1792 to a revolutionary force intrinsically present in the revolution since its beginning.[13] They argue that the source of the fear and savagery of the September Massacres was the imagined counter-revolution. Peter McPhee disagrees, suggesting that the massacres were a social conflict caused by the rival vision of the new society and the failure of revolutionary consensus. McPhee emphasises the real and present danger of the internal and external enemy republicans were facing and the panic with the fall of Verdun.[14]

The effect of the massacres was twofold: Europe learnt about the revolutionary violence and the Convention faced the realisation that the *sans-culottes* were a difficult force to restrain. The September Massacres did nothing to resolve the imminent threat that the Austro-Prussian armies posed to Paris. The Convention assembled for its first session on 20 September 1792, the day the French army stopped the Austro-Prussian advance towards Paris at Valmy.

THE NATIONAL CONVENTION

The inauguration of the National Convention elected under universal male suffrage brought with it the promise of fundamental change in the new society. The three momentous years of the Convention broke radically with the past. The work of the Convention can be seen as a first step towards establishment of a democratic republic, but also as a violent and destructive regime focused on self-preservation. The very nature of the National Convention was that it was born in crisis and it operated as a series of responses to crises. Many of the 749 of the Convention's deputies had sat in the Legislative Assembly or in the National Assembly, because there was no repetition of Robespierre's 'self-denying ordinance' of 1791 that had kept deputies from running for re-election. The deputies were predominantly lawyers and government officials. The majority of them were members of the bourgeoisie and two-thirds of them were under 45 years of age. The background of the deputies indicated that they had little in common with the Parisian *sans-culottes* or the mass of the peasant population. Perhaps more importantly they wanted to govern according to established legislative procedures and processes, whereas the *sans-culottes* often resorted to direct action. At the same time, peasants wanted to see the removal of the last vestiges of feudalism and were alienated by the anticlerical policies of Paris. The tenure of the Convention was thus characterised by tensions, both internal and external.

KEY INDIVIDUAL: GEORGES DANTON (1759–1794)

Danton was one of the leading figures of the radical stage of the revolution. A career lawyer, he became a leader of the Cordeliers early in the revolution and was recognised as a powerful speaker who was popular with the crowd. In August 1792, he became a member of the insurrectionary Paris Commune, which orchestrated the 10 August attack on the Tuileries Palace that resulted in the overthrow of the monarchy. Danton became minister of justice and was later elected a member of the Convention, the republican national assembly. From April to July 1793, he was a member of the Committee of Public Safety, established by the Convention as its executive governing body. Danton was a pragmatist and began to campaign for a conciliatory foreign policy. After July 1793 he left Paris. When he returned in November to pursue the relaxation of the revolution's emergency measures, Danton attacked what he saw as the dictatorship of the Committee of Public Safety. This final battle Danton lost. On 30 March 1794, he was charged with conspiracy against the revolution. After the mock trial, Danton was guillotined. Historians see him either as a great patriot or as a corrupt politician.

KEY INDIVIDUAL: MAXIMILIEN ROBESPIERRE (1758–1794)

Robespierre was one of the most influential figures of the revolution. Before he was elected as a deputy for the Third Estate to the Estates-General in 1789, Robespierre was a lawyer. His prominence grew steadily, initially in the Jacobin Club and later in the National Assembly and the Convention. He argued for universal male suffrage for the elections to the French legislature and opposed the war proposals of the Girondins of 1791 and 1792. After the overthrow of the monarchy he served as a deputy from Paris in the National Convention, demanding the execution of Louis XVI (January 1793) and the purge of the Girondins (May–June, 1793). On 27 July 1793, Robespierre was elected to the Committee of Public Safety where he opposed and successfully eliminated both the radical left (Jacques Hébert) and the moderates (Georges Danton and Camille Desmoulins); they were arrested and guillotined. Robespierre supported the enactment of the *Law of 22 Prairial* (10 June 1794), which gave the Revolutionary Tribunal extended powers and limited the judicial process to one of indictment and prosecution. His name became associated with the Reign of Terror.

Robespierre was arrested and summarily tried in response to the speech he made in the Convention on 26 July 1794 (8 Thermidor Year II), which was interpreted by the deputies as a threat of further purges. He was guillotined on 28 July. Robespierre's character has been the subject of great controversy. Was he the 'Incorruptible', as he was labelled, or 'incomprehensible', as Colin Haydon and William Doyle would have him?[15]

'This was a passionate man'—concluded Peter McPhee—'far from the emotionally stunted, rigidly puritanical and icily cruel monster of history and literature', who unlike most of his peers was 'not prepared to compromise the principles of 1789 in order to achieve stability, and in that lay his greatness and his tragedy'.[16]

KEY INDIVIDUAL: MARIE THÉRÈSE, PRINCESS DE LAMBALLE (1749–1792)

Marie Thérèse was a member of the House of Savoy. At the age of 17 she was married to Louis Alexandre, Prince de Lamballe, a descendant of Louis XIV. Two years later, in 1768, she became a widow when her husband, known for his libertine lifestyle, died of a venereal disease. Marie Thérèse joined the court of King Louis XV shortly before the marriage of his heir, Louis-Auguste, to Marie Antoinette. Her friendship with the dauphine and later queen became the subject of many scandalous publications, but Marie Thérèse remained a confidante of Marie Antoinette. She accompanied the royal family to the Tuileries Palace after the Women's March (5–6 October 1789), remaining with them until the attack on the palace on 10 August 1792. After their imprisonment in the Temple, Marie Thérèse was taken to La Force prison. The accounts of her death during the September Massacres vary in degree of horrible detail. Witness accounts suggest that on 3 September she faced a mock trial and was murdered, as were other victims of the vigilante violence on that day. Her severed head was carried about in an attempt to show it to Marie Antoinette at the Temple prison.

The painting *Death of the Princess de Lamballe* by Leon Faivre (1908) presents the reality of the September Massacres: a crowd storming a prison, armed men holding weapons, a woman pointing at the motionless, mutilated body of a woman on the ground, children witnessing the street violence, blood on the cobblestones and death. The painting offers the full colour of the Parisian street, people wearing clothing of all social classes.

DOCUMENT: ACCOUNT OF THE DEATH OF THE PRINCESS DE LAMBALLE BY RESTIF DE LA BRETONNE

The killing of the Princess de Lamballe was observed by the French novelist, Restif de la Bretonne (1734–1806).

I saw a woman appear, pale as her underclothing, held up by a counter clerk. They said to her in a harsh voice: 'Cry out: "Long live the nation!"' 'No! no!' she said. They made her climb onto a heap of corpses. One of the murderers seized the counter clerk and took him away. 'Ah!' cried the unfortunate woman, 'don't hurt him!' They told her again to cry out 'Long live the nation!' She refused disdainfully. Then a killer seized her, tore off her dress and opened her belly. She fell, and was finished off by the others. Never had such horror offered itself to my imagination. I tried to flee; my legs failed. I fainted. When I came to my senses, I saw the bloody head. I was told that it had been washed, its hair curled, and that it had been put on the end of a pike and carried under the windows of the Temple.[17]

DOCUMENT: MARIE-JEANNE ROLAND ON THE SEPTEMBER MASSACRES

Marie-Jeanne Roland (1754–1793), better known as Madame Roland, was a prominent supporter of the Girondins. She kept a salon where influential individuals of the Parisian political scene met. Her husband, Jean-Marie Roland, was a member of the Girondin ministry formed in March 1792; he resigned the day after the king's execution and was denounced in the Convention by Danton. Madame Roland was arrested on 1 June 1793, having helped her husband to escape from the capital. She wrote her memoirs during her captivity. She went to the guillotine on 8 November 1793 and is credited with the cry: 'Oh, Liberty! What crimes are committed in your name!'

MADAME ROLAND'S COMMENTS ON THE SEPTEMBER MASSACRES

The ministers emerged from the Council after eleven o'clock; we heard only next morning of the horrors committed during the night and which were still being committed in the prisons. Appalled by these abominable crimes, by our own inability to prevent them and by the evident complicity of the Commune and the General commanding the [National] Guard, we decided that the only course open to a responsible minister was to denounce them publicly with the utmost vigour, challenge the Assembly to put a stop to them and arouse the indignation of all good men, taking the risk of assassination if need be. But the massacres continued. At the Abbaye [prison] they lasted from Sunday evening until Tuesday morning; at La Force, longer; at Bicêtre, four days, and so on. I am now in the first of these three prisons myself and that is how I have heard the gruesome details; I dare not describe them. But there was one event which I will not pass over in silence because it helps to show how all this was linked and premeditated. In the Faubourg St-Germain there was a warehouse where they put prisoners for whom there was no room in the Abbaye. The police chose the Sunday evening just before the general massacre to move prisoners from this depot to the prison. The assassins were lying in wait; they fell upon the coaches, five or six in number, broke them open with swords and pikes and slew the men and women within, screaming there in the open street. All Paris witnessed these terrible scenes, carried out by a small number of butchers ... All Paris saw it and all Paris let it go on. I abominate this city. It is impossible to imagine Liberty finding a home amongst cowards who condone every outrage and coolly stand by watching crimes which fifty armed men with any gumption could easily have prevented. The forces of law and order were badly organised, and still are, because the power-hungry brigands were careful to oppose any form of discipline which might restrain them. But does a man need to receive orders from his officer and march in column of fours when it is a question of rescuing people who are having their throats cut? The fact is that the reports of conspiracies in the prisons, however improbable, and the constant propaganda about the people's will and the people's anger, held everyone in a sort of stupor and gave the impression that this infamous performance was the work of the populace, whereas in reality there were not above 200 criminals. It was not so much the first night that astonished me, but four days! And the ghoulish sightseers coming to watch the spectacle! I know of nothing in the annals of the most barbarous nation to compare with these atrocities.[18]

HISTORIANS ON THE RADICALISATION OF THE REVOLUTION

The period that began with the inauguration of the Legislative Assembly in October 1791 is seen by historians as the time of the further radicalisation of the revolution. The declaration of war and later the overthrow of the monarchy made it even more radical. Historians debate the reasons for the radicalisation of the revolution, and the overarching themes emerging in this debate are the issues of persisting social inequality seen as the basis of political empowerment of 'passive' citizens, and the issue of violence. None of the interpretations are over-simplistic, but some historians are more persuasive than others.

Peter McPhee acknowledged the fundamental significance of the events of 10 August by referring to them as the Second Revolution. Simon Schama suggested that it was not incidental that the radical path included the killings of 10 August because 'bloodshed was not the unfortunate by-product of revolution, it was the source of its energy. The verses of the "Marseillaise" and the great speeches of the Girondins had spoken of the *patrie* in the absolute poetry of life and death.'[19] In contrast, John F. Bosher argued that the crowd was manipulated 'mainly by educated leaders who approved of popular violence on ideological grounds'.[20] David Andress questioned this proposition, questioning why the crowd 'so imbued with violence' did not erupt decisively until 'enemy troops were well inside the national frontiers'. And perhaps ironically, he added, 'radical activists had decided to topple the monarchy to save the nation from its own treacherous leaders?'[21]

Yet, the violence of the Parisian crowd may have had different origins, the persisting political exclusion, as McPhee suggested. After 10 August, the disfranchisement of 'passive' citizens, concludes McPhee, was no longer defensible. He also argues that the popular insurrection that deposed Louis XVI on 10 August gave the clearest signal yet to the whole of Europe—'The Revolution was now armed, democratic and republican'.[22]

Adam Zamoyski suggested that Europe did indeed take that threat seriously—'Many of those who had welcomed the Revolution began to recant'.[23] On the other hand, if Europe received the news of the end of the French monarchy with horror, the French response was measured if muted. 'The most startling feature of the overthrow of the monarchy', notes McPhee, was 'the relative lack of anger or shock in most parts of the country: it was as if the aura of monarchy had evaporated with the King's attempt to flee 14 months earlier'.[24] Perhaps even more significantly, argues McPhee, 'the presence of the *fédérés* meant that it was the French people rather than the Parisians alone who had risen' on 10 August.[25]

The most hotly contested historiographical issue encountered in this chapter is the September Massacres. The opinions of historians are divided. They oscillate between explanations sought in violence being a necessary and integral part of the revolutionary action, or the violence as the force behind the revolution, unleashed at the time of need, always present, threatening and singularly persuasive. The violence of the revolution was, for Georges Lefebvre, a defence against violent counter-revolution. Similarly, even though the massacres were caused by fear and panic, John Hall Stewart argued, to 'the average Frenchman they doubtless seemed a regrettable but unavoidable necessity'.[26] These 'most atrocious killings' were, in the assessment of Donald Sutherland, 'pre-emptive strikes intended to prevent the junction of the internal and external enemies'.[27] William Doyle agreed, adding that in the paranoid atmosphere of Paris the revolutionary activists of the Commune sought revenge on those who in the past opposed them.[28] In contrast, Simon Schama pointed directly to the fact that the September Massacres 'exposed a central truth of the French Revolution: its dependence on organised killing to accomplish political ends'. Schama concluded, 'For however virtuous the principles of kingless France were supposed to be, their power to compel allegiance depended, from the very beginning, on the spectacle of death.'[29]

The horrific circumstances of the massacres cannot be denied, admits McPhee, but he reminds readers that the killings were not confined to Paris. In addition to political ideology, McPhee argues that the 'deeply entrenched social hatred' caused 'a desire to punish those alleged to be in league with the enemy now advancing through eastern France'.[30]

CONCLUSION

The hopes that the Legislative Assembly would deliver peace, growth and stability quickly evaporated when the deputies realised that the revolution needed to be defended from within and without. The challenges faced by the Legislative Assembly were in part a result of the unresolved issues of equality and political participation of 'passive' citizens. The early days of the Assembly were preoccupied with the potential threat of the French émigrés who lived across the Rhine in the German principalities. The fateful decision to declare war on Austria brought with it initial enthusiasm and a surge of patriotism, but in the long term the war losses and increasing paranoia about conspiracies and plots turned the public against the king. The passing of the 'men of 1789' was marked by the Champ de Mars massacre on 17 July 1792 and paved the way for Louis XVI to be deposed and the Republic to be declared in September 1792.

NOTES

1 *Le Journal des débats des Amis de la Constitution (Journal of the debates of Friends of the Constitution)*, 13–14 December 1791.
2 *Le Journal des débats*, 13–14 December 1791.
3 Schama, *Citizens*, 505–506.

4 *Les Révolutions de Paris*, nos. 214 and 215, 5–12 November 1793.

5 *La Patrie en Danger*, 11 July 1792.

6 Jeremy D. Popkin, *The Right-Wing Press in France, 1792–1800* (Chapel Hill: University of North Carolina Press, 1980); William Murray, *The Right-Wing Press in the French Revolution, 1789–92* (Woodbridge: Boydell Press, 1986).

7 Sutherland, *The French Revolution and Empire*, 137.

8 Philip G. Dwyer, *Napoleon. The Path to Power* (New Haven: Yale University Press, 2008), 99.

9 Micah Alpaugh, 'The Making of the Parisian Political Demonstration: A Case Study of 20 June 1792', *Proceedings of the Western Society for French History* 34 (2007): 115–133, here 131.

10 Hampson, *A Social History of the French Revolution*, 148.

11 Doyle, *The Oxford History*, 189–190.

12 McPhee, *Robespierre. A Revolutionary Life*, 125.

13 Furet, *The French Revolution, 1770–1814*, 114–115; Hampson, *A Social History of the French Revolution*, 153; Schama, *Citizens*, 587–588.

14 McPhee, *Liberty or Death*, 163.

15 Colin Haydon and William Doyle, eds, *Robespierre* (Cambridge: Cambridge University Press, 1999), 3–16.

16 McPhee, *Robespierre. A Revolutionary Life*, 231–232.

17 Restif de la Bretonne, *Les Nuits de Paris* (Paris, 1794), 421.

18 Marie-Jeanne Roland, *The Memoirs of Madame Roland*, 1793, translated by Evelyn Shuckburgh (London: Barrie & Jenkins, 1989), 70–71.

19 Schama, *Citizens*, 617–618.

20 John F. Bosher, *The French Revolution* (London: Weidenfeld and Nicolson, 1989), 178.

21 David Andress, 'The Course of the Terror, 1793–94', in *A Companion to the French Revolution*, ed. Peter McPhee (Chichester: Wiley-Blackwell, 2013), 294–309, here 294.

22 McPhee, *Living the French Revolution, 1789–1799*, 110.

23 Adam Zamoyski, *Phantom Terror. The Threat of Revolution and the Repression of Liberty, 1789–1848* (New York: Basic Books, 2014), 45.

24 McPhee, *Living the French Revolution, 1789–1799*, 110.

25 McPhee, *Robespierre. A Revolutionary Life*, 126.

26 John Hall Stewart, *A Documentary Survey of the French Revolution* (New York: Macmillan, 1951), 314.

27 Donald Sutherland, 'Urban Crowds, Riot, Utopia, and Massacres, 1789–92', in *A Companion to the French Revolution*, ed. Peter McPhee (Chichester: Wiley-Blackwell, 2013), 231–245, here 242.

28 Doyle, *The Oxford History*, 190.

29 Schama, *Citizens*, 637.

30 McPhee, *Living the French Revolution, 1789–1799*, 110.

5

THE TERROR AND THE THERMIDORIAN REACTION

The deputies to the National Convention that assembled in September 1792 faced a reality unforeseen in 1789, and made decisions uncalled for by the *cahiers de doléances*. The period of the Convention radically broke with the past as the deputies oversaw fundamental changes in the constitutional system of France now that the Constitution of 1791 was redundant. The men of the Convention were democrats and republicans and they proclaimed France a republic, which acted as a challenge to the whole of Europe. Theirs was the first attempt to lay the groundwork for the basic institutions of a democratic society. The situation the Convention faced often required its action to be drastic, improvised, decisive and far-reaching. The fate of Louis XVI divided the nation. The military crisis was one of the symptoms of growing internal dissent about the relationship between the national government and the provinces. In the course of its existence, the Convention's policies became repressive, but also reforming; the guarantees of social rights went far ahead of the times. Yet, there was no compromise between the revolutionary government and its opposition. When, in September 1793, terror became the order of the day, the popular movement triumphed even if the revolution began to 'devour its children'. Within the year, however, the abstract notions of republican virtue supported by terror were rejected. It seemed that by 1795 the revolution had truly run its course.

DOI: 10.4324/9781003157748-5

THE REPUBLIC

The National Convention proclaimed the abolition of the monarchy on 21 September 1792. Henceforth, France was a 'one and indivisible' republic. A year later, the Convention declared 22 September the first day of liberty and retrospectively introduced a new calendar with all public documents dated from the first year of the French Republic. The newly elected deputies faced many challenges. Among the most significant were the need to establish a new constitution, the continuing war and the need to decide the fate of Louis XVI.

From the beginning, the National Convention was divided along political and personal lines. The new cohort of deputies included journalists, writers and pamphleteers known, as Simon Schama observes, for the enormous influence they exerted through their publications. Among them were Marat, Desmoulins and Brissot. Their election to the Convention, in Schama's opinion, infused the debates with an unrestrained, critical journalistic style, the outcome of which was often theatrical, vicious oratory, with deputies gesticulating and shouting.

The best way of describing the two dominant factions in the Convention which emerged from the Jacobin Club is to use the factional names, the labels that had withstood the test of time: the Girondins and the Montagnards. The Montagnards were so called because they sat on the upper seats to the left of the president. The group of deputies who were to become the core of the Montagnards were the Parisian deputies and they included Robespierre, Danton and Marat. The membership of the Montagnards overlapped with the membership of the Jacobin Club, with Robespierre becoming the most influential man in both. For the Girondins, the more radical Montagnard group represented anarchy and prevented the development of a functioning republican system. The Girondins sat on the right of the president. In general, they represented the provincial wealthy property owners. Among their leaders were Brissot, Vergniaud, Roland and Condorcet. To the Montagnards, the Girondins were secret monarchists, elitist and uncaring about the common people.

The factions were not political 'parties' in the modern sense. Their membership fluctuated as the result of personal and political rivalries, with the Convention acting as a battlefield where the course and fate of the revolution was decided. It is not an over-statement, claimed Jonathan Israel, to say that 'the Revolution was divided by a schism philosophical, moral, ideological, and personal'.[1] Because of the range of motivations, it is not possible to give a precise number of deputies on either side. For example, Alison Patrick estimates that out of the 750 deputies, the Girondins could count on the support of approximately 180; the Montagnards relied on approximately 140 deputies, although another 160 would support them on various occasions; there were approximately 250 deputies of the Plain (see below).[2]

The conflict between the factions dated back to late 1791. The two factions clashed frequently from the first weeks of the meetings of the Convention. The Girondin leaders rose in the Convention to accuse the Montagnards of a plot to establish a dictatorship. The Montagnards responded in kind by accusing their opponents of conspiracy to restore the imprisoned king. To the general public, however, the Montagnards were seen as more committed to the issues that concerned the lower classes and in particular the *sans-culottes*. This view was influenced by Robespierre's speeches which were full of passionate idealism, his rhetoric more didactic, and his political stance uncompromising. Peter McPhee sees the Montagnards as more flexible and willing for the government to control the price of food.[3] In late 1792, for example, with food scarcity and food rioting, Robespierre responded to the hunger of the ordinary French by pronouncing that the most fundamental of all rights was the 'right of existence' and that all laws needed to support that right. Robespierre's factional colleague Louis-Antoine de Saint-Just explained this right simply: the supply of food is the link between the welfare of the people and their freedom. These two groups competed to win the votes of the undecided deputies, the Plain, who sat at the cross-benches and thus held the balance in the new assembly.[4]

DEBATE ON THE FATE OF THE KING

The question that further divided the Convention was what to do with Louis XVI. France was a republic now. His office was redundant and so was he. There was no question of simply letting him and his family go free, although some deputies considered keeping the king hostage; but the strategically decisive battle of Valmy on

22 September changed that. The majority of the deputies were discussing various options of a trial and execution. Robespierre took the straightforward position—Louis XVI should be executed without trial. He argued in early December 1792 that the people had judged the king guilty on 10 August and his execution was the natural outcome of their judgment; their liberty demanded it. Robespierre's ideas influenced the leadership of the Montagnards and the *sans-culottes*. The Girondins and the Plain wavered, canvassing different opinions and ideas. They argued that Louis' fate should be decided by a national referendum, that the death sentence should not be an option. In any case, the pressure for action against Louis outweighed the provisions of the existing law.

The fact that the 1791 Constitution gave the king legal immunity from prosecution was seen as inconvenient, but not insurmountable. In the end the Convention decided to give the king a trial and for the deputies to vote on his fate. It was a compromise between the Girondins and the Montagnards and the stage was thus set for a public spectacle. Louis XVI, now referred to by the Convention as Louis Capet, was indicted on 11 December 1792 and accused of 'a multitude of crimes' and violating 'the sovereignty of the people'. Contemporary witnesses observed that the trial did not have much to do with legal procedure. Louis was initially denied a lawyer and was not presented with any evidence. The defence team that prepared Louis' case worked under the leadership of Lamoignon de Malesherbes. The former Lord Chancellor later paid with his life for volunteering to take this role. The defence's argument rested on the proposition that the Convention had no legal authority to judge the king. They also argued that the king initiated the reforms aimed at a national revival when he summoned the dormant institution of the Estates-General in 1789. Louis told the deputies that his 'conscience reproached him for nothing'. The evidence used against Louis included the documents that were discovered in the king's private archives stored in a safe in the Tuileries Palace.[5] These documents were used to support the charges relating to the flight to Varennes, the massacre at Champ de Mars, and conspiring with Lafayette and Mirabeau. In the end, the majority of deputies were convinced that Louis was guilty of 'attempts against liberty and of conspiracy against the general security of the state'. The outcome of the trial appeared therefore to have an inevitable conclusion.

The deputies had still to decide on the king's punishment. The Girondins suggested several alternatives. Condorcet argued against the death penalty, reminding the deputies that their decision to execute Louis would only benefit France's enemies. From the left, Thomas Paine wanted to banish Louis to the United States to re-educate him.

DOCUMENT: CONDORCET'S SPEECH ON THE DEATH PENALTY

The last of the *philosophes*, Marquis de Condorcet was a gifted mathematician and a supporter of free trade and the abolition of slavery. He was also an advocate for public education and equality for women. Condorcet was an active deputy of the National Convention and was aligned with the Girondins. His strong voice in political debate brought him into conflict with the Montagnards and ultimately caused his death. Nevertheless, he saw the revolution as proof of the inevitability of progress.

They will tell the people that the Convention sacrificed Louis only to satisfy its vengeance; they will paint us as men greedy for blood; they will paint our revolution as leading to anarchy and disorder. Citizens, that is the real way to harm us, the one which the despots hold in their hands ... When I saw my colleagues climb on the podium to speak their minds, I noticed several, among the firmest patriots, pronounce the death penalty only in moans. Well! Abolish the death penalty for all private offences, while reserving the chance to examine whether it should be kept for offences against the State, because the questions here are different, raising considerations that do not count elsewhere. Until now you have shown proof of an active wish to maintain liberty; you have been accused of taking it too far. I do not suggest that you decrease it, but I ask that you add a measure of charity. Make haste to decree laws that will establish adoption; make haste to assure the fate of those children born outside wedlock; see to it that the labels 'abandoned children' and 'bastards' be no longer in use in the French language. The needs of the State oblige that taxes be established; ways exist to do so in order that these taxes do not burden the poor; make haste to see to it.[6]

THE JUDGMENT OF LOUIS

Finally, between 14 and 20 January, the Convention voted on four motions. The first was to decide Louis' guilt. There were 693 who voted 'yes', with 27 abstentions and no one against the motion. The second motion was to decide whether to hold a national referendum; 283 deputies voted for, 424 against, with 12 abstentions. The third motion was on the method of Louis' punishment: death or otherwise. The debate lasted 36 hours. Out of 721 votes only 361 voted unconditionally for the death penalty—a majority of just one. As the outcome of the vote on the third motion was so close, a fourth motion was put forward: should Louis be reprieved. In the final vote the Montagnards defeated the Girondins' appeal for leniency. It was rejected by 380 votes to 310. The Montagnards demanded that the penalty be carried out immediately.[7]

EXECUTION OF LOUIS XVI

On 21 January 1793, the king was taken from the Temple to the square renamed Place de la Révolution, now known as Place de la Concorde. The Paris Commune, fearing a demonstration if not a rescue attempt, decided to shut the city gates and 1,200 guards were assigned to accompany Louis' coach to the scaffold. The king tried to make a final speech. He proclaimed his innocence and forgave all those who were guilty of his death—the rest of his words were drowned out by the sound of the drums. With the fall of the guillotine's blade the revolution progressed far beyond the demands of the *cahiers de doléances*. Traditionally, the phrase 'Le Roi est mort, vive le Roi!' was used to announce the death of a king of France, stressing the continuity of the monarchy as an institution. When Louis XVI's head was held aloft, the crowd below shouted 'Vive la Nation!'[8] The Convention's position was now represented by the words printed on republican posters and propaganda: Liberty, Republic or Death. There was no turning back.

BRITISH COMMENTARY ON THE DEATH OF THE KING

Three weeks after the execution of Louis XVI and a week after the French declaration of war on Britain, a coloured etching by James Gillray, entitled *The Zenith of French Glory*, was published in Britain.

Drawn by a British caricaturist who created a number of works ridiculing the events of the revolution, the image clearly mocked the events unfolding in Paris. The blood of the revolution's victims exudes from this image as the shocked viewer slowly takes in the details of the satire. The scene is full of 'obscene exaggeration, a superabundance of narrative, and juicy brutality'.[9] Prominent in the foreground is an impressive example of a filthy *sans-culotte*. He is playing an accompaniment to the work of the guillotine on a violin. The face of the *sans-culotte* is sneering. As in other works of James Gillray, *sans-culottes* is taken almost literally here. He hardly has any trousers and he is sitting with a naked behind on top of a lantern as if on a chamber pot. He rests his foot on the head of one of the churchmen hanged on the lamppost turned into a gallows. Hanging from another lamp is a judge in the full robes of office. To the right of the *sans-culotte* is a blasphemous portrayal of the crucifix with the words above the crucified body of Jesus 'King of the Jews' replaced with a card 'Goodnight Sirs'. Beyond the square, the revolutionary anarchy devours a church shown with its dome aflame. The crowd is portrayed as an amorphous mass wearing liberty caps.

THE WAR OF THE FIRST COALITION

On 23 January 1793, the Convention issued a proclamation announcing the death of the former king with the ringing words that the tyrant was no more, and claimed that the French people were now united in their pursuit of liberty and fraternity. It was addressed to the French people but was received across Europe with shock and disbelief.

The death of Louis did not end the factional struggle that divided the Convention. The decision to execute Louis sealed the division between the Montagnards and the Girondins. In the minds of Parisians the Girondins' attempts to spare Louis' life made them supporters of the monarchy. The lack of compromise resulted in prolonged instability, which affected France's ability to deal with crises, both internal and external. All European courts reacted with horror to the news of the execution of Louis XVI and broke off diplomatic relations with France. France responded by declaring war on Britain and the Netherlands on 1 February 1793. With other monarchs joining the war, an anti-French coalition was formed.

In late 1792, the French enjoyed a series of early successes. For example, the French troops annexed Savoy on 27 November. In the north-east the French advances were partly due to withdrawal of Prussian troops from the front as Frederick William of Prussia shifted them east in order to secure Prussian participation in the Second Partition of Poland and the port of Gdańsk. Unopposed, the French revolutionary armies progressed eastwards with little resistance and carried with them the principles of liberty and equality. In practical terms, this meant introducing reforms already in force in France: the abolition of tithes, feudal dues and the nobility—all forms of privilege. Their mandate, William Doyle observed, was 'in the name of peace, help, fraternity, liberty, and equality, to assist all peoples to establish "free and popular" governments, with whom they would then co-operate'.[10] The excitement of spreading the principles of the revolution, however, started to evaporate as the tide of war turned against France.

On 18 March 1793 at Neerwinden, the French army, led by Charles Dumouriez, was defeated by a coalition army, ending the French invasion of the Austrian Netherlands. As a result, the French army retreated through Brussels on 24 March. The Austrians regained Belgium and the Rhineland as the Spaniards entered France from the south. Dumouriez, whose conviction in the revolution was shaken by the judicial murder of the king, attempted to rally his troops to march on Paris against the Convention and to restore the Constitution of 1791 with the infant Louis XVII as king. Unsuccessful, he defected to the enemy on 5 April 1793, leaving the French armies in disarray.

The defection of Dumouriez, a high-ranking military leader and hero of the first great victories at Valmy and Jemappes and a factional associate of the Girondins, provided the Montagnards with cause to criticise their rivals. The Montagnards used Dumouriez's defection as evidence that the Girondins could not be trusted. The public increasingly feared that the counter-revolution would attack, not from outside France, but from within. The suspicion that there were traitors working against the revolution made a measured political debate extremely difficult.

FACING THE DANGERS AT HOME

The declaration of the Republic by the Convention, the war of the first coalition, the execution of Louis XVI and the unfinished constitution put France on the path of extraordinary measures. As early as October 1792, in response to the September Massacres, the Convention established the Committee of General Security and granted it policing powers. Danton argued that such an institution was needed to prevent the excesses of the revolutionary *journées* and vigilante justice, which demonstrated its power during the September Massacres. With the civil war in the Vendée and military losses on the frontiers, the Montagnards were becoming increasingly powerful. The deputies of the Plain, argues Peter McPhee, were no longer prepared to support the Girondins, and the Montagnards' constructive proposals for dealing with the crisis were accepted. A new 'emergency concept of law' and 'order that was rooted in considerations of "public safety"', according to Peter Jones, 'was starting to take over, and it had no time for procedural niceties. Indeed, the highly decentralised local government system that the committees of the National Assembly had devised in 1789–90 now appeared to be a luxury that the revolution could barely afford.'[11]

The measures created to enable a centralised response to the unfolding situation included the creation of powerful committees and positions. The Convention established the Committee of General Security in October 1792 to oversee internal security of the Republic. Its members were responsible for policing and dealing with suspected counter-revolutionaries, non-juring priests, as well as hoarders and speculators. The suspects were then brought before the Revolutionary Tribunal to decide whether they were guilty of the suspected crimes. One of the committee's more prominent members was Joseph Fouché, who was responsible for the maintenance of an extensive network of spies.

In March 1793, a Revolutionary Tribunal was created to dispense 'revolutionary justice'. From September 1793 it comprised 16 examining magistrates, with a jury of 60 and a public prosecutor. The notion of revolutionary justice demanded that the trials were fast-tracked and this necessarily limited the independence of the judges and the rights of defendants. Initially, those brought before the tribunal could expect a verdict with a range of penalties; however, after the enactment of the Law of 22 Prairial Year II (10 June 1794), if the charges were not dropped, the only penalty was death. Peter McPhee provides the statistics in regard to the sentencing of the tribunal: from March 1793 until September, only 66 of the 260

(25 per cent) accused were sentenced to death; in the final three months of 1793, 177 of the 395 (45 per cent) accused were sentenced to death.[12]

In the face of the growing opposition to the policies of the Convention, on 9 March 1793 a new institution of Representatives on Mission was established. The Convention sent almost 100 of its deputies as emissaries to the *départements*. The Representatives on Mission were responsible for ensuring local compliance with the Paris decrees. In particular, they coordinated the support of the war effort. Their role as enforcers of the will of Paris effectively terrorised the population.

The Convention decreed on 21 March 1793 that every commune, and in the cities every *section*, was to have a committee of surveillance. These 'police committees' were to be composed of 12 elected members and were primarily responsible for maintaining a record of the foreigners resident in their locality, for identifying and arresting suspects, and for issuing certificates of loyal and patriotic citizenship.

The Convention also needed an executive body that could coordinate the work of other agencies. On 25 March, on the initiative of Bertrand Barère, a Committee of Public Safety was established. The committee began its work on 7 April 1793, with a membership of nine deputies and a mandate that was renewable monthly. Danton, who was elected to the committee, took on the leading role, pleading for unity and reconciliation, yet Barère was to be its longest serving member. Between March and May 1793, the deputies gave the committee executive powers to supervise the army and coordinate the provision of supplies both for the army and the general population. The membership of the committee was expanded to 12 deputies in July 1793, and the Law of 14 Frimaire Year II (4 December 1793) granted the committee full executive powers. It was in the expansion that Robespierre joined the committee and quickly became its de facto leader. The centralisation of the government functions in the hands of the members of the Committee of Public Safety meant that from December 1793 they not only formulated policy, but also effectively controlled its implementation through direct supervision of the armed forces, foreign policy and, through the Representatives on Mission, the local authorities in the *départements*.

The mounting war toll was addressed by the Convention on 24 February 1793 with a decree conscripting 300,000 extra men into the revolutionary army. The Montagnards, supported by the deputies of the Plain, proposed this as an emergency measure. The *Levée en masse* applied to all French male citizens aged 18 to 40 years, unmarried or widowed, without children. The implementation of the levy was generally successful in the south-east and east of France and around Paris. In the south and west of France, however, it provoked armed rebellions. In the region of the Vendée the rebellion turned into a civil war in 1793.

UPRISING IN THE VENDÉE, 1793

The people of the Vendée region had a range of grievances that were ignored or could not be addressed by Paris. In 1790 and 1791, their opposition to the *Civil Constitution of the Clergy* was evident, with 90 per cent of the local priests refusing to take the Clerical Oath. The Church played an integral part in the lives of the people of the Vendée, with the parish priests serving an important social, political and economic role and providing the cornerstone of the community's identity. The revolution did not change life for the better for the peasants, and perhaps the execution of Louis XVI in January 1793 further alienated them. The tenant farmers were hostile towards the enterprising pro-revolutionary bourgeoisie in the region who benefited from the nationalisation of Church lands. Heavier taxes, a decline in trade in textiles, and resentment of the reform of the Church further disenchanted the local people about the revolutionary leaders in Paris. Historians generally agree that while the conscription order from Paris set off the uprising, the region exploded in violence because of broader grievances against the revolution. In essence, the people of the Vendée responded to the revolution that they saw as destroying the fabric of their everyday lives.

The uprising in the Vendée began with the peasants' opposition to conscription and quickly turned into insurrection. Between March and December 1793, peasants, artisans and weavers formed the Catholic and Royal Army led by local nobles. On 11 March 1793, they captured the town of Machecoul, killing the National Guard and the constitutional priest. By June 1793, their army had grown to 40,000. The civil war was fought by both sides with unrelenting cruelty. The rebels captured several small towns in the region and attempted to seize the port city of Nantes, which could ensure the arrival of external support.

When the hostilities started in the Vendée in March 1793 the French revolutionary armies faced defeat in the Austrian Netherlands and the Convention was preoccupied with the external threat. In August, however, the Convention decided to crush the Vendée Rebellion. The deputies saw the revolt as treason and the insurgents as irrationally attached to the archaic *ancien régime*, the past characterised by tyranny, superstition and ignorance. For François Furet it became the 'most symbolic conflict that pitched Revolution and *ancien régime* against one another'.[13]

Consequently, the Convention used extreme methods to subdue the Vendée Rebellion: mass drownings of prisoners in the Loire River; the burning of entire villages, together with the massacre of their inhabitants. This merciless slaughter was consistent with the revolutionary ideology of its leaders who gradually degraded opponents, concludes Simon Schama, and were incapable of contemplating any compromise.[14] Estimates suggest that 220,000–250,000 men, women and children, over a quarter of the population of the region, lost their lives in the Vendée between 1793 and 1794. Reynald Secher went as far as to call these massacres genocide, an assessment not shared by either Peter McPhee or Simon Schama.[15] The revolution was faced with both external and internal threats and its leaders responded as have many other societies during civil war. In the Vendée, the revolution unleashed a deadly cycle of extreme violence. Historians continue to debate whether the violence was the revolution's self-defence, or was the fuel that fed the revolution's rapacious appetite for change if not destruction.

'The Vendée is no more', General François Westermann reported to the Convention in December 1793, 'we did not take any prisoners … pity is not revolutionary'. After the region had been pacified, between December 1793 and May 1794, General Louis-Marie Turreau's 'infernal columns' exacted further revenge on the region. It was a strategy of scorched earth: 'all villages, farms, woods, heathlands, generally anything that will burn, will be set on fire', wrote Turreau.[16] General Jean-Baptiste Kléber notified Paris that 'the enemy's destruction was now a certainty' and admitted that 'pen refused to describe the atrocities which we inflicted on these wretches'.[17]

Decades after the rebellion, in an attempt to glorify the royalist resistance against the revolution, King Louis XVIII commissioned a portrait of Henri de la Rochejaquelin (1772–1794), the youngest general of the Catholic and Royal Army. The painting presents a striking example of heroic bravery, a handsome fighter astride a barricade or fortification, fighting with one hand, the badge of the Sacred Heart pinned on his breast, and the flag of the Catholic and Royal Army behind him.

POPULAR RADICALISM AND THE SPLIT IN THE CONVENTION

The Vendée Rebellion was not the only problem to distract the Convention from pursuing the war effort. The cyclical food shortages that had plagued the *ancien régime* continued to ravage France and in 1793 the Convention had to deal with a worsening economic crisis: the 1792 grain harvest was poor; the army's food requisitioning and the British blockade of French ports added further pressure; food prices soared, again resulting in inflation, which diluted the value of *assignats*. The economic repercussions were typical: price rises outpaced wage increases; popular protests ensued; the food crisis deepened the divide between the Girondins and the *sans-culottes* and their leaders. For the Girondins, the *sans-culottes* were incited to action by radicals such as Marat and Jacques Roux, the leader of the *enragés*.

The struggle between the moderates and radicals in the Convention also spilled into the *départements*. The moderates and radicals competed for control of major regional centres and by May 1793 the Girondins' allies controlled the administration of Lyon, Marseille, Bordeaux and Caen. The conflict was also debated in the newspapers, which criticised the undemocratic influence of Paris on the Convention. Why, they asked, should the Parisian *sans-culottes* enjoy preferential treatment and the provinces be ignored?

In June, Marseille proclaimed itself to be 'in a legal state of resistance' to the National Convention, and its own Revolutionary Tribunal sentenced 30 members of the Jacobin Club to death. The city of Toulon followed. This rising became known as the Federalist

Revolt. In this revolt the regional manufacturing and trade centres demanded that Paris respect their local autonomy and freedom of trade. They rejected the representatives from Paris, who arrived in the *départements* with limitless powers, as representing Convention's centralism. To counter that centralism, they demanded the abolition of the Revolutionary Tribunal and the Committee of Public Safety, and if all else failed, the calling of new elections.[18] Those who supported the Federalist Revolt felt aggrieved by the influence that the *sans-culottes* exerted on deputies in Paris but rebelled against the 'range of emergency measures', including regulation of the market, conscription, and greater police powers.[19]

The Convention rejected any notion of 'federalism' as contrary to the principle of French unity. The Republic was one and indivisible. Consequently, the reprisals against the Federalist Revolt were brutal. Lyon was subjected to a siege and its population suffered widespread famine. On 12 October 1793, the Committee of Public Safety decreed that the city's fortifications and the houses of its rich citizens should be razed to the ground in the city's 'war on liberty'. The population suffered reprisals, with executions taking place between August and October. At least 26 people were guillotined each day. In December 1793, the Representatives on Mission ordered mass shootings during which 360 victims were executed in groups fired on by a cannon. By April 1794, the casualties reached 2,000. The cities of Bordeaux, Marseille and Nantes were subjected to the same treatment. In this confrontation between the Convention and the mercantile middle class, argues Simon Schama, the bourgeoisie became the main casualty.[20]

VICTORY OF THE MONTAGNARDS

The disagreements and the nature of the debate between the Girondins and the Montagnards became more and more aggressive. The Girondins accused the Montagnards of provoking the *sans-culottes* to commit the atrocities of September 1792. When Condorcet presented the Convention with a new constitutional proposal to allow popular referenda to repeal legislation in February 1793, the Montagnards rejected the draft legislation as threatening the primacy of Paris. The Girondins responded in March 1793 with an attempt to convict the Montagnard deputy, Marat, before the Revolutionary Tribunal, accusing him of inciting *sans-culottes* to violence and rioting against rising food prices. Their strategy backfired when, on 24 April 1793, Marat was acquitted, and the demonstrations turned against the Girondins. In the popular etching 'Marat's Triumph', Jean-Paul Marat was depicted as crowned with laurel, and carried on the shoulders of his supporters who were celebrating his acquittal by the Revolutionary Tribunal.

The Girondin leaders misjudged the public mood. Marat was a hero of the *sans-culottes*. Yet they continued to provoke the *sans-culottes* and the Paris Commune by describing them as anarchists and blood-drinkers. They faced the response of the Montagnard leaders and the radical *sans-culottes* of Paris in May and June. On 31 May 1793, the Paris *sections* staged another insurrection led by the *sans-culottes*. They surrounded the Convention and demanded the expulsion of 29 Girondin deputies. The *sans-culottes* demanded their enemies be silenced.[21] The Plain again sided with the Montagnards to prevent what they perceived as the danger of internal breakdown and external threat. This decision needs to be put in the context of the events of April and May of 1793. The revolution faced a combination of crises: military, social, economic and political. Foreign armies had entered France and fighting continued on French soil. The civil war in the Vendée proved to be more than a temporary distraction and it engaged significant resources of the Republic. The economic downturn caused further disenchantment among the population. The rule of the Convention from Paris faced opposition from a large proportion of departmental authorities. The intimidated Convention gave in to the demands of the Paris Commune and the *sans-culottes*. The 29 deputies were arrested, including two ministers; one of the Girondin leaders, Roland, fled.[22] The Montagnards were in control of the Convention. The events of 31 May to 2 June 1793 enabled the Montagnards to enact a new constitution, but they also set a precedent: no deputy of the National Convention could enjoy immunity.

On 24 June, the deputies endorsed a new constitution. The Constitution was essentially the work of Robespierre and contained truly revolutionary guarantees of social rights and popular control over a unicameral legislative assembly elected by direct, universal male suffrage.[23] In Article 21, the Constitution guaranteed all citizens either employment or sufficient welfare benefits for those who were unable to work, and free public education. The right of the public to dissent when the 'government violates the rights of the people' by means of insurrection was confirmed in Article 35. The provisions were far ahead of their time, but even though the Constitution was accepted in August 1793 by a national referendum, it never came into effect, as France entered the period of the 'revolutionary government'.

No immunity, however, could have saved the Montagnard deputy and radical journalist Jean-Paul Marat. On 13 July, Marat was killed by Charlotte Corday, a Girondin supporter from the Federalist town of Caen. In order to meet Marat, she had written to him, promising to give him the names of traitors to the Republic. She visited Marat at home and killed him with a single stab to the chest while he was sitting in a bath to treat a painful skin disease. Corday gave herself up to the police and confessed, explaining her motivation: she wanted to stop Marat's incessant promotion of violence and to prevent civil war. She 'knew he was ruining France' and decided to kill 'one man to save a hundred thousand'.[24] Corday demonstrated no remorse, was sentenced to death on 17 July and executed the same day. The death of the 'Friend of the People' gave the revolution one of its most iconic martyrs. Within months of Marat's murder, Jacques-Louis David portrayed the murdered Jean-Paul Marat lying dead in a bath on 13 July 1793, presumably shortly after his murder by the young noblewoman from Normandy.

DOCUMENT: *DECLARATION OF THE RIGHTS OF MAN AND THE CITIZEN*, 26 AUGUST 1793

The original *Declaration of the Rights of Man and the Citizen* adopted by the National Assembly on 26 August 1789 included universal rights, but by 1793 it had become associated with the 'men of 1789' such as Lafayette. In 1793, the National Convention revised the *Declaration of the Rights of Man and the Citizen* and included it as the preface to the new Constitution.

The French people, convinced that forgetfulness of and contempt for the natural rights of man are the sole causes of the misfortunes of the world, have resolved to set forth these sacred and inalienable rights in a solemn declaration, in order that all citizens, being able constantly to compare the acts of the government with the aim of every social institution, may never permit themselves to be oppressed and degraded by tyranny, in order that the people may always have before their eyes the bases of their liberty and their happiness, the magistrate the guide to his duties, the legislator the object of his mission. Accordingly, in the presence of the Supreme Being, they proclaim the following declaration of the rights of man and citizen.

1   The aim of society is the general welfare. Government is instituted to guarantee man the enjoyment of his natural and inalienable rights.

2   These rights are equality, liberty, security, and property.

3   All men are equal by nature and before the law.

4   Law is the free and solemn expression of the general will; it is the same for all, whether it protects or punishes; it may order only what is just and useful to society; it may prohibit only what is injurious thereto.

5   All citizens are equally admissible to public office. Free peoples recognise no grounds for preference in their elections other than virtues and talents.

6   Liberty is the power appertaining to man to do whatever is not injurious to the rights of others. It has nature for its principle, justice for its rule, law for its safeguard. Its moral limit lies in this maxim: Do not do to others that which you do not wish to be done to you.

7   The right of manifesting ideas and opinions, either through the press or in any other manner, the right of peaceful assembly, and the free exercise of worship may not be forbidden. The necessity of enunciating these rights implies either the presence or the recent memory of despotism ...

13 Every man being presumed innocent until he has been pronounced guilty, if it is thought indispensable to arrest him, all severity that may not be necessary to secure his person ought to be strictly repressed by law ...

15   The law ought to impose only penalties that are strictly and obviously necessary: the punishments ought to be proportionate to the offence and useful to society.

16   The right of property is the right appertaining to every citizen to enjoy and dispose at will of his goods, his income, and the product of his labour and skill.

17   No kind of labour, tillage, or commerce may be forbidden the industry of citizens.

18   Every man may contract his services or his time; but he may not sell himself nor be sold; his person is not an alienable property. The law knows of no such thing as the status of servant; there can exist only a contract for services and compensation between the man who works and the one who employs him.

19   No one may be deprived of the least portion of his property without his consent, unless a legally established public necessity requires it, and upon condition of a just and previous indemnity.

20   No tax can be imposed except for the general advantage. All citizens have the right to participate in the establishment of taxes, to watch over the employment of them, and to cause an account of them to be rendered.

21   Public relief [of poverty] is a sacred debt. Society owes maintenance to unfortunate citizens, either procuring work for them or in providing the means of existence for those who are unable to labour.

22   Education is needed by all. Society ought to favour with all its power the advancement of the public reason and to put education at the door of every citizen.

23   The social guarantee consists of the effort to assure to each the enjoyment and preservation of his rights; this guarantee is based upon national sovereignty …

29   Each citizen has an equal right to participate in the formation of the law and in the selection of his representatives or his agents.

30   Public functions are essentially temporary; they cannot be considered as distinctions nor rewards, but as duties.

31 The offences of the representatives of the people and of its agents ought never to go unpunished. No one has the right to consider himself more inviolable than others ...

33 Resistance to oppression is the consequence of the other rights of man.

35 When the government violates the rights of the people, insurrection is for the people, and for every portion thereof, the most sacred of rights and the most indispensable of duties.

LEVÉE EN MASSE, 23 AUGUST 1793

The defeat of the Federalist revolts gave the Montagnard-dominated Convention the opportunity to address the issue of the influence and impact of the radical Paris Commune and the Paris *sections*. Even though the Convention had secured relative stability in the provinces through a variety of harsh measures, the deputies were not able to control the streets of Paris. The Convention still faced the agitation of the radical press, which only added to the atmosphere of crisis. The journalist Jacques Hébert questioned the Convention's decisiveness in dealing with traitors. Written in oath-strewn vernacular, his *Le Père Duchesne* became the bestselling paper. In addition to demanding harsher measures against hoarders, Hébert demanded the extension of price controls to 'all goods of first necessity'. These demands were shared by Jacques Roux, a radical associated with the Jacobins and Girondists, and the newspaper, *L'Ami du peuple*. They all called for merciless use of the guillotine to eliminate all opposition. The Terror was the answer. The deputies gave in to the demands and attempted to pacify the situation by introducing the death penalty for hoarding grain, among a series of new measures.

On 23 August 1793, the Convention voted in the *Levée en masse*. This decision to create a national conscripted army was, in Simon Schama's assessment, born out of desperation, but if successful would give the Convention the ability to suppress all internal revolts and defeat foreign intervention.[25] This decree was the first instance of conscription in modern history and expressed the state's right to require all citizens to meet a national emergency. This groundbreaking measure called on all French people to rally to the defence of the Republic. The Convention decree was made in response to pressure from the *sans-culottes* and the realisation that the volunteer army was dwindling in numbers. While it did stop short of universal conscription, it did amount to the mobilisation of the populace in defence of the nation. All unmarried men and widowers between the ages of 18 and 25 were called upon to enlist while married men and women were encouraged to assist in the manufacture of arms and materials. In 1792 the French army included approximately 155,000 men and its numbers increased significantly with the levy of 300,000 in March 1793. At least 300,000 soldiers were mobilised by the *Levée en masse*, bringing the French army to number around 750,000 men.[26]

On the same day as the *Levée en masse* was decreed, journalist Théophile Leclerc, who had succeeded Marat at *L'Ami du Peuple*, published an 'Appeal to the Guillotine', taking aim at the internal enemies of the revolution, attacking the government of the day as sacrificing the interests of the people to the greed of the bourgeoisie. Leclerc wrote that, 'if the National Convention really desires the salvation of their fatherland', they should prove it by conscripting all *sans-culottes*, closing toll-gates and shops and ceasing all activity except for the manufacture of arms. Above all, the Convention should ensure that all citizens remained committed to the cause by letting 'the popular tribunals' be formed by the 'best of the citizens' and 'two guillotines be set up permanently on the Place de la Revolution'. The people, having been armed, would then form in platoons and attack the homes of all 'hoarders, speculators, suspects, egoists, persons who have grown rich since the Revolution, the plunderers of the Revolution in general!'[27]

The radicalism of Théophile Leclerc was matched by Jacques Roux, the leader of the *enragés*, the most militant *sans-culottes*. It had its origins in the suffering of the urban working class he witnessed himself. Roux argued that ordinary people were starving because profiteers were hoarding food supplies, and he began his campaign for speculators to be punished by death as traitors. Hence, the *enragés* demanded an active government intervention by instituting control of the prices of essential goods. Their ideas, which seemed radical in early 1793, gained acceptance as the events of the year unfolded, and culminated in the attack on the Convention on

4–5 September 1793, making them 'virtually the political masters of Paris'.[28] They also found their supporters among members of the Paris Commune, including Jacques-Rene Hébert and the Society of Revolutionary Republican Women.

The militarisation of the citizenry which involved the women workers producing clothing also exerted pressure on the Convention by their petitioning for improvements in the working conditions. In addition to economic postulates, women's rights to public office and to bear arms were also campaigned for by 'a family of sisters', the Society of Revolutionary Republican Women, led by Claire Lacombe and Pauline Léon. Their declared mission was to 'instruct themselves, to learn well the Constitution and laws of the Republic, to attend to public affairs, to succour suffering humanity, and to defend all human beings who become victims of any arbitrary acts whatever'.[29]

Whilst some men praised women of the Society for 'breaking the links in the chain of prejudice', such as those which confined women to the narrow sphere of their households, others, for example, members of the Jacobin Club, attacked them as 'counter-revolutionary sluts' who make 'a revolution over coffee and sugar'.[30]

THE TERROR IS THE ORDER OF THE DAY

The participants of the Parisian insurrection incited by Jacques Roux on 4 September 1793 marched on the Convention the following day with a range of economic demands. The organisers wanted to force the Convention to create a revolutionary army made up of civilians to punish hoarders and seize the food to feed the people of Paris. This revolutionary *journée* coincided with the arrival of reports that Cap Français, the main port of the Caribbean colony of Saint-Domingue, was destroyed by fire in the most extensive case of urban violence in the entire course of the revolution, and the news that Toulon had opened its harbour and city to the British fleet.[31] In the atmosphere of emergency, noted Schama, patriotism took primacy over questions of prices and supplies: 'It was no hard thing, then, to decree that since the Convention and the Committee of Public Safety had a shrewd idea that they would be its executors.'[32] The *enragés*' cause found its direct expression in the Law of the Maximum enacted by the Convention on 29 September 1793. The *sans-culottes* seemed to have forced the Convention to adopt their policies for the second time in three months without resistance—in order to ensure the safety of the Republic, its real and imagined enemies were to be terrorised.

The Convention declared on 5 September 1793 that the government would not hesitate to use force against its own citizens to ensure compliance with the national laws and to protect the unity of the Republic. Danton spoke in the Convention that France was 'in a real and active state of revolution'. He called for the Convention to recognise that the true patriots, who earned a living by the sweat of their brow, were absent from the *section* meetings, and because of their absence, conspiracies took place. Danton demanded that the Convention 'therefore decree that two large section-meetings be held each week' and that any 'man of the People' who attends will receive renumeration for the time spent away from work.[33] He endorsed the demand of the protesters to create a revolutionary army, but proposed for the army to be organised by the Committee of Public Safety, and therefore controlled by the government.

REVOLUTIONARY GOVERNMENT AND THE TERROR

The range of emergencies faced by the Republic meant that the Convention's day-to-day executive tasks were handled by the Committee of Public Safety. After the defeat of the Girondins, the Committee's membership changed, with a number of the Montagnard leaders, such as Robespierre and Saint-Just, replacing more moderate deputies. With the influential moderate Danton leaving the Committee, its policies became more radical. The Committee increasingly performed the function of an executive branch of government, with some members assigned to particular government departments or tasks. For example, Lazare Carnot was in charge of the war strategy and army in general. The policies of the Committee were carried out by the Representative on Mission or specially appointed agents. In the months that followed the declaration that 'terror is the order of the day' (5 September 1793), the Convention decreed the government of France would remain 'revolutionary until the peace' (10 October 1793)—revolutionary, that is dictatorial. The same decree suspended the 1793 Constitution, placing all government bodies and the army under the control of the Committee of Public Safety, which had to report weekly to the Convention. The law, argued John Hall Stewart, had fundamentally altered the nature of government in France. The citizens of the Republic had almost all individual rights suspended and were now governed by a revolutionary dictatorship. The Reign of Terror had begun.

Among the extraordinary measures decreed by the Convention was the Law of Suspects enacted on 17 September 1793; it provided for setting up of surveillance committees in every *département* to expose the 'unpatriotic' and to terrorise them.[34] Individuals suspected of counter-revolutionary activity could be jailed indefinitely. Following the introduction of the Law, the Revolutionary Tribunal tried and sentenced to death a number of prominent political figures. Among the first to be executed was Marie Antoinette, who was guillotined on 16 October. The 37-year-old former Queen of France was memorialised by Jacques-Louis David, seated with her hands bound behind her back in a tumbrel on the way to the guillotine, in a drawing that is pitilessly frank in contrast to the apologetic heroism of David's 'Death of Marat'. Jacques Hébert in *Le Père Duchesne* expressed his views differently: 'The bitch was audacious and insolent right to the very end'.[35] Marie Antoinette's execution was followed by the deaths of the 21 Girondin leaders (31 October), Olympe de Gouges (3 November), the former Duke of Orléans, Philippe Égalité (7 November), Madame Roland (8 November), and the 'men of 1789'—Bailly (12 November) and Barnave (29 November). The executions of such high-profile individuals emphasised the resolve of the Convention to eradicate all possible counter-revolution. Indeed, claims Schama, these executions were the reflection of the nature of the revolution itself, which at every stage of its development was defined by armed conflict, violence and riot.[36]

According to the Law of Suspects a broad array of individuals could be considered to pose a threat to the revolution: those who emigrated as a result of the revolution even though they may have returned to France; former nobles and their families or agents of the émigrés who had not steadfastly shown their devotion to the revolution; those who had shown themselves to be supporters of tyranny or federalism and enemies of liberty; public officials who had been suspended or dismissed from their positions by the National

Convention; those who were unable to justify their means of existence and the performance of their civic duties; and those who had been refused certificates of revolutionary patriotism.

The Law of Suspects whilst seen as excessively harsh and severe was designed to quell the insecurity of the people of Paris, argues Peter McPhee, where long-established neighbourhoods were unsettled by the influx of newcomers, both civilians and soldiers. The city at the heart of the revolution was 'crackling with a potent mixture of rumour, optimism and suspicion'. Lies, feuds and denunciations were rife 'yet the activities of the section authorities were self-consciously legal and "correct"'.[37]

Another of the extraordinary measures decreed, the Law of the Maximum, was enacted on 29 September 1793. It provided for maximum prices on a range of foodstuffs including wheat and flour and gave the government the right to requisition supplies from suppliers. The main purpose of the law was to set price limits, preventing inflationary price rises in order to secure continued access to the food supply. For the food producers and suppliers it meant imposition of restrictions on their capacity to make profits. The Convention's growing fear of the *sans-culottes* outweighed its strong support for free-market principles.[38]

REVOLUTIONARY CULTURE

The revolutionaries were full of hope that the France they were creating would be a truly new society—a clear break from the *ancien régime*. The new society was to be built on new civic principles and a new revolutionary culture. Establishing the new order within meant that France was to regenerate itself. The revolutionaries also pursued uniformity, which, for example, targeted France's many local dialects. They argued that the opposition to the revolution was caused by linguistic diversity, which prevented people's full understanding of the new values propagated by Paris. Even the old forms of address were to be abandoned, with preference given to the simple *citoyen* (citizen), in an attempt to change the language usage that inadvertently propagated class differences. The new France was, after all, a national community of equal citizens. The traditional culture was to be replaced by new symbols and new values. Public buildings and official documents were embellished with slogans such as 'Liberty, Equality, Fraternity, or Death'.

Nonetheless, the new society was infused with the old symbols, often drawn from Roman tradition, with new revolutionary meaning. Simple items such as playing cards featured new revolutionary motifs, with the figures of Liberty or portraits of the *philosophes* in place of kings and queens. New decorations, new costumes for officials and public festivals became part of the cultural campaign of the Convention.

On 5 October 1793, the Convention made another radical step towards breaking from the past and replaced the Christian calendar with a new revolutionary one. The new calendar was meant to demonstrate that the revolution opened a new era in human history. Societies had introduced calendars in the past but this one was to be truly revolutionary. It was meant to change the behaviour of people by replacing the old feast days associated with old rituals. Years were to be counted from the proclamation of the Republic on 22 September 1792, and accordingly 1793–1794 became Year II. In the broader sense it reaffirmed the Convention's intention of imposing 'order'. The new calendar was based on the scientific achievements of the age and exemplified the simplicity that came to be deemed a virtue. The year opened on the equinox of 22 September and was divided into 12 months, each of 30 days which were in turn divided into ten-day weeks. Each day had ten hours, composed of ten minutes and a hundred seconds. The months were given names related to nature: Nivôse was the month of snow, Frimaire the month of frosts. There were five national holidays called the *sans-culottides* but no Sundays or Christian saints' feast days, reflecting the secular nature of the new society.

Arguably, according to the higher wisdom of nature, people had been meant to count in tens, since they had been created with ten fingers. For all the rhetoric, the revolutionary calendar, allegedly based on the laws of nature, was also technically defective, and various adjustments were made to fix it before it was abolished by Napoleon in December 1805. The introduction of the new calendar complemented the reform of weights and measures and the introduction of the metric system on 1 August 1793. The new calendar was part of the deliberate de-Christianisation but, like the abandonment of Catholicism in France, it never quite worked.

Over the course of 1793, the anticlerical attitudes of the popular movement grew. Open hostility towards the Catholic Church turned into efforts to suppress the Christian religion altogether. The majority of the deputies of the Convention, including Robespierre, were afraid that the de-Christianising campaign would further worsen conflict over religion. His approach was essentially pragmatic—Robespierre admitted that 'if God did not exist, it would be necessary to invent Him'.[39] The excesses of the de-Christianisation practised by militant *sans-culottes* went on initially without any control. In November 1793, they turned Paris's Notre Dame Cathedral into a Temple of Reason, and a fortnight later all Paris churches were closed by the Commune. The campaign extended to the countryside, with wholesale destruction of Catholic symbols: images and statues of saints were damaged; cemeteries were desecrated; Christian worship was ridiculed, with republican masses sung where 'the blood of kings, the true substance of republican communion', was shared; monks and nuns were often forced to marry in secular marriage ceremonies. In the provinces, Representatives on Mission, such as the former priest Fouché, undertook similar if not more enthusiastic actions.

De-Christianisation divided the Jacobins in Paris, with Danton expressing his disgust and Robespierre his revulsion towards the Festivals of Reason, which he thought were 'ridiculous farces'. In the end, argues Georges Lefebvre, Robespierre feared that de-Christianisation was atheism in disguise, which was immoral and which alienated many, including supporters of the revolution. The most ardent supporters of de-Christianisation were the Hébertists, the radicals who supported the popular journalist Jacques Hébert. Their success united Robespierre and Danton who now decided to curb the militancy of the Paris Commune.

THE REVOLUTIONARY GOVERNMENT

The extensive executive powers of the Committee of Public Safety made it the real heart of the government. The Committee's membership and its mandate were subject to vote by the Convention every 30 days. On 4 December 1793, the Convention took another step towards the centralisation of power in Paris by passing the Law on Revolutionary Government of 4 December 1793, also known as the Law of 14 Frimaire Year II.

The Law of 14 Frimaire Year II consolidated the earlier legislation instituting the Terror and redefined the relationship between the Convention and the Great Committees, the Revolutionary Tribunal and the surveillance committees. The committees' remit of authority was clearly defined. The Committee of Public Safety controlled the ministers, appointed generals and conducted foreign policy while also enforcing central government's policies through local government in the *départements*. The Committee of General Security was in control of police and internal security, supervised surveillance committees and managed the operation of the Revolutionary Tribunal. The role of the National Convention was now at the heart of both legislative and executive government but stripped of most of its power, as it had delegated full executive power to the two Great Committees.

The reasons for the enactment of the Law on Revolutionary Government were both economic and political. In Albert Soboul's view, the deputies aimed at establishing the absolute authority of the Committee of Public Safety over all aspects of the life of the nation, a trend that had been apparent since 2 June.[40] The Law is often referred to as the 'Constitution of the Terror', perhaps because it combined the earlier decrees, which established the institutions of the Terror, and at the same time specified the relationship between these various branches of the revolutionary government. In the view of Simon Schama, the Law of 14 Frimaire Year II ended the effective lawlessness of the various revolutionary institutions by providing strict interpretation of the principles of operation of the revolutionary government and enforcing accountability with a system of checks and balances.[41] The surveillance committees were now required to report every ten days on their activities. All officials, including the Representatives on Mission, were to enforce the Convention's directives without altering their provisions and were prohibited from acting outside their jurisdiction. In the absence of an operational constitution, the Law of 14 Frimaire Year II set out the organisation of government, giving the national government authority to remove and replace local administrators. It was an attempt to give the Terror a human face by enforcing accountability of public officials.

DOCUMENT: CAMILLE DESMOULINS ON TERROR

Desmoulins launched his newspaper *Le Vieux Cordelier* the day following the enactment of the Law of 14 Frimaire Year II. The first two issues, approved by Robespierre, targeted the Hébertists and de-Christianisation, but Desmoulins was attacked in the Jacobin Club for having written sympathetically about the death of the Girondins—'they die as republicans, as Brutus died'. The title of the newspaper *Le Vieux Cordelier* (The Old Cordelier) was deliberate as Desmoulins wanted to distance himself from the editorial line taken by the new Cordeliers controlled by Hébert and his supporters.

No longer do we have a paper that tells the truth, or at least the whole truth. I re-enter the arena with all the honesty and courage for which I am known. A year ago we were ridiculing, and with good reason, the so-called freedom of the English, who do not have unrestricted freedom of the press, and yet what honest man would today dare to compare France with England as regards freedom of the press? See with what audacity the *Morning Chronicle* attacks Pitt and his conduct of the war. What journalist in France would dare to criticise the blunders of our committees, of the generals, of the Jacobins, of the ministers, and of the Commune, in the way that the opposition criticise that of the British ministry? And I, a Frenchman, I, Camille Desmoulins, cannot have the freedom of an English journalist! I feel indignant at this. And do not tell me that we are in the middle of a revolution and that in a revolution it is necessary to suspend the liberty of the press. I have a storehouse of truths, which I will not open up entirely, but I will dispense just enough to save France and the Republic, one and indivisible.[42]

DOCUMENT: ROBESPIERRE ON REVOLUTIONARY GOVERNMENT

Robespierre, the leading member the Committee of Public Safety, is one of the most recognisable revolutionaries. Historians vary in their assessment of Robespierre's achievements and ideas: Norman Hampson attributes to Robespierre the ability to express the radicalism of Paris; Ruth Scurr questions his 'complete self-delusion'; Jeremy Popkin regards Robespierre as a gifted politician and restrained; to Peter McPhee he was a passionate man; for David Jordan, he represented an apologist for political ruthlessness; George Rudé understands Robespierre as the guiding spirit of the revolution; and according to François Furet, he personified the revolution itself.[43]

Robespierre's fall from power, condemnation and death had perhaps more to do with his own vision of an ideal republic, the vision that all too often was misunderstood as indifference to the human cost of making it happen. In a speech on 25 December 1793, Robespierre argued that a dictatorship was necessary to achieve the liberties that were the object of the revolution. The speech reflected the circumstances of 1793; at that time the revolution had to fight for its survival with both an internal and an external enemy. It had to take extraordinary measures to maintain the unity of the state by forcing the unity of the nation. Robespierre explained the principles of 'revolutionary government'. Revolutionary government had to be founded on terror he maintained, because of the extraordinary task ahead of it— the success of the revolution. The terror, he argued, had to be moderated by high moral standards.

The theory of revolutionary government is as new as the Revolution which brought it into being ... It is the function of government to guide the moral and physical force of the nation towards the object for which it was established. It is the function of constitutional government to maintain the Republic; the object of revolutionary government is to establish it. Revolution is the war of liberty against its enemies; the Constitution is the government of a victorious and peaceful liberty. The revolutionary government needs an extraordinary activity precisely because it is at war. It is subjected to less uniform and less rigorous rules because the circumstances in which it finds itself are tempestuous and shifting, and especially because it has been obliged to constantly deploy new and rapid resources to meet new and pressing dangers. The principal concern of the constitutional government is civil liberty, and that of revolutionary government, public liberty. Under a constitutional government, it is almost enough to protect individual liberties against abuses from the State; under a revolutionary government, the State is obliged to defend itself against the factions which attack it. Revolutionary government owes good citizens the protection of the State; to the enemies of the people, it owes only death.[44]

ELIMINATING THE OPPOSITION

National unity was one of the preoccupations of the Montagnards, who engaged in unmasking the counter-revolutionary activity they blamed for the revolution's continuing difficulties. In their attempts to bring the provinces in line with Paris, some Representatives on Mission applied the principle that the 'terror is the order of the day' with extreme cruelty. To cement the submission of the Vendée to the Convention its troops killed civilians, burned villages and fields. The executions of the 'men of 1789' and other prominent republicans in October and November 1793 were also typical of this uncompromising battle between the new and the old. About this time, two new factions formed among the Jacobins: they became known respectively as the Hébertists and the Dantonists after their leaders, Hébert and Danton. Both these factions, states Marisa Linton, opposed the Committee of Public Safety, for different reasons. Hébert was the new spokesperson for the *sans-culottes* and he favoured even greater radicalisation of the revolution. He called for the continuation of the Terror against counter-revolutionaries, implementation of policies benefiting *sans-culottes* and forcible de-Christianisation. Danton and his supporters, on the other hand, argued for the reverse: the Terror needed to be dismantled and the power of the Paris Commune and *sans-culottes* militants curtailed, and an amnesty should be offered to counter-revolutionaries. This final demand gave Danton and his followers the label of the 'Indulgents' because they called for 'indulgence' (remission of punishment for sin) for people identified as counter-revolutionaries.[45]

In early 1794, both factions were eliminated. Their show trials dominated March and April 1794, the period of the revolution often referred to as the Great Terror. First was the trial of the most prominent spokesman of the Parisian *sans-culottes* movement, the journalist Jacques Hébert; second, the trial of Danton and Camille Desmoulins, who wanted to stop the revolution because, they argued passionately, it had gone far enough. The trials and the executions of the Hébertists and Dantonists only accelerated the pace of the Terror.

Jacques Hébert was the most prominent voice of the Paris *sans-culottes* movement. His journal, *Le Père Duchesne*, became the voice of radical patriotism. In 1793, Hébert and his supporters were instrumental in realising the key demands of the Parisian *sans-culottes*. They succeeded in the Convention imposing the Law of the Maximum and the drive for de-Christianisation. They called for the continuation of the Terror and harsh treatment of all counter-revolutionaries. They were also behind the attack on the Convention on 4–5 September 1793. This event in particular demonstrated the force of the 'general will' and the ability of the crowd to exert pressure on the Convention.

The enactment of the Law of 14 Frimaire Year II, regulating the structures of the revolutionary government, on 4 December 1793 was precisely designed to prevent any attempts to impose the 'general will' on the Convention. The Committee was now determined to prevent any form of factionalism, to end the de-Christianisation campaign and above all to prevent Hébert from becoming a source of alternative power to the Committee. When on 4 February 1794, the day the Convention voted for the abolition of slavery, Hébert called on *sans-culottes* to support his insurrection against the unnamed faction, Robespierre's patience was wearing thin, argues Marisa Linton. And he acted to prevent the revival of popular agitation. On 5 February Robespierre addressed the Convention stressing the primacy of public interests above all individual interests.[46] On 13 March, Hébert and his followers were arrested by the Committee of Public Safety. They were tried on trumped-up charges. Hébert was guillotined on 24 March.

The removal of Hébert brought an end to the economic policies forced upon the Convention by the Hébertists. Neither the Law Against Profiteers of 26 July 1793, providing for the death penalty against hoarders, argues Peter McPhee, nor the Law of the Maximum had been successful. They had discouraged free trade by penalising both retailers and consumers. An improvement to the supply of goods was the aim of a new Law of 12 Germinal Year II (1 April 1794), which removed restrictions on the retail trade. The aim of the law, in Robespierre's words, was 'to prevent fraud but not discourage trade'.[47]

Robespierre's speech of 5 February 1794 was, for McPhee, his attempt to respond to Danton, Camille Desmoulins and the Indulgents by presenting the Terror as virtue's necessary companion. Danton, Desmoulins and a group of deputies began arguing for an end to the Terror. Desmoulins criticised the Committee of Public Safety in his paper, *Le Vieux Cordelier*, and similarly Danton argued that the revolution had to stop with the restoration of democratic government under the provisions of the Constitution of 1793. Now was the time, they argued, to allow people to go back to their normal lives. Danton proposed the establishment of a Commission of Clemency to review the lists of arrested suspects. In late March, meetings between Robespierre and Danton did not resolve the situation. Robespierre remained convinced that Danton was involved in a conspiracy against him and the other members of the Committee of Public Safety. On 30 March 1794, Danton, Desmoulins and others were arrested. Their trial was rigged, with the procedure changed to prevent Danton speaking. They went to the guillotine on 5 April 1794. This execution gave the signal that no revolutionary politician would be spared in the Terror. The Committee of Public Safety, observed François Furet, silenced all opposition.

FESTIVAL OF THE SUPREME BEING

Robespierre made a speech on 7 May 1794 (18 Floréal Year II) on the relationship between the principle of the Republic and religion and morality. He talked about the popular revolutionary festivals and about the need for establishing a cult of the Supreme Being. Subsequently, the decree of the Convention established a new revolutionary cult, a state religion that acknowledged the existence of the Supreme Being and the immortality of the human soul. Importantly, the new law guaranteed freedom of worship to all religions. The cult was both a political strategy and an expression of Robespierre's idea that both civic unity and morality needed a form of public worship and celebration.[48]

On 8 June 1794 (20 Prairial Year II), Robespierre presided over the Festival of the Supreme Being to inaugurate the new state religion. This celebration was designed by the artist Jacques-Louis David to show the nation's spiritual unity with loyalty to revolutionary principles. Robespierre opened the festival, which was well attended, with a ceremonial rejection of atheism by burning its effigy. An artificial rock was erected at Champ de Mars, renamed the 'Field of Unity'. A tree of liberty was set up on the rock, as was a statue of Hercules on top of a Greek column.

DOCUMENT: ROBESPIERRE ON 'ETERNAL JUSTICE'

This speech of 5 February 1794 was made in the context of the conflicting calls by Danton for the end of the Terror and by Hébert for increased severity of the Terror. Robespierre outlined his vision of a society born out of the reign of Terror. 'What is the goal towards which we are heading?', he asked the deputies. The goal was clear—'the peaceful enjoyment of liberty and equality' enabled by 'the reign of that eternal justice from which the laws have been engraved not on marble and stone but in the hearts of all men'.

What is the goal towards which we are heading? The peaceful enjoyment of liberty and equality, the reign of that eternal justice from which the laws have been engraved not on marble and stone but in the hearts of all men, even in the heart of the slave who forgets them or of the tyrant who denies them. We want an order of things in which all base and cruel passions will be unknown, and all generous and charitable feelings watched over by the laws; where ambition is the desire to merit glory and to serve the country; where distinctions are born only of equality itself; where the citizen is responsible to the magistrate and the magistrate to the people, and the people to justice; where the country assures the well-being of each individual, and where each individual enjoys with pride the prosperity and glory of the fatherland; where all its members grow by constant exchange of republican sentiments and by the need to merit the esteem of a great people; where the arts are decorations of the liberty that ennobles them; commerce, the source of public prosperity, and not just of the monstrous opulence of a few families.

In our country, we want to substitute morality for egotism, probity for honour, principles for customs, duties for proprieties, the rule of reason for the tyranny of fashion, contempt of vice for contempt of misfortune, pride for insolence, greatness of soul for vanity, love of glory for love of money, good folk for good company, merit for intrigue, genius for wit, truth for brilliance, the charm of happiness for the boredom of sensuousness, the greatness of man for the pettiness of the great; a people magnanimous, powerful, happy, for a people amiable, frivolous and wretched, that is to say, all the virtues and all the miracles of the republic for all the vices and all the absurdities of the monarchy ...

Now what is the fundamental principle of democratic or popular government, that is to say, the essential force that maintains and inspires it? It is virtue: I am speaking of public virtue, which brought about so many wonders in Greece and Rome, and which must produce even more astounding ones in republican France: of that virtue that is none other than love of the fatherland and of its laws ...

If the mainspring of popular government in time of peace is virtue, the mainspring of popular government in time of revolution is at the same time virtue and terror; virtue, without which terror is intolerable; terror, without which virtue is powerless. Terror is nothing other than justice, prompt, stern and inflexible; it is therefore an emanation of virtue; it is not so much a particular principle as a consequence of the general principle of democracy applied to the most urgent needs of our Country. It has been said that terror is the mainspring of despotic government. Would ours then resemble a despotism? Yes, just as the sword that shines in the hand of the heroes of liberty resembles that with which the satellites of tyranny are armed. If the despot rules his brutalised subjects by terror, he is right as a despot. Tame the enemies of liberty by terror, and you will be right as the founders of the Republic. The government of the Revolution is the despotism of liberty against tyranny.[49]

THE GREAT TERROR

Two days after the Festival of the Supreme Being, the Convention's decree expanded the list of political crimes to include 'criticism of patriotism'. The verdicts of the Revolutionary Tribunal were limited to death or acquittal. Trials could be conducted for groups of defendants accused of the same crime. The right to a public defence was also curtailed. In addition, the deputies' immunity from arrest was revoked. The streamlined procedures made the passing of the death sentence easier and quicker. It is no surprise that the Law of 22 Prairial Year II (10 June 1794) unleashed the so-called 'Great Terror'.[50] The pace of executions accelerated, with 1,376 victims executed in Paris in six weeks. The Law also had other consequences. The deputies of the Convention began to fear for their own security. Ironically, the impulse to end the Terror was the war, in particular the decisive French victory at the battle of Fleurus on 26 June 1794. Following this key victory, French troops crossed the border with Belgium and re-entered Antwerp; in the south-east they succeeded in repelling the Spanish and the Savoyards. The victories gave rise to celebrations in Paris, attracting hundreds of thousands of people; Parisians attended the night-time illuminations in the Tuileries Gardens and a series of commemorative picnics, with neighbours setting up tables in the streets to share meals. The patriotic festivals were held at the time when hundreds of 'conspirators' were going to their deaths at the guillotine.

> For if the Year II of the Revolution was marked by spectacular military victories, by an advance of the ideals of social justice, and by moments of deeply felt sentiments of brotherhood, it was also a period of oppressive fear and suspicion and of ever-greater numbers of executions.[51]

Some of the moderate deputies, including friends of Danton, began quietly rejecting Robespierre's rhetoric of a moral revolutionary society built on Terror.

The experience of the Terror was undeniably traumatic, but its impact was uneven across France. The areas of major insurrections or borderland regions where suspicion of collaboration ran high were particularly affected. Estimates of how many people were killed as a result of the Terror differ significantly, from 15,000 to more than 100,000.[52]

THE FALL OF ROBESPIERRE

The showdown between Robespierre, his supporters and their opposition in the Convention was brought on by the differences between the Committee of Public Safety and the Committee of General Security about the allocation of responsibility. When the attempt at reconciliation between the two committees failed in July 1794, Robespierre decided to take the conflict to the floor of the Convention. On 26 July 1794 (8 Thermidor Year II) Robespierre gave a speech in which he denounced a plot that he said was directed against him, threatening unnamed deputies. Fear of the guillotine mobilised Robespierre's opponents and on the following day in the Convention they unexpectedly accused Robespierre of instituting dictatorship. Robespierre was prevented from replying, with the deputies voting overwhelmingly in favour of his arrest. In the hours that followed, Robespierre and his supporters relocated to the building of the Paris Commune, the Hôtel de Ville, and attempted to rally the Paris *sections* to their cause. But it was no use. The *sans-culottes* had lost trust in Robespierre with the execution of the Hébertists and they refused to support him. On 28 July 1794, the Convention's troops recaptured Robespierre and several of his supporters, including Saint-Just. They were guillotined the same day.

Throughout France the supporters of the Terror were disconcerted and the majority of the population could not believe that Robespierre was a traitor to the Republic like Hébert and Danton.[53] After his death, his enemies turned his revolutionary rhetoric against Robespierre and made him the man responsible for the 'worst excesses, if not the entire system, of the Terror'—the tyrant, the man of blood. It seemed that the majority rejected his case for continuing the Terror: 'The guilty complain of our rigor— the country, more justly, complains of our weakness'.[54] Thus the revolution had turned against its most fervent supporters; 28 July marked the beginning of the end for the revolution.

THE THERMIDORIAN REACTION

The execution of Robespierre and his supporters brought forward the end of the Reign of Terror. Initially there was some confusion over whether the Convention deputies who rose against Robespierre would undo his method of government. Such an expectation, according to Albert Soboul, seemed a reasonable conclusion. The removal of Robespierre released the wave of responses against the Terror and the radical revolution. It could not be controlled or restrained by those who plotted against Robespierre. On 29 July, the Convention made changes to the composition of the Committee of Public Safety: a quarter of the Committee were to stand down every month and were not eligible for immediate re-election. The same rules for all the Convention's committees followed. On 1 August the Law of 22 Prairial was repealed and on 10 August the members of the Revolutionary Tribunal were arrested. These changes were reflected in the numbers of people guillotined in Paris over the rest of the year—only 40 executions were carried out.

The flow-on effect resulted in reduction of the surveillance committees from 48 to 12 in Paris. On 11 August the Committee of Public Safety was stripped of the power of control of the government. On 24 August 1794, the Paris Commune was abolished and replaced with an executive responsible for the administration of the city reporting to the Convention. The fundamental structures of Terror had been undone as no longer necessary.[55]

Over the next years the central question of how to retract the worst excesses committed during the Reign of Terror remained a major issue. Thousands of prisoners arrested under the Law of Suspects were released from prisons, and those who had overseen the massacres of rebels in the provinces were tried and executed. On 18 September 1794, the Convention decided to cease supporting any religion in France and stopped the wages of the constitutional Church, with the effect that, for the first time ever in France, the separation of Church and state became reality. On 12 November 1794, the Convention ordered the closing of the Jacobin Club in Paris and symbols of the radicalism, including the busts of Marat placed in public spaces after his assassination, were destroyed. The return to stability of civic life did not mean that France was to restore the monarchy or that the nobility were back in power. 'Thermidorians brought back', wrote François Furet, 'that new race of political men that the Feuillants had managed to personify for one summer alone—conservative revolutionaries, the Revolution was leaving the shores of utopia to discover the strength of personal interests'.[56]

The attitude towards the working class hardened. The laws governing work and economy were seen as necessary to restore law and order. The egalitarian divorce law of 1792 and the 1793 law granting illegitimate children the same inheritance rights as legitimate heirs were repealed.

THE END OF THE REVOLUTION—DEFEAT OF THE *SANS-CULOTTES*

The political changes introduced in the wake of the Thermidorian reaction were accompanied by dismantling of a number of the revolution's social and economic policies. The Convention removed price controls on 24 December 1794. Between August and December 1794, the *assignats* rapidly lost all value due to inflation which occurred as the price of bread increased sharply. During an exceptionally harsh winter (the worst of the whole century) food prices soared as supplies of grain ran short with the frozen River Seine shutting down transport. By April 1795 prices had risen to 750 per cent above 1790 levels.[57] The popular movement reacted with two demonstrations on 12–13 Germinal Year III (1–2 April 1795) and 1–4 Prairial Year III (20–23 May 1795). Both protests involved large crowds converging on the Convention demanding 'bread and the Constitution of 1793'. Nonetheless, they had no influential leaders and even though the insurrection turned violent and had some support from the former Montagnard deputies it was to be the last major day of action of the popular movement. The National Guard dispersed the crowd and martial law was declared in Paris. In fact, the defeat of these demonstrations hastened the removal of everything associated with the radical phase of the revolution. This was the date, declared Georges Lefebvre, 'which should be taken as the end of the Revolution. Its mainspring was now broken.'[58] In any event, there was no return to the *ancien régime* and the hopes of some deputies for a constitutional monarchy were dashed with the death in prison of the child-king Louis XVII on 8 June 1795.

THE GILDED YOUTH AND THE WHITE TERROR

At the time of the Thermidorian reaction the right-wing press re-emerged. Even fashion reflected these changes, with the abandonment of dressing to look like *sans-culottes*. The flashy display of wealth returned, with elegant clothes that emphasised status. The usage of the courtesy style term 'Monsieur' instead of the revolutionary 'Citizen' also returned as the preferred form of address. William Doyle discusses the emergence of squads of anti-*sans-culottes* vigilantes, *muscadins* and *merveilleuses*, and *jeunesse dorée*—the so-called 'Gilded Youth'.[59] They were recently released prisoners, petty bureaucrats, the sons of the well-to-do, who patrolled the streets in gangs, taking revenge into their own hands. Like the *ancien régime* dandies, they flaunted expensive clothes considering themselves the antithesis of the *sans-culottes*. They wore their hair in the so-called 'victim style', powdered and braided at the back of the head, in contrast with the short and unpowdered haircuts of the 'patriots'. In imitation of counter-revolutionary leaders, they wore coats with black collars, and all that was missing from an outright declaration of counter-revolution was a white cockade. They harassed those who had supported the Terror whom they dubbed 'terrorists' and disrupted their political meetings. As a result of pressure from the 'Gilded Youth' and other groups, the Paris Jacobin Club was closed down by the decree of 12 November 1794 (22 Brumaire Year III).[60]

Outside Paris, similar counter-terror movements emerged, often referred to as 'White Terror', implying that these movements had been inspired by the royalists. Seen as a response to the excesses of revolutionary Terror, 'White Terror' was directed towards officials who were in the past loyal to the revolutionary Convention, the Jacobins, those who persecuted refractory clergy, and *sans-culottes*. In Lyon, punishment was demanded of the former 'terrorists', who were publicly identified. This vigilante justice was motivated by revenge for the brutal treatment received at the hands of its victims when they had been in power in the years before. It was characterised by anarchy and dispensed by armed mobs and gangs through lynching and abductions.[61]

THE CONSTITUTION OF 1795

The changes that followed the overthrow of Robespierre on 28 July 1794 did not immediately result in elections to a new legislature. The Convention, elected in September 1792, continued to govern France until October 1795. The Convention prepared a new constitution which was closer in its ideals to the Constitution of 1791 than to the egalitarian Constitution of 1793 but reflected the principles of 'liberty, equality, security and property' as the core rights of man.[62] The Constitution of 1795 whilst reflecting a more conservative outlook reaffirmed the abolition of slavery and the granting of citizenship to the blacks in the colonies, against the protests of white colonists; a decade before the slave trade, but not slavery itself, was banned in Britain and seven decades before the United States of America abolished slavery.

The Constitution was approved by the Convention on 22 August 1795. It included a declaration of rights that omitted equality of birth or citizens' entitlement to welfare; the right of resistance to oppression was also removed.[63] The citizens' 22 rights were balanced by nine duties. Citizenship with full voting rights was restricted to male taxpayers. The deputies to the national legislature would be chosen by electoral assemblies which only citizens owning or renting substantial property were eligible to attend. Elections were to be annual, rotating one-third of the deputies each time. The parliament was to be bicameral, composed of two chambers or 'Councils'. The lower chamber, the Council of Five Hundred, would initiate all legislation, and the upper, the Council of Elders, with 250 members aged over 40 and married or widowed, could only pass or reject legislation coming from the lower chamber. The Directory of five members chosen by the Council of Elders from a list presented by the Council of Five Hundred was to hold the executive power; one of the directors was to retire each year. Neither directors nor the ministers they appointed could be deputies.[64]

The Constitution was later approved by a popular referendum. Ironically, it would also give a pretext for a counter-revolutionary uprising. The contentious issue was the requirement for two-thirds of the deputies for the new Councils to be elected from among the outgoing deputies of the Convention. Dissatisfaction was particularly strong in Paris and an armed insurrection occurred on 5 October 1795 (13 Vendémiaire Year IV). The Convention used the regular army to fight the counter-revolutionary demonstrators. The suppression of this insurrection marked the last mass rebellion of the revolutionary period.[65]

CONCLUSION

This chapter explored issues that emerged during the radical phase of the revolution, from the declaration of the Republic on 22 September 1792 to the referendum that endorsed the Constitution of 1795. During this period, there was a dramatic increase in the influence of the popular movement, the *sans-culottes*, which culminated in the Constitution of 1793, the most democratic of the revolutionary constitutions. The political differences between the Girondins and Montagnards resulted from their different visions of France and were only overcome by the destruction of the Girondins. The threats to the unity of the Republic as well as the war of the first coalition prevented the Republic from implementing this visionary document. The Reign of Terror further impeded efforts to build a society based on the *Declaration of the Rights of Man and the Citizen*. With the intensification of obsession with conspiracies and traitors, the revolution turned inward against itself—or as Pierre Vergniaud remarked—'devoured its own children': first the Girondins, then the Hébertists, Danton and his supporters and lastly Robespierre. The major change in policy between this period and the one that preceded it was the redefinition of the relationship between the government and the *sans-culottes*. After July 1794, the Convention revoked almost all the measures instituted in 1793 and 1794 in response to pressure from the popular movement. The Constitution adopted in 1795 radically reduced the political participation rights of the lower classes. The experience of unlimited democracy influenced the Convention, which established a constitutional system dominated by the prosperous and educated. This was the price of stability, where social order was reconciled with a republican form of government.

NOTES

1 Jonathan Israel, *Revolutionary Ideas. An Intellectual History of the French Revolution from The Rights of Man to Robespierre* (Princeton: Princeton University Press, 2014), 287.
2 Alison Patrick, 'Political Divisions in the French National Convention, 1792–93', *The Journal of Modern History* 41, no. 4 (1969): 422–474, here 427, 436.
3 McPhee, *Liberty or Death*, 171.
4 McPhee, *Liberty or Death*, 171.
5 Sian Reynolds, *Marriage and Revolution. Monsieur and Madame Roland* (Oxford: Oxford University Press, 2012), 243–245.
6 Speech of Marquis de Condorcet, in Dwyer and McPhee, *The French Revolution and Napoleon*, 73.
7 Doyle, *The Oxford History*, 196; Joseph Trapp, *Proceedings of the French National Convention on the trial of Louis XVI, late King of France and Navarre*, 2nd edn (London: Murray Kearsley Wenman and Co., 1793).
8 Adam Zamoyski, *Holy Madness. Romantics, Patriots and Revolutionaries 1776–1871* (London: Weidenfeld & Nicolson, 1999), 1.
9 Rolf Reichardt and Hubertus Kohle, *Visualizing the Revolution. Politics and Pictorial Arts in Late Eighteenth-Century France*, trans. Corinne Attwood (London: Reaktion, 2008), 194.
10 Doyle, *The Oxford History*, 199.
11 Jones, *The French Revolution 1787–1804*, 67.
12 McPhee, *Liberty or Death*, 230.
13 Furet and Ozouf, *A Critical Dictionary of the French Revolution*, 165.
14 Schama, *Citizens*, 585–599.
15 Jean-Clément Martin, 'The Vendée, Region of Memory', in *Rethinking France*, ed. Pierre Nora (Chicago: University of Chicago Press, 2001), 383–408; Jean-Clément Martin, 'The Vendée, Chouannerie, and the State, 1791–99', in *A Companion to the French Revolution*, ed. Peter McPhee (Chichester: Wiley-Blackwell, 2013), 246–259; Reynald Secher, *A French Genocide. The Vendée*, trans. George Holoch (Notre Dame: University of Notre Dame Press, 2003); McPhee, *Liberty or Death*, 176–177.

16 Dwyer and McPhee, *The French Revolution and Napoleon*, 101–102; Arno J. Mayer, *The Furies. Violence and Terror in the French and Russian Revolutions* (Princeton: Princeton University Press, 2000), 339–340.

17 Dwyer and McPhee, *The French Revolution and Napoleon*, 101–102; Mayer, *The Furies*, 340.

18 Paul R. Hanson, *The Jacobin Republic under Fire. The Federalist Revolt in the French Revolution* (University Park: Pennsylvania State University Press, 2003), 99–122.

19 Doyle, *The Oxford History*, 242.

20 Schama, *Citizens*, 620–622.

21 Doyle, *The Oxford History*, 228–229.

22 Doyle, *The Oxford History*, 235.

23 McPhee, *Robespierre. A Revolutionary Life*, 156; Doyle, *The Oxford History*, 244.

24 Cited in Olivier Coquard, *Jean-Paul Marat* (Paris: Fayard, 1993), 410.

25 Schama, *Citizens*, 646.

26 Paul R. Hanson, *Historical Dictionary of the French Revolution*, 2nd edn (Lanham: Rowman & Littlefield, 2015), 70, 81, 200, 277, 342; McPhee, *Liberty or Death*, 210–211.

27 Théophile Leclerc, 'The Appeal to the Guillotine', *L'Ami du peuple*, 23 August 1793, in Gilchrist and Murray, *The Press in the French Revolution*, 282–284.

28 McPhee, *Liberty or Death*, 224.

29 Cited in McPhee, *Liberty or Death*, 225.

30 Cited in McPhee, *Liberty or Death*, 226.

31 Popkin, *A New World Begins*, 356.

32 Schama, *Citizens*, 757.

33 Proceedings of the National Convention (5 September 1792), in Baker, *The Old Regime and the French Revolution*, 348.

34 McPhee, *Liberty or Death*, 213.

35 Cited in Schama, *Citizens*, 675.

36 Schama, *Citizens*, 676.

37 McPhee, *The French Revolution*, 125.

38 Stewart, *A Documentary Survey of the French Revolution*, 498–500.

39 McPhee, *Robespierre. A Revolutionary Life*, 175.

40 Albert Soboul, *The French Revolution, 1787–1799* (New York: Vintage Books, 1975), 356.

41 Schama, *Citizens*, 687.

42 *Le Vieux Cordelier*, no. 1, 15 Frimaire II (5 December 1793), 5–6, 7, in Gilchrist and Murray, *The Press in the French Revolution*.

43 Popkin, *A New World Begins*, 415; McPhee, *Robespierre. A Revolutionary Life*, 231; David P. Jordan, 'Robespierre', *The Journal of Modern History* 49, no. 2 (1977): 282–291; Norman Hampson, *The Life and Opinions of Maximilien Robespierre* (London: Duckworth, 1974), 127; Furet, *The French Revolution, 1770–1814*, 142–150; Ruth Scurr, *Fatal Purity. Robespierre and the French Revolution* (New York: Metropolitan Books, 2006), 344.

44 Speech by Robespierre, 25 December 1793, in Dwyer and McPhee, *The French Revolution and Napoleon*, 105.
45 Marisa Linton, *Choosing Terror. Virtue, Friendship, and Authenticity in the French Revolution* (Oxford: Oxford University Press, 2013), 194–195.
46 Linton, *Choosing Terror*, 288–289.
47 McPhee, *Robespierre. A Revolutionary Life*, 190.
48 Scurr, *Fatal Purity*, 347–348.
49 *La Gazette nationale* (or *Le Moniteur universel*), no. 139, 19 Pluviôse II (7 February 1794); 3rd series, vol. 6, pp. 402, 404, in Gilchrist and Murray, *The Press in the French Revolution*, 297–298.
50 Scurr, *Fatal Purity*, 328.
51 Tackett, *The Coming of the Terror in the French Revolution*, 324.
52 Colin Jones, *The Longman Companion to the French Revolution* (Hoboken: Taylor and Francis, 2014), 121.
53 Georges Lefebvre, *The French Revolution from 1793 to 1799*, trans. John Hall Stewart and James Friguglietti, 2n edn (London: Routledge, 1967), 136.
54 Scurr, *Fatal Purity*, 344–345.
55 Doyle, *The Oxford History*, 282.
56 Furet, *The French Revolution, 1770–1814*, 153.
57 McPhee, *The French Revolution*, 158.
58 Lefebvre, *The French Revolution from 1793 to 1799*, 145.
59 Doyle, *The Oxford History*, 284, 294.
60 Victor Barrucand, ed., *Mémoires et Notes de Pierre-Réné Choudieu* (Paris: Plon, 1897), 292–300, in Richard Cobb and Colin Jones, *Voices of the French Revolution* (Topsfield: Salem House Publishers, 1988), 234.
61 Popkin, *A New World Begins*, 439–441.
62 McPhee, *Liberty or Death*, 296.
63 Micah Alpaugh, *The French Revolution. A History in Documents* (London: Bloomsbury Academic, 2020), 237–238.
64 Dwyer, *Napoleon. The Path to Power*, 171–172.
65 Doyle, *The Oxford History*, 320.

6

EPILOGUE
Revolutionary ideals and the rise of Napoleon

During 1793 Jeanne-Louise (Nanine) Vallain painted an allegory of the French Revolution and her painting was hung in the meeting hall of the Jacobin Club in Paris. It is easily recognisable as a personification of Liberty, who is represented as a solemn, seated woman, wearing clothing associated with ancient Rome and holding a pike with a red Phrygian cap of liberty in her left hand; in her right hand, she holds an unrolled scroll, which reveals the *Declaration of the Rights of Man and the Citizen*. A bound bundle of wooden rods, the fasces, lie just behind the scroll. These are usually bound around the pike to symbolise the administration of justice. Perhaps it is significant that Liberty, or more accurately the Republic, is strong enough to hold the pike alone in her hand, like her British counterpart Britannia, who holds the trident. At her bare feet lie symbols of vanquished monarchy, broken chains, the inverted crown of a deposed monarch and the mutilated feudal registers of seigneurial dues.

Like so much art of the period, this is an allegorical image, personalising freedom, fairness, law and order. It certainly neatly summarises the achievements of the revolution and may well have struck a chord in post-Robespierre France as the revolution entered the period of the Directory, the longest period of a continuous revolutionary government. This chapter of history was closed on 9 November 1799 when Napoleon Bonaparte took charge as the First Consul. When, in 1804, Napoleon decided to abandon the republican façade and crowned himself Emperor, the revolution, arguably, was truly over.

DOI: 10.4324/9781003157748-6

THE OUTCOMES OF THE REVOLUTION

With the enactment of the Constitution of 1795, the leaders of the Republic were hoping that their country would enter a period of stabilisation and prosperity. Louis XVI's brother was proclaimed Louis XVIII, but because he was in exile there was no real prospect of the restoration of the Bourbon dynasty to the French throne. France was to remain a republic for the foreseeable future. It was obvious that the revolution had caused deep and permanent changes in French society. With the benefit of hindsight, it can safely be said that many of the changes made during the revolution were never reversed.

The French Revolution began in 1789 with the assertion of political rights by the Third Estate and hopes for a constitutional settlement to benefit the whole nation. Through 1789 to 1795 the revolutionary ideals were challenged, refined, altered and rejected. The Constitution of 1795 resembled more its predecessor enacted in 1791 than the Constitution of 1793. In 1795, it was impossible to predict that power would be seized in 1799 by one of the republican generals, Napoleon Bonaparte.

The freedoms heralded in 1789 formed the foundation of the enduring concept of rights: French citizens have the right to do 'all that is not forbidden by the law'. With this concept taking hold in the consciousness of the nation, there was no going back to a society based on the corporate privilege of the *ancien régime*. Similarly, the idea that all people are equal prevented a return to the inequities of privilege based on hereditary social status. The protection of property rights also broke away from the *ancien régime* and benefited sections of the bourgeoisie and the peasants. The sale of the former Church lands and some of the noble estates broke the monopoly of the old elites. A return to any or even some form of feudal reciprocity was unthinkable; the new landholders replaced the old privileged groups and would protect their rights against the workers. Property rights were an extension of the individual freedoms proclaimed by the revolution. The new society was characterised by the new cultural values, with its elites drawing on elements of bourgeois and aristocratic values.

The 1789 demands for a constitution were the expression of a need for a written legislative instrument to delineate the relationship between the government and the citizens. The *Declaration of the Rights of Man and the Citizen* enshrined the idea of representation as the underlying belief of sovereignty vested in the nation. These principles were never reversed, even if the subsequent regimes restricted some aspects of the electoral process; from this point, taxes were approved by a legislative body and not decreed without consultation.

The revolution reshaped France's administrative structures according to the principles of rationality, uniformity and efficiency. The *parlements*, the provincial assemblies, the tax barriers, tolls and customs duties, internal borders, together with all forms of local, provincial and regional privilege, were irrevocably gone. Post-revolutionary France was developing a centralised and uniform administration of government, justice and education. This included a single set of laws for the whole of France, the civil registration of births, marriages and deaths, and the division of France into *départements*. In that respect, the proposals of the *cahiers des doléances* were realised and France has become a unified nation.

The secularisation of the society, the freedom to practise one's own religion or no religion at all, was another right that proved lasting. There was no longer a question of the religious observances of minorities such as Protestants and Jews being denied. In the wake of the revolution, the censorship of books was not re-established, but different forms of control of the popular press remained in place for much of the nineteenth century.

Attempts to change the political, social and economic set-up of any society evoke passion and dissent, and often result in violence. The revolution's constant was the presence of violence at every major stage. The defence against real and imagined enemies consumed much of the revolution's energy. Its responses demonstrated that ideology can result in dictatorship for which survival means the silencing of all opposition, uniformity and centralisation—all in the name of the greater good. The experience of the Terror is just one of the examples.

The French Revolution provides more questions than answers because of its transformative nature. Peter McPhee argues that the best measure of the outcomes of the revolution is to compare and contrast the 1789 *cahiers des doléances* with the characteristics of

French society in 1795.[1] The changes introduced by the revolution that stood the test of time were those that reflected the central grievances expressed in the *cahiers*, among them popular sovereignty, civil equality, careers based on merit and utility, and the end of the last vestiges of feudalism.

NAPOLEON BONAPARTE (1769–1821)

The story of the rise of Napoleon Bonaparte is remarkable and astonishing, and closely tied to the revolution itself. For many historians, Napoleon is a product of the revolution, a promoter of its values and a symbol of its end. When the Constitution of 1795 was enacted, Napoleon was 26. Four years later he had reached the position of First Consul, which made him the ruler of France, and his military prowess made him one of the greatest leaders in world history. The period of the Directory, which lasted longer than any other revolutionary regime since 1789, gave Napoleon a chance for success. His early military successes in Toulon and Paris and the support of Parisian politicians resulted in Napoleon's appointment as the commander of the French armies in Italy in 1796. His career and meteoric rise were launched by the success in the campaigns of 1796–1797 when his troops defeated the Piedmontese and the Austrians. In 1798, the Directory felt threatened by the glory of the young general and instead of pursuing plans to invade England, sent Napoleon to Egypt so that he was away from Paris. The expedition was to deal a blow to the British by cutting the trade route to India, but the destruction of the French fleet by the British navy admiral Horatio Nelson made the continuation of the French mission in Egypt untenable. On his return to France in October 1799, the growing unpopularity of the Directory and the instability of the political factions enabled Napoleon to depose the Directory in a coup on 9 November 1799 (18 Brumaire Year VIII). The Directory was replaced by a three-man executive called the Consulate, with Napoleon as the First Consul. In 1801, Napoleon signed a concordat normalising France's relations with the papacy. The 1802 referendum approved Napoleon's indefinite tenure of office and two years later France was proclaimed an Empire. Napoleon crowned himself Emperor. In a certain sense, Napoleon, who had come from a fairly humble background, had risen, on merit, to become the equivalent of a king, but one who ruled, seemingly, in the name of the people.

Under Napoleon's rule, many aspects of the revolutionary reforms continued. In 1804, he introduced the Civil Code of 1804 to unify and standardise France's local law codes. The code protected property rights and guaranteed religious liberty and equality for all adult males. But women's rights were diminished significantly: their role was reduced to domestic functions, although Napoleon introduced protection for single mothers and abandoned children. The rights of workers were also constrained in favour of employers.

Napoleon used military service as a means of social transformation and mobility, with the result that the French army maintained higher morale. His personal charisma inspired almost fanatical loyalty among his soldiers. During the prolonged military conflict in Europe, Napoleon was undefeated on land. In 1805, when Austria refused to remain neutral in Napoleon's conflict with Britain, he took Vienna and defeated the combined Austrian and Russian forces at Austerlitz on 2 December 1805. The defeat of Prussian forces at Jena and Auerstadt followed and Russia's army was crushed at Friedland. The peace treaties ensured Napoleon's total domination of Europe.

Napoleon's approach to the territories under his control was pragmatic. He reorganised the conquered territories to create states dependent on France, as with the Confederation of the Rhine, which combined almost all the German states except Austria and Prussia. The Holy Roman Empire was disestablished in 1806. In Italy Napoleon annexed some of the territories directly to France and established the kingdoms of Italy and Naples. In the annexed territories and the satellite states Napoleon insisted on abolishing serfdom and seigneurial dues, introduced constitutions, codified a set of laws and granted civil rights to Jews and religious minorities. These changes were very much in keeping with the spirit of the French Revolution, but they also encouraged the growth of nationalism in Germany and Italy, laying the foundations for their respective unification as nation states in the nineteenth century.

With the establishment of the alliance between Britain and Russia against France, Napoleon invaded Russia in 1812 with the Grand Army of 600,000 men. He advanced as far as Moscow, which was left undefended but set on fire by the departing Russians. With the French armies' morale at its lowest, Napoleon ordered a retreat in October 1812. In the cold, lacking provisions and facing Russian guerrilla tactics, the Grand Army was reduced to 100,000 troops by December 1812. The French defeat at the Battle of Leipzig in October 1813 brought the war into France. Deserted by his own generals, Napoleon abdicated in March 1814 and agreed to go into exile on the island of Elba. After his abdication, the younger brother of the executed Louis XVI, the Count of Provence, was placed on the French throne and reigned as Louis XVIII until his death in 1824. In early 1815, Napoleon returned to France. He rallied the troops and public support for his restoration as he faced the war with the coalition led by Russia and Britain. His armies were defeated at Waterloo on 18 June 1815. After the defeat Napoleon was permanently detained on the island of Saint Helena, off the coast of West Africa. He died there at the age of 52.

CONCLUSION

Napoleon's rule is a remarkable conclusion to the French Revolution. His position as Emperor certainly suggests that the ideas and values of the revolution had been abandoned and that there was a return to a system resembling the *ancien régime*. This is seemingly confirmed by the restoration of the House of Bourbon and the coronation of Louis XVIII in 1814. As noted above, however, France never really returned to the conditions of the old order. The principles of democracy, liberty, merit, equality and sovereignty of the people have been an enduring aspect of French politics since 1789. Even today the revolutionary declaration 'Liberty, Equality, Fraternity' remains the national motto and the Tricolour the flag of France's Fifth Republic. Moreover, the events and values embodied in the French Revolution have spread far beyond the nation of France. The values enshrined in the United Nations Declaration of Human Rights, for example, have much in common with the *Declaration of the Rights of Man and the Citizen*. Indeed, the very ideas of rights, citizenship, secular society, free speech, merit, rule of law, popular sovereignty and democracy in the Western world have been fundamentally shaped by five tumultuous years of French history.

Given that these ideas continue to shape and drive events in the world today, it is possible to say that the French Revolution may be over, but the revolution is yet to end.

NOTE

1 McPhee, *Liberty or Death*, 369.

HISTORIANS AND THE FRENCH REVOLUTION

The French Revolution is studied and interpreted as an example of how societies change, how ideas take shape and how historical events produce a chain of events with far-reaching effects. The ways in which historians interpret the French Revolution often serve as models for the understanding of other great historical events.

Shortly after the revolution, accounts of the events were often produced with a commentary attempting to understand what had happened. For example, Adolphe Thiers (1797–1877) wrote a multi-volume *History of the French Revolution*, published between 1823 and 1827. Thiers was fascinated by the ideals of 1789, but found it difficult to reconcile them with the violence of the Reign of Terror. Jules Michelet (1798–1874), on the other hand, insisted that the revolution had a popular dimension and argued in his *History of France* (1833–1867) that events of such magnitude and impact could not be understood without examining the role of the common people. Alexis de Tocqueville's (1805–1859) attempt to analyse the revolution in *The Old Regime and the Revolution* (1856) moved away from just a narrative of the events towards an appraisal. Tocqueville's conclusions highlighted the continuities of the revolution in creating a unified and uniform national state, a process he argued started with the reforms of the 1770s and 1780s introduced by the Crown. Far more influential than Tocqueville was Hippolyte Taine (1828–1893) whose *The Origins of Contemporary France* (6 vols, Paris, 1876–1893) gave strength to the view that the Enlightenment free-thinkers destroyed the stability of pre-revolutionary France by desacralising monarchy, undermining the Church, and challenging the established social order. Among the critics of this interpretation

DOI: 10.4324/9781003157748-7

was Alphonse Aulard (1849–1928) who edited collections of documents and contributed significantly to later interpretations. In contrast to Tocqueville, Aulard argues that the revolution broke the tradition of the *ancien régime*. He concludes that the revolutionaries of the radical phase of the revolution gave true meaning to the ideals of 1789, because they attempted to implement democracy and republicanism.

Aulard's approach established a basic framework for thinking about and understanding the revolution; he argued that the revolution was a sharp break with the *ancien régime* and that the revolution was an essential and unavoidable step in establishing France as a modern democracy and a secular state. The ideals of 1789 and the subsequent reforms could only be realised in the radical measures instituted after 1792. The Terror was thus necessary in defeating the opposition within France and abroad. As a general rule, historians who follow this interpretation also accept that the bourgeoisie were the beneficiaries of the changes.

The most prominent historians who contributed to the classical interpretation of the French Revolution, quoted in this book, are Georges Lefebvre and Albert Soboul. Lefebvre demonstrated that peasants were capable of articulating their own concerns, which could be distinguished from the demands of other groups. His publications include *The Great Fear of 1789* (1932) and *The Coming of the French Revolution* (1939, English translation published in 1946). Lefebvre argues that the course of the revolution can be explained as the interplay between the four social classes: the aristocracy, whose resistance to the reforms proposed by the Crown set the revolution in motion; the bourgeoisie, who set the revolutionary programme; the peasantry, whose uprising in 1789 threatened other classes into abolition of feudalism; and the urban working class, who radicalised the revolution after 1792.

Albert Soboul's publications redefined the membership of the radicalised urban militants, the *sans-culottes*, to include shopkeepers, artisans and others who held their own political ideas, often independent of the bourgeois leaders. The research by George Rudé in *The Crowd in the French Revolution* (1967) showed that the violence perpetrated by the *sans-culottes* had a purpose and expressed a definite political agenda. Richard Cobb's examination of the Terror, translated into English in *The People's Armies* (1987), gave voice to the revolutionary experiences of ordinary people, including *sans-culottes*. He argues that the diversity of individual experiences is far more telling than the presumption of class conflicts.

Yet some historians began to question the idea that the revolution was an expression of social conflict. Alfred Cobban in *The Myth of the French Revolution* (1955) disagreed with Lefebvre and Soboul and argued that the bourgeoisie were in fact social climbers who worked hard to obtain venal offices and were threatened by the reforming monarchy. The call for a revision of the classic approach was taken up by François Furet who, in *Interpreting the French Revolution* (1981), argued against the dogma of applying class struggle to eighteenth-century France. In his view, the revolution did not assist in the transition of feudal France to capitalism, but rather stunted its nascent growth. For Furet, there was no class conflict but a rivalry of various pressure groups for participation in the political process. The new regime operated very much like the old one. This line of argument seems to be reflected in the conclusions reached by Keith Baker in *Inventing the French Revolution* (1990).

William Doyle's reconsideration of *The Origins of the French Revolution* (1980) indicated a return to political history. He offered his detailed political narrative in *The Oxford History of the French Revolution* (1989; 3rd edition 2018), where he argued that the 'outbreak owed more to accident and political miscalculation than to social conflicts';[1] and in which he concluded that a profound cultural transformation of French society by the revolution was simply not worth the human cost; the revolution was 'in every sense a tragedy'.[2] Other successful narrative histories of the revolution were produced by Simon Schama (*Citizens: A Chronicle of the French Revolution*, 1989), Peter McPhee (*Liberty or Death. The French Revolution*, 2016), Jeremy Popkin (*A New World Begins. The History of the French Revolution*, 2019) and, within a wider timeframe and context, Adam Zamoyski in his *Holy Madness. Romantics, Patriots and Revolutionaries 1776–1871* (1999). Two of these, Schama and McPhee, offer completely different conclusions about the significance of the revolution. Schama's assessment focuses on the violence of the revolutionary experience, which 'connected social distress with political change'.[3] According to Schama, the revolution was destined to fail because of the disproportionate hopes it created, and its key outcome was the human loss. On the other hand, Peter McPhee stresses widespread social change as the outcome of the extended revolutionary upheaval. He argues that changes in the life of the bourgeoisie, women, peasants, the Catholic clergy, the former nobles, and France as a nation were profound, long-lasting and never to be reversed. The changes, maintains McPhee, affected not just private lives, but also institutional and public life, with the principles of rationality, uniformity and efficiency now firmly embedded.[4] Jeremy Popkin, an authority on the revolution in Haiti, offers a modern approach in his broad narrative which incorporates his vision of the role played by revolutionary women and the debate about race, colonial politics and the abolition of slavery.

The classical and the revisionist approaches, and political history were followed by the 'third way' of interpreting the revolution. Historians agree that the revolution was a major crisis in France's history, but they are looking for ways of understanding the origins and impact of 1789 as more than just a political event. This 'cultural history' includes works by Robert Darnton, David Garrioch, Lynn Hunt, Peter McPhee, Mona Ozouf, Caroline Weber, and Timothy Tackett.[5] In defining the revolution, these historians underline new language and forms of dress, intellectual history, a redefinition of gender roles, new patterns of behaviour, new relationships between social groups, instead of the high-level actions of political actors and class. The areas of research broaden to include the experience of women and slaves, who had previously often been treated as marginal. There is broad agreement that the revolution gave an opportunity for women's political participation and extended their rights, even if the definition of these rights was restricted. The work of Joan Landes, *Women and the Public Sphere in the Age of the French Revolution* (1989), is the notable exception: she argues that the revolution was deeply anti-women.

The economic interest as the key motivation for individuals was examined by John Markoff in *The Abolition of Feudalism* (1996) and Timothy Tackett in *Becoming a Revolutionary* (1996) and most recently by Rafe Blaufard in *The Great Demarcation: The French Revolution and the Invention of Modern Property* (2016), where he reminds about the fundamental nature of ownership within the revolutionary context.

There is also more research on the influence of various political factions and their support network. Gary Kates's 1985 work on *The*

Cercle Social, the Girondins, and the French Revolution analysed the origins, rise to power and ideology of the leaders of the Girondin factions and their impact. Ideas that brought about the Terror were always subject to contested interpretations. These include consideration of the nature of fear of real and imagined plots in *Conspiracy in the French Revolution* (2007), edited by Peter Campbell, and David Andress's *The Terror* (2006), and revolutionary violence in Michel Biard's *Terror: The French Revolution and Its Demons* (2021). Marisa Linton's examination of the impact of personalities of the key participants in her *Choosing Terror: Virtue, Friendship, and Authenticity in the French Revolution* (2013) highlights the affective nature of relationships and personal dilemmas of those who participated in and led the revolutionary struggle. Similarly, two new biographies of Robespierre, by Ruth Scurr and Peter McPhee, delve into new ways of understanding revolutionary leaders, as do biographies of the revolutionary partners the Rolands by Siân Reynolds in the innovative *Marriage and Revolution* (2012) and Philippe Girard's *Toussaint Louverture: A Revolutionary Life* (2016).

An intriguing proposition can be found in Micah Alpaugh's work, *Non-Violence and the French Revolution: Political Demonstrations in Paris, 1787–1795* (2015); Alpaugh argues that the episodes of violence need to be seen in the context of otherwise unrecognised popular non-violent demonstration. For Ronen Steinberg, the violence of the Terror traumatised the French and he examines its aftermath though the suffering and distress in *The Afterlives of the Terror* (2019). These themes are now also present in works which bring together research on the global significance of the Revolution, for example Bailey Stone's *Reinterpreting the French Revolution. A Global-Historical Perspective* (2002), *The Age of Revolutions in Global Context, c. 1760–1840*, edited by David Armitage and Sanjay Subrahmanyam (2010), and *The French Revolution in Global Perspective*, edited by Suzanne Desan, Lynn Hunt and William Nelson (2013).

Among the collections of essays presenting the variety of approaches to the revolution are recent handbooks and companions such as *The Oxford Handbook of the Ancien Regime* (edited by William Doyle, 2012), *A Companion to the French Revolution* (edited by Peter McPhee, 2013), and *The Oxford Handbook of the French Revolution* (edited by David Andress, 2015).

Interpretations of the French Revolution today are far more diverse because they take a complex range of issues into account. Historians argue that the nature of revolutionary change escapes simple explanation. The revolution was a complicated process with a high loss of life and much suffering. The path of the revolutionaries involved crises of their own making, such as the reform of the Church, and others that were the inevitable responses to change. The revolution that began with the *Declaration of the Rights of Man and the Citizen*—despite the fact that it excluded women and 'passive' citizens—opened a new chapter of history and paved the way for freedom and equality to triumph.

NOTES

1 Doyle, *The Oxford History*, 446.
2 Doyle, *The Oxford History*, 427.
3 Schama, *Citizens*, 292, 307; McPhee, *Liberty or Death*; Popkin, *A New World Begins*.
4 Peter McPhee, *A Social History of France, 1789–1914*, 2nd edn (Basingstoke: Palgrave Macmillan, 2004), 90–107.
5 Robert Darnton, *Pirating and Publishing. The Book Trade in the Age of Enlightenment* (New York: Oxford University Press, 2021); Lynn Hunt, *Politics, Culture, and Class in the French Revolution* (Berkeley: University of California Press, 1984); Mona Ozouf, *Festivals and the French Revolution* (Cambridge, MA: Harvard University Press, 1988); Tackett, *The Coming of the Terror in the French Revolution*; Garrioch, *The Making of Revolutionary Paris*; Caroline Weber, *Queen of Fashion. What Marie Antoinette Wore to the Revolution* (New York: H. Holt, 2006).

GLOSSARY

absolutism, absolutist system a system of government in which the monarch is the ultimate authority of state.

ancien régime French term for old, in the sense of former, regime; used to describe the system of government and life before the revolution.

aristocratic revolt a period immediately following the Assembly of Notables, which met in February 1787 and refused to endorse the reforms proposed by Louis XVI aimed at reducing the Crown's budget deficit by introducing a uniform land tax. The revolt was characterised by resistance of the privileged estates through the *parlements* and widespread, popular unrest in Paris and the provinces in support of the *parlements*, whose powers were limited by the king's edict of May 1788. The revolt came to an end with the reappointment of Necker as finance minister, and the king's decision to summon the Estates-General for May 1789.

armée révolutionnaire an armed force of Jacobins and *sans-culottes* raised in late summer 1793 to spread the revolution in the countryside and to force farmers to release their stocks of grain for Paris and other towns. Disbanded after the executions of the Hébertists in 1794.

artisans skilled craft workers making, for example, clothing, household items and sculptures.

Assembly of Notables a gathering of eminent individuals (notables) summoned to advise the monarch. It was convened in February 1787, and again in November 1788.

assignats interest-bearing bonds based on the value of confiscated church property that became paper money after April 1790. They rapidly lost value, and by 1795 were almost worthless.

August Decrees the result of the deliberations of the Assembly between 4 and 11 August 1789, on the reform and dismantling of the feudal system. The Assembly abolished feudal dues on 4 August, but in the following week made a distinction between 'personal servitude', which was abolished outright, and property rights, for which peasants had to pay compensation. Its immediate effect was the renunciation of noble and clerical privilege.

benefices church offices that provided ministers with a revenue-rewarding church.

bicameral having two chambers (in a parliament or legislative body).

Bourbon dynasty the ruling house of France, a branch of the Capetian dynasty. The first Bourbon king of France and the direct ancestor of Louis XVI was Henry IV who ruled from 1589 to 1610. Spain and Luxembourg currently have Bourbon monarchs.

bourgeois the original meaning of bourgeois was 'citizen of a town'. By 1789, the term was used to describe the middle classes. During the revolution, it referred to the urban upper middle class of the Third Estate: professionals such as lawyers, doctors, bankers, brokers, manufacturers and office holders in the bureaucracy.

Breton associated with Brittany, a region in north-west France.

Brunswick manifesto published on 25 July 1792 by the commander of the Austro-Prussian forces invading France, it threatened summary justice for the inhabitants of Paris if any harm was to come to the royal family. The manifesto galvanised the *sans-culottes* into a popular insurrection that overthrew the monarchy on 10 August 1792.

cahiers de doléances lists or books of grievances, drawn up in early 1789 by representatives of each of the three estates. They exposed problems inherent in the political and social system and contained proposals to be acted on by the deputies to the Estates-General.

Civil Constitution of the Clergy, 12 July 1790   a law that aimed at reform of the administrative structures of the Roman Catholic Church in France, but which in effect subordinated the Church to the government, making it a national church.

Committee of General Security the Committee of General Security was one of the two leading government committees established in 1793. It was a body charged by the Convention with policing state security throughout the country, issuing passports and prosecuting foreign agents. It oversaw revolutionary justice.

Committee of Public Safety the more prominent of the two leading government committees established in 1793 and responsible for both internal and external affairs. Consisting of 12 members, it functioned as the executive branch of government from April 1793 to October 1795. It was disbanded in 1795.

Constitution of 1791 the Constitution accepted by Louis XVI in September 1791. It provided for France as a constitutional monarchy; the separation of powers, with the National Assembly as the legislative body, the king at the head of the executive branch and the judiciary independent of the other two branches. It ceased to be operational on 10 August 1792.

Constitution of 1793 also known as the Jacobin Constitution. It included provision of welfare and public education, the right to rebel when the government violates the rights of the people, and vote by universal male suffrage. Its implementation was postponed 'until peace'.

Constitution of 1795 also known as the Constitution of the Year III, it was ratified on 22 August 1795 and remained in effect until the coup of 18 Brumaire (9 November 1799). It established a liberal republic with a bicameral legislature and a five-member executive government known as the Directory.

convoke   to call together or summon a meeting.

Cordeliers   the radical revolutionary club of the Cordeliers was founded in April–May 1790 under the leadership of Danton, Marat and Hébert. It attracted many members because of the low fees and its radical rhetoric. It also welcomed women to its meetings, which were each attended by about 400 people. Hébert's newspaper, *Le Père Duchesne*, became its mouthpiece. It lost power and influence after the Terror and was discredited and closed in March 1794.

corvée   in-kind tax of unpaid work on land or roads or aid given to troops by peasants for a specified number of days each year.

Declaration of the Rights of Man and the Citizen, 26 August 1789   passed by the National Assembly, it proclaimed the fundamental principles on which French society is based, famously starting with the pronouncement that 'Men are born and remain free and equal in rights'.

denounced   publicly condemned.

Directory   a committee of five directors chosen by the Council of Five Hundred and approved by the Council of Ancients as the executive branch of government. It was in power from 26 October 1795 to 10 November 1799.

divine right   a political doctrine of royal legitimacy which maintains that a monarch is subject to no earthly authority, deriving the right to rule directly from the will of God. It is often expressed in the phrase 'by the grace of God'.

duchy   territory ruled by a duke or duchess.

edicts   laws or royal decrees enacted by the king on his own authority.

emancipation   the process of being set free from legal, social or political restrictions.

émigrés   people who leave their own country in order to settle in another, usually for political reasons.

encyclical   a letter written by a pope to a particular audience, usually bishops. The official title of an encyclical is generally the first two or three words of the letter's Latin text.

Encyclical *Charitas*, 13 April 1791   Pope Pius VI's response to the reform of the Church in France addressed to the French bishops in which the head of the Roman Catholic Church condemned the *Civil Constitution of the Clergy* as heretical and schismatic.

ennoblement   the act of conferring of nobility and the induction of an individual into the nobility.

estates   also known as orders, the three groups that divided French society until the revolution: the First Estate, the clergy; the Second Estate, the nobility; the Third Estate, the commoners. Membership of an estate determined social status, opportunity and privilege.

Estates-General   the consultative assembly comprising representatives of the three estates of the realm: clergy, nobility and commoners. The Estates-General were summoned by Louis XVI for May 1789 to consider the reform of the taxation system. The emancipation of the deputies of the Third Estate led to the Estates-General transforming into the first revolutionary legislature, the National Assembly, in June 1789.

expropriated   when private property is taken by a government to be used for the benefit of the public.

faubourg   a suburb or a district, especially one in Paris.

federalism, federalists   the federalist movement was particularly influential in Caen, Bordeaux, Lyon and Marseille. In contrast to the Vendée insurgents, the federalists proclaimed their loyalty to the revolution and the Republic, but objected to the disproportionate influence of the *sans-culottes* and the dominance of Paris over the provinces.

féderés   citizen soldiers who came to Paris from the provinces for the Festival of the Federation in July 1790, and again on 14 July

1792. Many were from Marseille and participated in the uprising of 10 August 1792. Some returned home; others went on to join the regular army at the front.

feudalism   a societal structure based on the relationship between sections of the population (lords, vassals and serfs) and based on the holding of land in exchange for service or labour.

Feuillants   constitutional monarchist deputies who split from the Jacobins over a petition to depose Louis XVI after the flight to Varennes in June 1791. They formed their own club, named after the monastery of the Feuillant monks in which they met.

franchise   the right to vote.

gabelle   tax on salt.

généralités   the administrative divisions of France under the *ancien régime*, which served as a framework for royal administration.

Girondins   a group of deputies in the Legislative Assembly, with some from the Gironde region, in south-west France. They were one of the two major factions in the National Convention (the other being the Montagnards). They opposed the Jacobins in 1793. Many of the Girondins were supporters of the 1793 'federalist revolt' against the Convention. They were expelled from the Convention during the Reign of Terror; their leaders were arrested, tried and guillotined in October 1793. The term was rarely used prior to 1793; their opponents often called them Brissotins, after their most prominent spokesman, Jacques-Pierre Brissot.

Hébertists   followers of Hébert, a journalist and prominent member of the Cordeliers Club. They were anti-Christian and, during the de-Christianisation campaign, they turned several thousand churches, including Notre Dame, into Temples of Reason.

Indulgents   informally led by Danton, who together with his supporters was accused of winding back the Terror and being 'indulgent' towards counter-revolutionaries.

insurrection   a revolt against legitimate authority.

intendant   holder of administrative office.

Jacobins   a revolutionary club that met in a former Jacobin monastery, the debating centre of increasingly radical revolutionary ideas. Its branches spread all across France and Europe. The Jacobins rose to political dominance in Paris and in many provincial cities. Because of its association with the policies of the Terror, the Convention ordered the Paris club to close in November 1794.

journées   the French word for 'days'; here referring to revolutionary days of action.

judicial murder   a death sentence that is legal, but unjust.

Law of 14 Frimaire Year II   enacted on 4 December 1793 and known as the Constitution of the Terror, it consolidated all previous Terror legislation and streamlined the administration of the Republic by clarifying the relationship between government bodies and delineating their roles.

Law of the Maximum, 29 September 1793   the law that provided for maximum prices of foodstuffs and gave the government the right to requisition goods from suppliers. Its main purpose was to set price limits, thus preventing rising food prices.

Legislative Assembly   a single-chamber parliament elected under the constitutional monarchy of 1791–1792, and ended with the elections to the National Convention.

Lettres de cachet   letters signed by the king, countersigned by one of his ministers and issued under the sovereign's seal; they contained orders directly from the king, often to enforce arbitrary actions, such as authorising imprisonment without trial.

Levée en masse   decree enacted on 23 August 1793, it was the first instance of conscription in modern history and expressed the state's right to require all citizens to meet a national emergency.

libertine   a person, especially a man, who freely indulges in sensual pleasures without regard to moral principles.

Lit de justice   a royal session of the Parlement of Paris presided over by the king to ensure registration of the king's edicts.

livre   the basic unit of currency of France until 1795. Other units included the *Louis* (gold coin) = 24 *livres*, *écu* (silver coin) = 6 *livres* = 120 *sols*, 1 *livre* = 20 *sols*, 1 *sol* = 12 *deniers*.

Montagnards   the name of the Montagnard faction derived from the location (high at the back) of the seats in the National Convention its members occupied. They were the main faction opposed to the Girondins. Estimates of the number of Montagnards vary considerably, from 140 to 300, and a significant proportion of their membership belonged to the Jacobin Club. They were supported by the Paris Commune and by the *sans-culottes*; of the 24 deputies elected from Paris, 21 were Montagnards. The Montagnards came to dominate the Convention in 1793, but lost influence with the demise of Robespierre.

Muscadins   also known as the 'Gilded Youth', these were anti-Jacobin youth from wealthy families. They wore flamboyant clothes and, after the fall of Robespierre, violently attacked his sympathisers, supporters of the Terror and the *sans-culottes*.

National Assembly   the National Assembly, after July 1789, the National Constituent Assembly, and often simply called the Assembly, was a direct successor of the Estates-General. It emerged as the national representative body after 17 June 1789 when the deputies of the Third Estate and some deputies of the other estates proclaimed themselves the National Assembly. After initial opposition, Louis XVI recognised the National Assembly on 27 June 1789 when he requested all three estates to unite as one body. The National Assembly served as the legislature from 1789 to 1791.

National Convention   this single-chamber assembly was elected in September 1792 and proclaimed the Republic. The 745 deputies were divided between Girondins and the more radical Montagnards, with a large number of crossbench members (the Plain) in between. It remained in session until October 1795.

National Guard   a citizens' militia formed in July 1789 in the Paris districts and other cities to maintain order, protect property against mob violence, and guard against counter-revolutionary plots.

nobility of the robe   nobles, such as magistrates, court officials and bureaucrats, who acquired their noble status from holding office, often a venal office.

nobility of the sword   old and established noble families, who could trace their lineage back to the Middle Ages. They often owed their status to their service to the Crown, often, in battle.

non-juring clergy   *see* refractory clergy

pamphlet   a publication, ranging from a single page to as long as a book, that was a popular way of communicating political ideas.

Paris Commune   the revolutionary municipal government of Paris formed in July 1789 by an insurrectional committee composed of 144 delegates—three from each of the 48 *sections* of the city. It was opposed by the Girondins, who tried to curb its growing influence on the Assembly and later on the Convention. In 1793, the Paris Commune and the Jacobins ousted Girondin members from the Convention.

parlements   the appellate courts of law in France. The function of the 13 *parlements* was to administer justice and to register, remonstrate and publish royal edicts.

patriotic cockade or the Tricolour   a red, white and blue arrangement of ribbons worn on clothes or a hat to indicate support for the revolution.

peasant   the word 'peasant' derived from the Old French word *paisent*, meaning 'someone who lives in the country'. Peasants made up approximately 80 per cent of the population.

philosophes   intellectuals and writers of the eighteenth century, such as Voltaire, Montesquieu, Rousseau and Diderot, who advocated the use of reason instead of custom, tradition, faith or superstition as the basis for the organisation of society. They were the key contributors to the Enlightenment.

Phrygian cap of liberty   a soft, conical red cap associated with freed slaves in ancient times as a symbol of their newly acquired freedom; came to symbolise liberty in revolutionary France.

pike   a weapon with a steel or iron point on a long wooden shaft.

Plain   the centre, crossbench or non-aligned faction in the Convention, which sat in the flat middle area of the chamber and generally remained uncommitted to the opposing Montagnards and Girondins.

polarised   forced to take opposing points of view.

Prince of the Blood   the status of a 'prince of the blood' belonged to the king's brothers and cousins, who were members of the Bourbon dynasty but did not belong to the immediate family of the king. The rank of 'prince of the blood' entitled its holder to a seat on the king's council and in the Parlement of Paris.

radical   an individual or group focused on altering existing structures of society in fundamental ways, often through violent means.

ratify   to give formal consent to, making an edict officially valid.

reactionary   opposing political or social progress or reform.

recalcitrant   resisting authority, not compliant.

red cap of liberty   *see* Phrygian cap of liberty

refractory or non-juring clergy   clergy who refused to take an oath of allegiance to the *Civil Constitution of the Clergy*.

Representatives on Mission   deputies sent from Paris by the National Convention who were entrusted with considerable powers of repression in the provinces, especially during the Terror. They also recruited men for the army. After June 1793, they were appointed by the Committee of Public Safety. One of their tasks became the suppression of the federalist revolt.

royal prerogative   customary authority, privilege and immunity belonging to the king alone.

sans-culottes   revolutionaries who made a virtue of their plain dress, in contrast to that of the nobility and the bourgeoisie. They were mostly workers, shopkeepers, petty traders, craftsmen and the poor, and wore trousers instead of the breeches and stockings of the higher classes.

schism   a split or division between groups of people usually within a religious denomination.

sections   the 48 areas or divisions into which Paris was divided for administrative purposes; they replaced the former 60 districts. Each was run by a revolutionary surveillance committee and was able to organise armed men, mostly *sans-culottes*. Other cities also had their *sections*. *Section* assemblies played a major role in shaping uprisings and influencing the government.

sovereignty   supreme power, the authority to govern itself, the power to rule.

summary justice   punishment of suspects without trial.

surveillance committees   surveillance or watch committees were formed in each *commune* in March 1793 to maintain public security and order. They often took the place of local government in the districts and were controlled by extreme Jacobins.

taille   a direct land tax imposed on each household and based on how much land it held.

corvée   a service of unpaid labour imposed for the upkeep of public roads.

Tennis Court Oath, 20 June 1789   an oath sworn by the deputies of the Third Estate 'not to separate, and to reassemble wherever circumstances require, until the constitution of the kingdom is established'.

tithes   historically, a tithe was a compulsory tax paid to the Roman Catholic Church, at the rate of one-tenth of produce at the time of harvest, and paid in kind, for example in agricultural products.

unicameral   referring to a legislative body with a single legislative chamber.

venal office a public office or position sold by the Crown to raise money. The key offices conferred on their holder personal noble status that became hereditary, generally after three generations. This practice was an important avenue of social mobility for the bourgeoisie and a source of income for the Crown.

vingtième direct tax on income levied during the American War of Independence (1778–1783) until 1786.

What Is the Third Estate?, 1789 a political pamphlet written by Abbé Sieyès. It called for the Estates-General to be genuinely representative by providing the Third Estate with double representation and called for the voting procedure to be by head and not by order.

BIBLIOGRAPHY

Alpaugh, Micah. *The French Revolution. A History in Documents*. London: Bloomsbury Academic, 2020.

———. 'The Making of the Parisian Political Demonstration: A Case Study of 20 June 1792.' *Proceedings of the Western Society for French History* 34 (2007): 115–133.

Andress, David. 'The Course of the Terror, 1793–94.' In *A Companion to the French Revolution*, edited by Peter McPhee, 294–309. Chichester: Wiley-Blackwell, 2013.

———. *French Society in Revolution, 1789–1799*. Manchester: Manchester University Press, 1999.

———. *Massacre at the Champ De Mars. Popular Dissent and Political Culture in the French Revolution*. Rochester: Boydell Press, 2001.

Auguste, Louis. *Réflexions sur mes entretiens avec M. le Duc de la Vauguyon*. Paris: J. P. Aillaud, 1851.

Baker, Keith Michael, ed. *The Old Regime and the French Revolution*. Edited by John W. Boyer and Julius Kirshner, University of Chicago Readings in Western Civilization, vol. 7. Chicago: University of Chicago Press, 1986.

Beales, Derek. *Joseph II*. Cambridge: Cambridge University Press, 1987.

Blackman, Robert. 'What Was "Absolute" about the "Absolute Veto"? Ideas of National Sovereignty and Royal Power in September 1789.' *Journal of the Western Society for French History* 32 (2004): 123–139.

Bosher, John F. *The French Revolution*. London: Weidenfeld and Nicolson, 1989.

Burke, Edmund. *Revolutionary Writings. Reflections on the Revolution in France and the First Letter on a Regicide Peace*. Edited by Iain Hampsher-Monk. New York: Cambridge University Press, 2014.

Cobb, Richard, and Colin Jones. *Voices of the French Revolution*. Topsfield: Salem House Publishers, 1988.

Cobban, Alfred. *A History of Modern France: The Old Regime and the Revolution, 1715–1799*, 2 vols, vol. 1, Harmondsworth: Penguin, 1957.

———. 'The "Parlements" of France in the Eighteenth Century.' *History* 35, no. 123/124 (1950): 64–80.

———. *The Social Interpretation of the French Revolution*, 2nd edn. Cambridge: Cambridge University Press, 1999.

Coquard, Olivier. *Jean-Paul Marat*. Paris: Fayard, 1993.

Darnton, Robert. *The Literary Underground of the Old Regime*. Cambridge, MA: Harvard University Press, 1982.

———. *Pirating and Publishing. The Book Trade in the Age of Enlightenment*. New York: Oxford University Press, 2021.

———. *What Was Revolutionary about the French Revolution?* Waco: Baylor University Press, 1990.

Doniger, Wendy. *The Ring of Truth and Other Myths of Sex and Jewelry*. New York: Oxford University Press, 2017.

Doyle, William. *Aristocracy and Its Enemies in the Age of Revolution*. Oxford: Oxford University Press, 2009.

———. *The French Revolution. A Very Short Introduction*. Oxford: Oxford University Press, 2001.

———. *Old Regime France*. Oxford: Oxford University Press, 2001.

———. *The Oxford History of the French Revolution*, 3rd edn. Oxford: Oxford University Press, 2018.

Dwyer, Philip G. *Napoleon. The Path to Power*. New Haven: Yale University Press, 2008.

Dwyer, Philip G., and Peter McPhee, eds. *The French Revolution and Napoleon. A Sourcebook*. London: Routledge, 2002.

Fitzsimmons, Michael. 'The Principles of 1789.' In *A Companion to the French Revolution*, edited by Peter McPhee, 75–90. Chichester: Wiley-Blackwell, 2013.

———. *The Remaking of France. The National Assembly and the Constitution of 1791*. Cambridge: Cambridge University Press, 1994.

Furet, François. *The French Revolution, 1770–1814*. Translated by Antonia Nevill. Oxford: Blackwell, 1996.

———. *Interpreting the French Revolution*. Translated by Elborg Forster. Cambridge: Cambridge University Press, 1981.

Furet, François, and Mona Ozouf, eds. *A Critical Dictionary of the French Revolution*. Cambridge, MA: Belknap Press, 1989.

Garrioch, David. *The Making of Revolutionary Paris*. Berkeley: University of California Press, 2002.

Gilchrist, John T., and William J. Murray, eds. *The Press in the French Revolution; a Selection of Documents Taken from the Press of the Revolution for the Years 1789–1794*. Melbourne: Cheshire, 1971.

Goodwin, A. 'Calonne, the Assembly of French Notables of 1787 and the Origins of the "Revolte Nobiliaire".' *The English Historical Review* 61, no. 240 (1946): 202–234.

———. 'Calonne, the Assembly of French Notables of 1787 and the Origins of the "Revolte Nobiliaire" (Continued).' *The English Historical Review* 61, no. 241 (1946): 329–377.

Gruder, Vivian R. *The Notables and the Nation. The Political Schooling of the French, 1787–1788.* Cambridge, MA: Harvard University Press, 2007.

Hampson, Norman. *The Life and Opinions of Maximilien Robespierre.* London: Duckworth, 1974.

———. *A Social History of the French Revolution.* London: Routledge, 1966.

Hanson, Paul R. *Historical Dictionary of the French Revolution,* 2nd edn. Lanham: Rowman & Littlefield, 2015.

———. *The Jacobin Republic under Fire. The Federalist Revolt in the French Revolution.* University Park: Pennsylvania State University Press, 2003.

Hardman, John. *The French Revolution. The Fall of the Ancien Regime to the Thermidorian Reaction, 1785–1795.* New York: St. Martin's Press, 1982.

———. *Overture to Revolution. The 1787 Assembly of Notables and the Crisis of France's Old Regime.* Oxford: Oxford University Press, 2010.

———. 'The Real and Imagined Conspiracies of Louis XVI.' In *Conspiracy in the French Revolution,* edited by Peter Robert Campbell, Thomas E. Kaiser and Marisa Linton, 63–84. Manchester: Manchester University Press, 2007.

Harris, Carolyn. *Queenship and Revolution in Early Modern Europe. Henrietta Maria and Marie Antoinette.* New York: Palgrave Macmillan, 2016.

Harris, Robert D. 'French Finances and the American War, 1777–1783.' *The Journal of Modern History* 48, no. 2 (1976): 233–258.

Haydon, Colin, and William Doyle, eds. *Robespierre.* Cambridge: Cambridge University Press, 1999.

Hunt, Lynn. *The French Revolution and Human Rights. A Brief Documentary History.* Boston: Bedford Books of St. Martin's Press, 1996.

———. *Politics, Culture, and Class in the French Revolution.* Berkeley: University of California Press, 1984.

Israel, Jonathan. *Revolutionary Ideas. An Intellectual History of the French Revolution from the Rights of Man to Robespierre.* Princeton: Princeton University Press, 2014.

Jones, Colin. *The Longman Companion to the French Revolution.* Hoboken: Taylor and Francis, 2014.

Jones, Peter M. *The French Revolution 1787–1804,* 2nd edn. Hoboken: Taylor and Francis, 2014.

Jordan, David P. 'Robespierre.' *The Journal of Modern History* 49, no. 2 (1977): 282–291.

Kates, Gary. *The Cercle Social, the Girondins, and the French Revolution.* Princeton: Princeton University Press, 2014.

Lefebvre, Georges. *The Coming of the French Revolution.* Translated by Robert R. Palmer. New York: Vintage Books, 1947.

————. *The French Revolution*. London: Routledge, 1962.

————. *The French Revolution*. Translated by Elizabeth Moss Evanson. London: Routledge, 2005.

————. *The French Revolution from 1793 to 1799*. Translated by John Hall Stewart and James Friguglietti, 2nd edn. London: Routledge, 1967.

Linton, Marisa. *Choosing Terror. Virtue, Friendship, and Authenticity in the French Revolution*. Oxford: Oxford University Press, 2013.

Marchione, Margherita, Stanley J. Idzerda and S. Eugene Scalia, eds. *Philip Mazzei. Selected Writings and Correspondence*, 2 vols. Prato: Edizioni del Palazzo, 1983.

Margerison, Kenneth. *Pamphlets and Public Opinion. The Campaign for a Union of Orders in the Early French Revolution*. West Lafayette: Purdue University Press, 1998.

Markoff, John. *The Abolition of Feudalism: Peasants, Lords, and Legislators in the French Revolution*. University Park: Pennsylvania State University Press, 1996.

————. 'The Claims of Lord, Church, and State in the Cahiers de Doléances of 1789.' *Comparative Studies in Society and History* 32, no. 3 (1990): 413–454.

Martin, Jean-Clément. 'The Vendée, Chouannerie, and the State, 1791–99.' In *A Companion to the French Revolution*, edited by Peter McPhee, 246–259. Chichester: Wiley-Blackwell, 2013.

————. 'The Vendée, Region of Memory.' In *Rethinking France*, edited by Pierre Nora, 383–408. Chicago: University of Chicago Press, 2001.

Mayer, Arno J. *The Furies. Violence and Terror in the French and Russian Revolutions*. Princeton: Princeton University Press, 2000.

Maza, Sarah. 'Politics, Culture, and the Origins of the French Revolution.' *The Journal of Modern History* 61, no. 4 (1989): 704–723.

McPhee, Peter. *The French Revolution, 1789–1799*. Oxford: Oxford University Press, 2002.

————. *Liberty or Death. The French Revolution*. New Haven: Yale University Press, 2016.

————. *Living the French Revolution, 1789–1799*. New York: Palgrave Macmillan, 2006.

————. *Robespierre. A Revolutionary Life*. New Haven: Yale University Press, 2012.

————. *A Social History of France, 1789–1914*, 2nd edn. Basingstoke: Palgrave Macmillan, 2004.

Mercier, Louis-Sébastien, Christophe Cave and Christine Marcandier-Colard. *L'an 2440 Rêve s'il en fut jamais*. Introd. et notes par Christophe Cave et Christine Marcandier-Colard. La Découverte-Poche Littérature. Paris: Éd. la Découverte, 1999.

Mounier, Jean-Joseph. *Délibération de la ville de Grenoble, du samedi 14 Juin 1788*. Grenoble: [s.n.], 1788.

Murray, William. *The Right-Wing Press in the French Revolution, 1789–92.* Woodbridge: Boydell Press, 1986.

Ozouf, Mona. *Festivals and the French Revolution.* Cambridge, MA: Harvard University Press, 1988.

Paine, Thomas. *The Political and Miscellaneous Works of Thomas Paine,* 2 vols. London: R. Carlile, 1819.

Patrick, Alison. 'Political Divisions in the French National Convention, 1792–93.' *The Journal of Modern History* 41, no. 4 (1969): 422–474.

Popkin, Jeremy D. *A New World Begins. The History of the French Revolution.* New York: Basic Books, 2019.

———. *The Right-Wing Press in France, 1792–1800.* Chapel Hill: University of North Carolina Press, 1980.

Reichardt, Rolf, and Hubertus Kohle. *Visualizing the Revolution. Politics and Pictorial Arts in Late Eighteenth-Century France.* Translated by Corinne Attwood. London: Reaktion, 2008.

Reynolds, Sian. *Marriage and Revolution. Monsieur and Madame Roland.* Oxford: Oxford University Press, 2012.

Riquetti, Honoré Gabriel. *Speeches of M. de Mirabeau the Elder.* Translated by James White. London: J. Debrett, 1792.

Roche, Daniel. *France in the Enlightenment.* Translated by Arthur Goldhammer. Cambridge, MA: Harvard University Press, 1998.

Rousseau, Jean-Jacques. *The Plan for Perpetual Peace, on the Government of Poland, and Other Writings on History and Politics.* Translated by Christopher Kelly and Judith Bush. The Collected Writings of Rousseau. Edited by Christopher Kelly. Hanover: Dartmouth College Press, 2005.

Rudé, George. *The Crowd in the French Revolution.* London: Oxford University Press, 1967.

———. *The French Revolution.* London: Weidenfeld and Nicolson, 1988.

———. *Revolutionary Europe 1783–1815.* London: Fontana, 1985.

Schama, Simon. *Citizens. A Chronicle of the French Revolution.* London: Penguin, 1989.

Scurr, Ruth. *Fatal Purity. Robespierre and the French Revolution.* New York: Metropolitan Books, 2006.

Secher, Reynald. *A French Genocide. The Vendée.* Translated by George Holoch. Notre Dame: University of Notre Dame Press, 2003.

Shapiro, Barry M. *Traumatic Politics: The Deputies and the King in the Early French Revolution.* University Park: Pennsylvania State University Press, 2009.

Shapiro, Gilbert, and John Markoff. *Revolutionary Demands. A Content Analysis of the Cahiers de Doléances of 1789.* Stanford: Stanford University Press, 1998.

Soboul, Albert. *The French Revolution, 1787–1799.* New York: Vintage Books, 1975.

———. *A Short History of the French Revolution, 1789–1799.* Berkeley: University of California Press, 1977.

Soulavie, Jean-Louis. *Historical and Political Memoirs of the Reign of Lewis XVI*, 6 vols. London: G. & J. Robinson, 1802.

———. *Mémoires historiques et politiques du règne de Louis XVI*, 6 vols. Paris: Treuttel et Würtz, 1801.

Stewart, John Hall. *A Documentary Survey of the French Revolution*. New York: Macmillan, 1951.

Stone, Bailey. *Reinterpreting the French Revolution. A Global-Historical Perspective.* Cambridge: Cambridge University Press, 2002.

Sutherland, Donald. *The French Revolution and Empire. The Quest for a Civic Order.* Oxford: Blackwell, 2003.

———. 'Urban Crowds, Riot, Utopia, and Massacres, 1789–92.' In *A Companion to the French Revolution*, edited by Peter McPhee, 231–245. Chichester: Wiley-Blackwell, 2013.

Tackett, Timothy. *The Coming of the Terror in the French Revolution*. Cambridge, MA: Belknap Press, 2015.

Terjanian, Anoush Fraser. *Commerce and Its Discontents in Eighteenth-Century French Political Thought*. Cambridge: Cambridge University Press, 2013.

Trapp, Joseph. *Proceedings of the French National Convention on the Trial of Louis XVI, Late King of France and Navarre*, 2nd edn. London: Murray Kearsley Wenman and Co., 1793.

Weber, Caroline. *Queen of Fashion. What Marie Antoinette Wore to the Revolution.* New York: H. Holt, 2006.

Wollstonecraft, Mary. *A Vindication of the Rights of Men. A Vindication of the Rights of Woman. An Historical and Moral View of the French Revolution*. Edited by Janet Todd. Oxford: Oxford University Press, 2008.

Young, Arthur. *Travels During the Years 1787, 1788, and 1789*. Bury St. Edmunds: J. Rackham, 1792.

Zamoyski, Adam. *Holy Madness. Romantics, Patriots and Revolutionaries 1776–1871.* London: Weidenfeld and Nicolson, 1999.

———. *Phantom Terror. The Threat of Revolution and the Repression of Liberty, 1789–1848.* New York: Basic Books, 2014.

INDEX

Printed in the United States
by Baker & Taylor Publisher Services